Seventh-day Adventist Christian: Do You Know Who You Are?

A Curiously Hard Question
at a Most Critical Time

Max Hammonds, MD, MPH, MHA

TEACH Services, Inc.
PUBLISHING
www.TEACHServices.com • (800) 367-1844

Copyright © 2015 Max Hammonds
Copyright © 2015 TEACH Services, Inc.

ISBN-13: 978-1-4796-0497-5 (Paperback)
ISBN-13: 978-1-4796-0498-2 (ePub)
ISBN-13: 978-1-4796-0499-9 (Mobi)

Library of Congress Control Number: 2015906540

Published by

TEACH Services, Inc.
PUBLISHING
www.TEACHServices.com • (800) 367-1844

Contents

Foreword

I have never prayed so much and so hard over any written work—or sermon, for that matter—as I have this book. The chapters of this manuscript began as sermons, most of them preached at the St. Petersburg Seventh-day Adventist Church when I was the head elder and, for a time, the unofficial lay pastor of that congregation. But the book began many years ago as a series of questions I had concerning this unusual Protestant denomination that I had joined and grown to love. The book was mostly centered around one question: Did they know who they were? Did they realize how much they knew, that other folk did not know?

Over the years, the ideas, the questions, and some of the answers became clearer as I fast forwarded through bookshelves of material that I assumed my fellow Seventh-day Adventists had read in their formative years in the denomination's school system, years that I had missed out on. The revelations of these books were astounding—the quality of the writing of Ellen White and others was awesome. *Do these people know what they have?*

To my utter dismay and sadness of heart, I began to realize that most did not know. In fact, most had no idea how far ahead their denomination was in organizational structure, financial soundness, unity of purpose and fellowship, solidness of doctrinal thought, spot-on historical referencing.

And so my writing outline began to grow. Do you know you are the Remnant? Do you know you are a Priest? The topics came and the sermons were written until the final result is the book you hold in your hands.

I ask you, the reader, a very personal question: Do you know who you are? Therefore, the writing style is up close and personal, a conversation and a dialog. I tried to avoid sounding preachy (which meant extensively rewriting the sermons), and I strictly avoided the scholarly style of footnotes and references.

As you read, you will notice that I purposefully capitalized such words as Remnant, People of God, Time of the End, Priest, Steward, etc. because I want to emphasize them as unique words that are not just any remnant or people of God or time of the end. My hope is that by capitalizing these words it will cause you to take note of our important mission and calling as a people. It is so easy to see ourselves as just any remnant, just any priesthood, just any stewardship. But it's deeper than that, which you will discover in this book.

And I expect you to participate as fully in the conversation as I do, as you ponder your answer to this very personal question: Do you know who you are?

If you are a Seventh-day Adventist, you will immediately notice that I have not inserted any Ellen G. White quotations to bolster my assertions. If you knew me personally (which I hope we can do sometime), you would know that I am an avid reader of Mrs. White's writings. Much of my understanding and many of the foundational ideas in this book will be familiar to those who also are her avid readers. But I take her at her word, which you will find quoted in only one place in this book—Chapter 12. "I exalt the precious Word before you today," she wrote. "Lay Sister White to one side. Do not repeat what I have said, saying, 'Sister White said this,' and 'Sister White said that.' Do not quote my words again as long as you live until you can obey the Bible. Find out what the Lord God of Israel says, and then do what He commands."

I believe that one of the problems in our Seventh-day Adventist culture is that we read only one prophet. We forget that the Holy Spirit worked through many different prophets, not just Isaiah or Joel or Ellen White. So I have taken her words to heart and have asked that you, the reader, learn what the Word has to say about who you are before you try to find out what the Spirit has said through the prophet of the Time of the End—Ellen G. White.

As I said at the beginning, this book is the Spirit's doing. I tried to listen and follow His lead. But I am not unique. God talks to everyone, but sadly, much of the time people don't listen. But I'll let you read Chapter 4–6 for the rest of the conversation on this topic.

Again, I must thank two extremely dedicated and warmly loved people who contributed much to this book: my friend, Steve Dickerson, who read each chapter hot from my e-mail files and dutifully corrected, edited, and questioned my words and my motives, and my wife, Carolyn, who suffered through yet another set of excuses as to why I had to spend my time writing instead of being with her.

In addition, I must thank Penny Estes Wheeler for doing the major editing and Scripture checking for the manuscript, a two-month task made more difficult by my hurried errors and faulty memory, and my daughter, Jacque Hammonds, for her artful illustrations and beautiful cover. And I want to thank the dedicated people at TEACH Services, Inc. for helping a struggling author (with no agent) through the arduous process of getting his book published.

However I was inspired and assisted, my writing, good or bad, is my own, and I take full responsibility for what I have written. Knowing full well that in the future, I will wish I could have expressed an idea more clearly or stated a concept differently, I leave it to you, the reader, and the Holy Spirit to interpret correctly what I wished to say.

This book is dedicated to my mother, Helen Louise Hammonds Rothston, and my wife, Carolyn Jo Wells Hammonds—the two lovingly stable influences in my convoluted life.

With prayers for the Holy Spirit to lead and bless you,

Max Hammonds, MD (retired)
Hendersonville, NC
July 16, 2013

Chapter 1

Introduction: Do You Know Who You Are?

"And I will give them a heart to know Me, for I am the Lord;
and they will be My people, and I will be their God,
for they will return to Me with their whole heart." Jeremiah 24:7

Hello. Come sit down next to me—right here—or in that chair across from me, if that's more comfortable. And welcome.

Or, more realistically, perhaps you're on a backpack trip and are sitting by a campfire—or on a commuter train going to work—or on an airplane at 30,000 feet on a trip to see your relatives in Idaho.

Actually, I don't know where you might be sitting. But I would like to talk with you up close and personal—as if we *were* sitting across from one another in a mountain retreat, before a fireplace, or at an early morning breakfast table. I would like to pretend that you are not reading a book—but that, in fact, we are having a very personal, face-to-face conversation.

I'm sorry. Please excuse me for being so blunt and forward since we've just met, but I really would like to talk with you about what is probably the most curiously hard question you'll ever have in regard to your life as a Seventh-day Adventist Christian. Our conversation will require deep personal discussion on my part and some close personal searching on your part.

Because, yes, this question pertains to *you*. Do you remember the famous quote from Socrates? (Yes, the philosopher from Athens, Greece, who was forced to drink hemlock poison.) The quote says: "Know thyself." This is the gist of the question I pose to you. *Do you know who you are?*

I'm not asking this question about your ethnic background, your sexual preference, your socio-economic status, or your career path. I'm asking this question as a fellow Seventh-day Adventist Christian. It's a question I've been pondering in one form or another for the last twenty or more years—about myself and about my Seventh-day Adventist friends.

I've heard that the three most important questions for most people are: where did you come from, why are you here, and where are you going? But I would like to suggest to you that my question encompasses and supersedes the other three: *Do you know who you are?*

Let me tell you a story about how I first became aware of this question. In the 1970s some friends and I established the Walla Walla Health Education Center at Walla Walla General Hospital. For those of you who work at the General now, you will not remember these efforts as they took place in the old hospital building on Bonsella Street in Walla Walla, Washington.

We set up our fledgling operation in the basement as there was no room anywhere else in the hospital. Our health classes were held in the basement; our board meetings were held in the basement; our special functions were held in the basement. Since that time the Walla Walla General Hospital has moved to a wonderful campus on South 2nd Avenue with a large auditorium and meeting rooms and enough parking to host large audiences. But at that time there was hardly room to turn around—in the basement.

Our governing board, which met every three months, included several prominent individuals from the community. At one particular meeting, about one year into our existence, we were discussing the name of the organization and whether it reflected the character and scope of the mission we had imagined for ourselves. One of the community leaders suggested that we include the moniker "Seventh-day Adventist" in our name to reflect the kinds of programs people could expect. Those of us who were Seventh-day Adven-

tists immediately and vigorously objected, then self-consciously tried to explain. We were concerned that the name would put people off, make them think we had a religious "hook" in what we were doing, and even raise up "prejudice" against the health center.

Then the community board member said something I'll never forget: "Don't you know who you are? We all know who you are. You've been in the community for decades, and we've come to expect a certain high level of performance in association with that name. Don't be ashamed of your name. We know who you are. Don't you know who you are?"

To this day the shock of that statement has never lost its punch. *Do you know who you are?*

After working—as physician, missionary, lay pastor, Sabbath School teacher, head elder, Pathfinder leader, writer, administrator—in the Seventh-day Adventist denomination for forty years, I'm still not sure that we, as Seventh-day Adventist Christians, know for certain how to answer that question. I'm not sure we collectively know who we are.

When asked to define who we are, too many of us stutter through a learned litany of unclear responses that include the Sabbath, the three angels, and certain health and social prohibitions. I suspect that the average member in the church can't answer with clarity and conviction the question: Do you know who you are?

Can you?

I'm not asking you this question in order to cleverly slip in a discussion of church doctrines, as vital as they are. I'm not asking it to compare you, favorably or unfavorably, with one of your fellow church members or to find fault with the church at large. I'm not about to bring up some esoteric and isolated fine point of doctrine or spring some radical new understanding on you. In fact, I think that the answer to my question has been with us for more than a century, actually, more like six millennia—ever since the Garden of Eden.

We live in momentous times in the history of this world and at a critical juncture in the history of our church. It is of paramount importance that we—as a people, as a church, and as individuals—know for ourselves who we are, why God has called us into existence as a church, and what our mission is in this world. Without a clear answer to this question, we will be unclear in our planning, unfocused in our mission, and uncommitted in our organizations.

I believe that the world needs to hear the messages that we have been directed by God to give. But it is only as we know *who we are* and *why we are here* that we can grasp the significance of the end time events to which we are witnesses and in which we will participate. And certainly the world will be confused and will not be interested in hearing *anything* that we have to share, of whatever value, if they sense that we don't know who we are.

In these little chats, these conversations, I want to suggest several biblical answers for my question. Please consider the answers, and their implications for your life. Pray about them. Let them roll around in your brain and bump into all the other ideas you have about God and church and what you're doing and why you're here—and who you are.

It's my prayer that these thoughts and ideas will spark thoughts and ideas in you. I also pray that, with our renewed sense of who we are, we—you and I, as well as our beloved church—will awaken to the urgings of the Holy Spirit. By His guidance and conviction, I pray that we will understand the significance of the times we live in and the role God has assigned the Seventh-day Adventist Church to play in them. I pray fervently that we will recapture the urgent passion for wit-

ness that marked the efforts of the founders of the Seventh-day Adventist movement.

Do you sense my passion and my urgency to discuss these things with you? I hope you do.

So as we begin, let me suggest a couple of ground rules.

First, because the Bible uses such widely differing metaphors in describing the Gospel, the Christian life, and God's People, I've given considerable thought as to how to arrange the topics for our little chats. In my own mind and very informally, I've organized the material into three general divisions:

1) the Seventh-day Adventist Christian and his/her relationship to God and how it's similar to what is generally understood and appreciated by all Christians,

2) scriptural metaphors for a Seventh-day Adventist Christian who has accepted a more serious, intensive, and intimate connection with God, and

3) last day events scenarios that describe the final mission of a Seventh day Adventist Christian.

You may or may not want to think in such an organized way as we work through our discussions. Because the flow from one division to the next and from one topic to the next seems, I think, to be a natural transition, the divisions may exist in my mind only to guide my own thinking and may not be of any use to you. If thinking in terms of these divisions helps in your own understanding, so much the better. If they don't help, you can ignore them.

Second, as you read these chapters and pretend with me that we are having a very private and personal conversation (as we are doing now seated here across from one another), I desire that you will think long and hard about the questions and issues inherent in the question I'm placing before you. And it's my prayer that our discussion will cause you to raise questions of your own, and that, with the guidance of the Holy Spirit, you will seek their answers in the Scriptures.

Third, let me set up one more ground rule—actually, it's a request. Please go get your Bible, right now. Yes, go get it. I'll wait right here until you get back. (See how up close and personal we are?) Are you back yet? Good for you, and thank you.

You see, all of our discussions (the chapters of this book) contain multiple Scripture references for the simple reason that my thoughts mean nothing if they are not *based on* the Word. And your understanding will mean nothing if you have not received these ideas and *processed them through* the Word. I will be "reading" these scriptures "aloud" to you. But I want you to read them for yourself. I want you to process them for yourself. I know this will be hard (especially if you're really on that backpack trip), but the blessing of your personal understanding will be worth it. So keep your Bible open and handy as we explore the various answers to what I think is the most basic, curiously hard question at this critical time in our church's history:

Seventh-day Adventist Christian, do you know who you are?

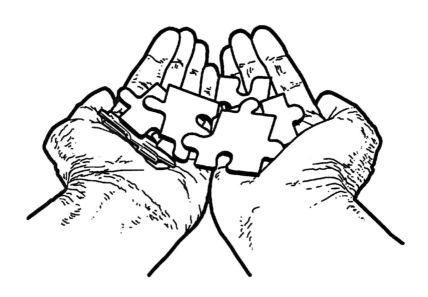

Chapter 2

Do You Know You Are a Greatly Beloved Saint?

"Blessed be the God and Father of our Lord Jesus Christ, who has blessed us with every spiritual blessing in the heavenly places in Christ, just as He chose us in Him before the foundations of the world, that we should be holy and blameless before Him. In love He predestined us to adoption as sons through Jesus Christ to Himself, according to the kind intention of His will, to the praise of the glory of His grace, which He freely bestowed on us in the Beloved."

Ephesians 1:3–6

For our very first, more complete conversation, I have a very simple message for you from the Lord. It's a one-word message. I can say it in one scripture verse. In fact, when I'm finished, I think you'll say, "Why didn't you just say so?"

Because, if I did it that way, you wouldn't believe me. It's as simple as that. So let's take a longer journey and explore the Scriptures along the way. Let's see where we end up and whether you'll believe me or not.

Open up your Bible there beside you (you do have it, don't you?) and turn to Ephesians 1:1. Read the greeting (aloud, if you like) that Paul writes to the Ephesians. "Paul, an apostle of Christ Jesus by the will of God, to the saints who are in Ephesus, and who are faithful in Christ Jesus ..." Did you see that? This letter is written to the saints *and* to the faithful.

Here's a little lesson in Greek that I learned just the other day. The Greek word *kai* is translated into English as "and." But it doesn't always mean "and also" as in, When I went to the beach, I took a book and an umbrella and a beach ball. In this example sentence, the "and" means "and also." When I went to the beach, I took a book *and also* an umbrella *and also* a beach ball.

In Greek, *kai* frequently means "therefore" or as we would say in English, "in other words" or "that is."

So let's read Ephesians 1:1 again with our new understanding. "To the saints who are at Ephesus—*in other words*—who are faithful in Christ Jesus."

Now look at the first two verses of Colossians (in your ever-present Bible), and read the greeting using our new translation skills. "… to the saints—*in other words*—the faithful brethren in Christ who are at Colossae …" From these two greetings we learn that the word "saint" is defined as those who are faithful.

Now let's read Philippians 1:1. "Paul and Timothy, bond-servants of Christ Jesus, to all the saints in Christ Jesus who are in Philippi, including the overseers and deacons …" It would seem that the saints in Philippi include some very holy people, the elders and the deacons.

That's what the word "saint" means. It comes from the same root word as sanctuary and sanctify. It means holy, set apart for God's special purpose. Yes, the elders and deacons are set apart—we call it ordained—by God through His church for God's special purpose.

Who are these saints to whom Paul is addressing his letters? Ephesians says that the saints include the faithful. Philippians says that the saints include holy people.

Oh, yes, let's not forget the Corinthians. Flip over to 1 Corinthians 1:1, 2: "Paul, called as an apostle of Jesus Christ by the will of God, and Sosthenes our brother, to the church of God which is at Corinth, to those who have been sanctified in Christ Jesus, saints by calling, with all who in

every place call upon the name of our Lord Jesus Christ, their Lord and ours …" And we discover again that saints are sanctified—set apart. Paul says that they are "saints by calling."

The words we've discovered so far that are used to describe these various people to whom Paul is writing include: faithful, holy, sanctified, called to be saints.

Let's look at one more scripture, Colossians 3:12–15. "And so, as those who have been chosen of God, holy and beloved, put on a heart of compassion, kindness, humility, gentleness and patience; bearing with one another, and forgiving each other, whoever has a complaint against any one; just as the Lord forgave you, so also should you. Beyond all these things put on love, which is the perfect bond of unity." Here is a description of the "chosen of God," the saints to whom Paul has been addressing all of his letters.

Wait a minute. You and I read one of our greetings from 1 Corinthians, didn't we? Aren't those the church members who were sleeping with their fathers' wives, taking each other to court, carousing in the local temples with the temple prostitutes, and fighting over the bread at communion?

The saints that you know—in the church where you grew up or in the church where you worship now—do they sound more like those described in Colossae or do they sound more like the Corinthians? Did Paul really address the Corinthians as saints?

H ave you ever been in love?
Yes, me too.

When my wife and I were married, we wrote our own wedding vows from the depths of our love. All of those emotionally charged words that you read in Song of Solomon, we said to each other. A lot of those sentiments made it into the wedding vows.

You know as well as I do that being in love is an intense feeling. It's an intense time, an intimate time. And the one you love is called—beloved. It signifies that this person is loved by someone. They are beloved.

But "beloved" doesn't have to describe just a male/female relationship. We also call our children beloved. Beloved can refer to other relatives as well, but that usually isn't the case—not generally with relatives.

Beloved can be a very special friend.

I have two male friends in North Carolina: Douglas and Arthur. They are closer to me than most of my siblings. They are my brothers in the sense that they know all about me. I can tell them anything, and have on occasion. I have their utmost confidence and trust, and they have mine. They hold me accountable, and they love me. And I love them, and I tell them so.

Please understand that we don't agree on everything. Art was a McCain Republican. I was an Obama Democrat. As you can imagine, we've had some very intense discussions, and we still don't agree. But those discussions were always with the knowledge that we loved each other.

In 1 Samuel 18:1 we read: "Now it came about when he had finished speaking to Saul, that the soul of Jonathan was knit to the soul of David, and Jonathan loved him as himself." This is the kind of relationship I have with Art and Doug. I love them as I love myself.

Have you ever been loved with that kind of love? Consider carefully before you answer. It might be a trick question.

Let me tell you about two men in the Bible who were greatly beloved by God. The first one was a young shepherd boy who defended his sheep against a lion and a bear and defended the honor of his God against the insults of a Philistine giant. In 1 Samuel 17:36 we hear David reminding King Saul that Goliath is taunting the Israelite army and insulting the God of Israel. Can you see Goliath up there on that far hill across the valley, shouting insults, cursing the God of Israel?

And David responded with a curse of his own. David's curse on Goliath tells you what was

And the one you love is called—beloved.

in David's heart, why he was not afraid to fight someone three times his size. You'll read it in 1 Samuel 17:46: "This day the Lord will deliver you up into my hands … that all the earth may know that there is a God in Israel."

This young man, probably around sixteen years old at the time, knew who God was. And God said to Samuel the prophet (as described in Acts 13:22), "I have found David the son of Jesse, a man after My own heart, who will do all My will."

Yes, I know, I'm talking about David, the man of great passion. David, the man who lusted after another man's wife, had her husband murdered, and was punished by the loss of four of his own sons.

But listen to what God says about him. Read 1 Samuel 16:7, the last part, which tells you about the way God views David *and* you and me. "Man looks at the outward appearance but God looks on the heart." In 1 Kings 14:8—notice there in the middle of the verse—God describes David as the man "who followed me with all his heart."

The very name "David" means "beloved." And God loved him *intensely*.

The second man greatly beloved by God was captured by Nebuchadnezzar during the first siege of Jerusalem by the Babylonian army. He was around eighteen years of age when he was taken to Babylon and educated at the University of Babylon along with his three friends. They distinguished themselves by graduating at the top of their class and became notorious by refusing to worship the gods of Babylon, even under the threat of death. This young man became the prime minister of Babylon, serving three different Babylonian kings, and continued to serve even when the regime changed and the Persians came to power.

Daniel was a very different kind of man than David. From his diet to his dress, from his daily prayers to his amazingly tactful speeches in the royal court, he was a young man under control. Daniel was not at all like David.

In the Scriptures, at least, we are never told of a sin committed by Daniel. In fact, when God wants to give Ezekiel an example of a righteous man (see Ezekiel 14), He mentions Daniel, along with Job and Noah.

Turn in your Bible to Daniel 9:22, 23 (NKJV) and notice how Daniel is described: "... O Daniel, I am now come out to give you skill and understanding. At the beginning of your prayers the commandment came out ... for you are greatly beloved." Can you imagine sweeter words to come from the mouth of God about you? "... for you are greatly *beloved*."

The man, whom God describes as righteous along with Noah and Job, has been praying and fasting, in sack cloth and ashes "for my sin and the sin of my people." And God sends Gabriel with a message for the man, Daniel. "Daniel, you are greatly *beloved*."

Two men—very much unalike—yet both are greatly beloved by God. How much are you loved by God? Do you know? Do you know who you are? So many of us don't know who we are.

There is an old country song, sung by the Statler Brothers, about who we are. The lyrics say that a certain man is a husband to his wife, a brother to his sister, a son to his mother, an employee to his boss, a neighbor to the man next door, a fishing buddy to his friends, and the list goes on and on. We fill many different roles in our lives. We are many different people in our lifetime.

But in the relationship that counts, in the relationship that is core to the existence of every Christian, it reads like this: "For in Him we live, and move, and have our being ..." (Acts 17:28).

In the relationship that is core to the very existence of every human being—to the Greeks in Athens, to the Christians in Corinth, to the members of your home church, and especially to you— what is *your* role in relationship to God?

In the eyes of God, who are you?

Do you know who you are?

Let me introduce you to one more person. For this part of our discussion, let's be aggressive Bible scholars. Open the Bible that I asked you to bring to our discussions, and let's look up these scriptures together.

In Isaiah 42:1, by what name is this Person called? "Behold, *My Servant*, whom I uphold."

Earlier, in Isaiah 11:1, Isaiah described him as: "A *shoot* will spring from the stem of Jesse, and a *branch* from his roots."

In Psalm 110:1 David calls Him "the Lord says to my *Lord*." What did it say? Yes, David calls Him Lord.

In Daniel 9:25, Daniel calls Him "*Messiah the Prince*."

In John 1:29, John the Baptist describes Him as "the *Lamb* of God."

In Revelation 19:16, John the Revelator describes Him as "KING OF KINGS AND LORD OF LORDS." (In all of the preceding verses, italics supplied.)

Lots of descriptions, and like you and me, He fills many different roles.

But who is He? When *God* speaks of Him, how does God describe Him? Turn to Mark 1:11 or Mark 9:7; God uses the same description in both scriptures. When God describes Jesus, He calls Him—what does it say?—"My beloved Son" Does Jesus know this? Does Jesus know *who He is* in this relationship with His Father?

Look at the parable of the owner of the vineyard in Mark 12:1. You know the story of the owner who planted a vineyard and put a wall around it and dug a winepress and put caretakers in charge of it and sent slaves to receive from the caretakers of the vineyard. But the caretakers beat some slaves and killed others and wounded others in the head and sent them away empty-handed. This was a familiar story to the hearers in Jerusalem.

Then in Mark 12:6 Jesus describes Himself in the story. He says, "He had one more to send, a beloved son." Yes, Jesus knows who He is in relationship with God. Jesus knows He is the Beloved Son.

Do you know who you are?

Now look up one more familiar scripture. Turn to John 3:16. Yes, I know that you know it. Turn to it anyway. Read it again—for the first time.

John 3:16 says, "For God so loved the world, that He gave His only begotten Son, that whosoever believes in Him, shall not perish, but have everlasting life."

God so loved the world that He gave—this Branch, this Servant, this Lord, this Messiah, this King of Kings— His own beloved Son as a sacrifice so that the world would not have to die but would have everlasting life.

Read it *aloud* again, right now, right where you are (wherever that is). But this time, put yourself in the verse. Make it personal. Where it says "the world," say "me" instead. Where it says

"whosoever," say "if I." Where it says "shall not perish," say "*I* shall not perish."

Okay—are you ready? Read it slowly. Read it from the NPV (New Personal Version).

"For God so loves *me* that He gave His only begotten Son, that *if I* believe in Him, *I* shall not perish but have everlasting life."

Do you need more evidence?

Romans 1:7 says, "To all who are beloved of God … called as saints …" Do you see the parallel, "in other words," structure there? Beloved of God *are* those who are called as saints. If you are not yet convinced that you are beloved, let's read it the other way around.

Jude 1:1 says, "To those who are the called, beloved of God the Father …"

Passionate as you are, like David, yet crying for the sins of yourself and your people, like Daniel; imperfect as you are, like the Corinthians, yet clinging to Jesus in faith, like the Ephesians—you are a saint. In the Grace-Faith Relationship with God, you are the beloved.

A saint is a special person set apart by God for His special purpose. The saint receives the gift of salvation. He grows by the power of the Spirit. He becomes like the Father in his character. And finally, in the judgment, is he condemned?

No!

You are loved. Intensely. Unreservedly. Sacrificially. Eternally.

Open your Bible and read it in Daniel 7:22: "Until the Ancient of Days came, and judgment was passed in favor of the saints of the Highest One, and the time arrived when the saints took possession of the kingdom." In the final judgment—the saints are given the kingdom! Praise the Lord!

But the first characteristic of a saint, the first qualification of a saint, is to know that he is greatly beloved. You are greatly beloved. God has emptied all of heaven—for you.

You are loved. Intensely. Unreservedly. Sacrificially. Eternally.

Do you know who you are?

You are a saint—and greatly beloved of God.

In a former church where I was a member, there was a young person named Joeh. That's not the actual name, of course, but since there is no "Joeh" in that church and J-o-e or J-o can be male or female, "Joeh" will do nicely. Joeh was in a relationship with another person when the two of them came visiting our church. But the relationship did not last. The other person left the church and joined themselves to someone else, leaving Joeh all alone.

Joeh stayed in our church and grew in our church until Joeh was helping in our church: leading a group Bible study, teaching a Sabbath School class, actively participating in the drama ministry, leading a food drive for the hungry, and heading up the prayer ministry of the church.

Joeh started a new prayer outreach called Ten Days of Prayer. It became a tradition that has lasted for years in that church. Every year, beginning on January 1, Joeh led the Prayer Ministry in hosting ten consecutive days of prayer. This was a nightly gathering where one of the church members was asked to give their testimony. The people responded with their own comments of affirmation. Then everyone prayed for each other.

After several years—please notice what I am saying—after *several years* during which Joeh arranged these Ten Days of Prayer meetings, Joeh stood up during the response time and said, "For the first time—tonight—I understand that Jesus loves me. I had always known that He loved all of you and that He loved the world. But for the first time in my life—tonight—I now know that He loves me."

Joeh had finally discovered what God had known all along—that Joeh was one of the saints and was greatly beloved.

Love begins with God. "In this is love, not that we loved God, but that He loved us …" (1 John 4:10). Do you remember our scripture at the beginning of this conversation? Do you see what it says? "… which He freely bestowed on us in the Beloved." Just as much as God loved Jesus, He loves you.

Do you know who you are? You are a saint, and greatly beloved by God.

And now I suggest that you take a little time to digest what we have just discussed. This plain, basic message comes as a shock to many Christians. So I'm going to suggest that you think about it and pray about it for a bit. When you have personalized this most basic piece of information about God, I'll be here, ready to welcome you to our next conversation.

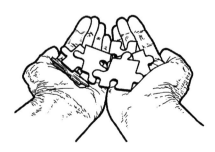

Chapter 3

Do You Know You Are a Christian?

"And when he [Barnabas] had found him [Saul], he brought him to Antioch. And it came about that for an entire year they met with the church, and taught considerable numbers; and the disciples were first called Christians in Antioch." Acts 11:26

Hi. Welcome back. I pray that you've taken a little time to think about our last conversation, to think about being a saint, to know that you are greatly beloved by God. It's a wonderful thing to know about yourself.

I'm glad you decided to return today because I wanted to share with you a second aspect of the answer to my question, *Do you know who you are?*, by telling you another story.

In the 1990s my daughter Jacque worked at a printing shop in Indianapolis that did work for many organizations and private individuals. One of these was a husband/wife team who printed a religious newsletter in which they warned people about various cults and religious heresies. During her interactions with them each month, she spoke about her religious experiences. They knew she was a Seventh-day Adventist.

Imagine her surprise when—one day—the newsletter's headline read "Are Seventh-day Adventists a Cult?" When the next issue came out and the headline was again about the Seventh-day Adventists being a cult, she confronted them with the questionable information they were asking her to print in their newsletter. Because she felt inadequate to speak to their issues, she asked me to respond to their newsletter articles.

I don't have copies of the newsletters, but I recall that the Seventh-day Adventists had made the list of "cults" with these people for several reasons. Here's part of what *I wrote* in reply to their newsletter articles, and reading this will reveal to you what they believed about us.

"The Adventist Church has published 'What Seventh-day Adventists Believe,' a scriptural study of our fundamental beliefs. Nowhere in anything we publish or espouse is there mention of the requirement for circumcision, of Levitical dietary laws still being in effect, of Jerusalem as a required and proper place of worship, of requiring tithe payment for church membership, or of observing Passover."

See what I mean? These people had some really strange ideas about what we as Seventh-day Adventists believe. And I propose to you that they aren't the only ones.

There are lots of people out there in the secular world who don't know who we are. In 2011 a popular weekly news magazine listed the following "facts" about Seventh-day Adventists: We have our headquarters in Utah, we require the keeping of Jewish holidays, we believe that Jesus is *not* God but only a good human being who was used by God, we believe in a negative religion because we *don't do* certain things.

So let me ask you: What *are* the basic beliefs of Christianity, the basic understandings that we have in common with Christians of all denominations—by which all may know that we are Christians? What beliefs do we, as Seventh-day Adventists, believe and hold in common with other Christians? Do you know?

Unlike the Apostle Paul, I'm not a "system" Seventh-day Adventist Christian. I'm not someone who was raised in the church from the time their binky was taken out of their mouth, someone who has attended church all their lives from Cradle Roll up and has seen all the picture rolls and heard all the favorite Adventist texts. I'm not someone who has attended church school from kindergarten on through college and professional school, someone who has taken communion every thirteenth Sabbath for their entire lives.

I'm not a system Adventist. I came into "the message" (I've been around long enough to have learned that phrase) at the ripe old age of twenty-eight. The first denominational book I read was *Daniel and the Revelation* by Uriah Smith. My second book was *The Great Controversy*. And I've been trying to catch up ever since.

And I've been asking: Do we look like other Christians? Do we act like other Christians? Are we really all that peculiar? Are we a cult, a religious sect, as some believe us to be? Are Seventh-day Adventists Christians?

To answer that question, let me share what I learned several years ago from a Seventh-day Adventist pastor: the five "Cs" of basic, mainstream, conservative Christian beliefs. Through the years they've proven to be very useful in understanding what a Christian is. They are:

Christ
the Cross
the Commandments
the Great Controversy
the Second Coming.

Seventh-day Adventists—like you and me—share these five principles with all other Christians. These are the bedrock of Seventh-day Adventist beliefs. I want you to know them in detail, to know their historical foundations and their Scriptural underpinnings so that you will know who you are. I want you to be able to tell others that you are a Christian when they try to convince you otherwise so that they will know—and you will know—that we as Seventh-day Adventists are Christians.

The first "C" stands for Christ.

To think about this first "C," consider our solar system. The sun stands at the center of our solar system. All nine planets (eight if you accept the loss of Pluto as a planet) rotate around the sun in defined orbits, held captive by the powerfully strong gravitational field of the sun. On our earth, the sun is the source of all biological and physical energy. According to our human understanding of biology, life in any form would be impossible without the sun. Our year and our day are determined by our relationship to the sun. The sun is the literal, and, for many, the figurative center of human lives.

In the same way, for many, Jesus is the literal and figurative center of the Christian religion. Yet for the first 250 years of early Christian history there was a struggle within Christianity concerning the nature of Jesus the Christ. Is He God or is He Man? Already at the end of the first century and the Apostolic Era, the Apostle John (1 John 4:2, 3a) recognized this struggle of trying to understand how Jesus could be both God and Man.

Here is the crux of the argument: Who is Jesus Christ; that is, is He God or is He Man? And here are the two polar opposite answers and their supporting arguments that people have come up with over the years.

If He is God, then He cannot die. Therefore, we have no sacrifice and we have no Savior, and thus, no way to deal with sin. If He is Man, then He cannot rise any higher than we can. He is not

> *This is the prime question in all of Christianity: Who is Jesus?*

our Creator, our Advocate, or our Judge. Therefore, we have no Lord and no way to achieve righteousness.

Do you see the problem? The nature of Christ has been at the center of almost every major schism in Christianity. This is the prime question in all of Christianity: Who is Jesus?

In AD 325 the Council of Nicaea debated this very question. While they spoke of other topics (like when to celebrate Easter), the very first topic for discussion was: Who is Jesus? Is He equal with the Father and is therefore God? (This was the Alexandrian position held by its main proponents who were from Alexandria.) Or is He a created being—the first and most perfect—and thus just a man? (This was the Arian position held by a church leader from Asia Minor named Arius—which some mainline churches of today still believe and follow.)

Can you see the council at Nicaea in all their ecclesiastical finery? The group included 318 bishop members along with their entourages, approximately 1,500 people, gathered in the large court where they met in Nicaea. And after several years of wrangling over the topic, they decided overwhelmingly that Jesus is God. Only two of the bishops supported Arius and voted for his position. And since that time the Nicaean Creed—which states that Jesus is "very God" as well as Man—has been the first of several foundation stones of Christianity.

What do Seventh-day Adventists believe about Jesus as the Christ? As good students of the Bible, Adventists read and believe Colossians 1:13–18. In essence it says that Jesus is God incarnate in Man and everything done on earth and in heaven is done for Him and through Him. Jesus Christ is the center of focus for everything "whether things on earth or things in heaven."

The sanctuary is not the focus.

Ellen White is not the focus.

The Sabbath is not the focus.

Jesus Christ is the focus and the central issue around which all other doctrines of the Christian Church revolve. Like the sun in our small solar system, everything in Christianity derives its energy from the Son, revolves around in the gravitational field of the Son, is held in place and given life by the Son. "He is before all things and in Him all things hold together" (Colossians 1:17).

This is not all I could tell you about this topic. But for brevity's sake I'll say that Seventh-day Adventists are Alexandrian Christians and agree with the decision at the Council of Nicaea. Seventh-day Adventists believe completely what it says in John 1:1, 14: "In the beginning was the Word, and the Word was with God, and the Word was God…. And the Word became flesh and dwelt among us, and we beheld His glory, glory as of the only begotten from the Father, full of grace and truth."

Is this what you believe? It is very definitely what Seventh-day Adventists Christians believe—that Jesus Christ is "very" God as well as "very" Man.

The second "C" stands for the Cross. Do you remember the shortest verse in the Bible? Open your Bible. (You did bring it back with you, yes?) Turn to John 11. There it is—verse 35: "Jesus wept."

But do you know why He wept? Back up and look at the story with me for just a moment, beginning in John 11:20. Do you see Martha rushing out to meet Jesus as He approaches the house? She blurts out, "Lord, if you had been here, my brother would not have died" (verse 21). And when Jesus says that Lazarus will rise again, she expresses her faith that Lazarus will rise in the resurrection.

Now look at verse 25. Do you see that Jesus is attempting to teach Martha something more? He tells her that He is the resurrection and the life and asks her if she believes Him. Martha replies, "I believe that you are the Christ, the Son of God" (John 11:27).

Do you understand what just happened?

Martha doesn't get it. Martha understands that the Messiah, the Anointed One, is God in human form, sent from the Father. And she understands

that Jesus is that One. But she doesn't understand that the Messiah is the Lamb of God and that the Messiah was sent by the Father to die so that those who believe that the Father sent Him will *not* have to die. Martha doesn't understand this and neither does Mary. In verse 32, when Mary comes out to meet Jesus, she repeats the very same words that Martha used.

Now look at verse 33. "When Jesus therefore saw her weeping, and the Jews who came with her, also weeping, He was deeply moved in spirit, and was troubled."

Why do you think He is deeply moved and troubled? Is it because Lazarus is dead?

No. Jesus knows He will resurrect Lazarus in just a few minutes.

Does Jesus cry because of the genuine sorrow of the sisters?

No. Jesus knows that there will be great rejoicing for them in just a few moments.

Then what's the reason for His tears?

Jesus looks around at all the people around the tomb. Some are genuinely sympathetic with the sisters for the loss of their brother who is, after all, the sole support of his sisters. Some are curious. Some are spies from Jerusalem sent by the priests. But none of them—*none of them*—knows who He is and why He has come to earth as the Messiah.

Jesus knows that after the resurrection of Lazarus some of these people will rush off to Jerusalem to tell the tale. He knows that the priests—those whose duty it is to give religious instruction to the people about God—will plot to kill Him *and* Lazarus to wipe out the evidence that Jesus is the Messiah. (Look this up for yourself in John 11:53; 12:10, 11.)

So He weeps.

From the time sin began, God has had a problem: How to condemn and eliminate sin from the universe and yet save the sinner that He loves, as in John 3:16—"For God so loved the world …"

Remember how often God has repeated this message. John 16:27 tells us, "For the Father Himself loves you …" First John 4:10 says, "In this is love, not that we loved God but that He loved us …"

And listen to the heart of God stating what His ideal for humans has always been. Found in Jeremiah 24:7, God says, "And they will be My people and I will be their God."

But how can God do this when He is a consuming fire (Hebrews 12:29) to all things evil and when God's people, whom He created and loves, are enmeshed in evil things? How can God, who loves the human beings He created, get close enough to demonstrate that love without killing that very Man whom He loves?

From the beginning, before there was sin, God was prepared with a plan to save those whom He loved. God was prepared for His own sacrificial death in place of the deaths of those He loved. God was prepared to meet the demands of His own righteous justice while, at the same time, saving those who are willing to accept this sacrifice, this incredible gift through His own righteous mercy (see Romans 3:26).

To be sure, certain things had to be in place before the ultimate sacrifice could be made. A substitute sacrificial system—the Sanctuary service—symbolizing the coming death of the Messiah was instituted until the "fullness of time" (Galatians 4:4). But the intention was always to do away with the symbolic ritual when the real sacrifice was made.

Therefore, on a hill outside of Jerusalem, in the year by man's reckoning of AD 31, the Son of God was crucified because "… God demonstrates His own love toward us, in that, while we were yet sinners, Christ died for us" (Romans 5:8). The ultimate expression of the love of God is the Cross. And from that Cross the reconciliation, the offer of peace, the offer of a renewed Covenant with God went out to the whole world.

What do Seventh-day Adventists believe about the Cross? Turn in your Bible and read John 3:16 with me. "For God so loved the world, that he gave His only begotten Son, that whosoever believes in Him shall not perish but have everlasting life." All Christians—including Seventh-day Adventist Christians—know and understand this verse. Yes, Seventh-day Adventists believe in the Cross.

The third "C" stands for the Commandments. (This one *may* stretch you just a bit, but let's try it.)

Have you ever eaten a box of Cracker Jack? Do you remember what was in the box, besides the caramel popcorn and peanuts? Yes, a prize. Do you remember tipping up the box and trying to find the prize before eating all the Cracker Jack? Well, this third "C" has a prize hidden in it—another "C." While we talk a bit more, see if you can guess what the hidden prize is.

The Commandments—there are ten of them and a lot more if you add all of the commandments, including:

- whom not to marry.

- how to bury your personal waste in the desert.

- how to cook your food, and many, many more that dealt with the practical issues of life in that time and place.

All these commandments are important. They are God's way of helping us interact with our world without getting hurt. These commandments are the instruction manual for living on this planet, and God expects us to follow them if we want to be safe. These are not the Ten Suggestions. They are the Ten *Commandments*.

Then Jesus bumps it up a notch in the Sermon on the Mount when He says that the intention of the heart, the motive behind following these commandments, is what's really important. He says that keeping the commandments is not just about behavior but about relationships: relationships with God and relationships with other people.

When asked directly "What is the great com-

Keeping the commandments is not just about behavior but about relationships.

---

mandment in the Law," what did Jesus say?

He quoted Deuteronomy 6:5, "You shall love the Lord your God with all your heart and with all your soul and with all your might," and Leviticus 19:18, "You shall love your neighbor as yourself." I can handle the sentiments of these two commandments. But Jesus bumps it up another notch when He adds, "I want you to be perfect, just like your Father in Heaven is perfect" (Matthew 5:48).

I don't know about you, but I think that this box of Commandment Cracker Jack is hard to swallow. (Do you like Cracker Jack? I always thought it was dry and a bit choke-y myself.)

Paul also found Commandment Cracker Jack hard to swallow, this business about trying to be good, about trying to be perfect. In Romans 7:14–18 Paul said, "I want to be good … and I even know what to do to be good … *but* I can't seem to do it."

Yes, I get the part about burying my waste in the desert. I can even deal with the good and bad food selections—most of the time. But when it comes to loving my neighbor, I'm in trouble.

I can't help but ask, Doesn't Jesus know who I am? Doesn't Jesus know that I'm one of those human beings who's described in Jeremiah 17:9:

"The heart is more deceitful than all else and is desperately wicked; who can understand it?" Doesn't Jesus know that I'm like Peter who said, "Go away from me, Lord, for I am a sinful man"? Can you relate to this? Do you know what this is like? Do you know who you are?

Oh, by the way, have you found the prize in this box of Commandment Cracker Jack yet? No? Okay, keep looking.

Now let me remind you of what Jesus told Nicodemus in John 3:3 (paraphrased and amplified)—"I don't want you to do this on your own. I don't want you to do this in the state you are in. I want you to start over. I want you to be born again."

Peter describes this same idea—with some extra details—to the crowds at Pentecost: "Repent, and let each of you be baptized in the name of Jesus Christ for the *forgiveness* of your sins; and you shall receive the gift of the *Holy Spirit*" (Acts 2:38). Peter says that when you are born again you get two gifts right at the starting point.

Tell me, what are they? Look at the text. What are they?

God tells us that when we are born again, we get two gifts: "Moreover, I will give you a *new heart* and put a *new spirit* within you … And I will put *My Spirit* within you and cause you to walk in My statutes" (Ezekiel 36:26, 27). Look at the text. What are the two gifts? Have you found the prize yet? What is it? What's the hidden "C"?

Concerning this new heart God says, I will "… put My law within them, and on their heart I will write it" (Jeremiah 31:33). Who does the writing?

And whom does Jesus ask the Father to send and abide with us? (See John 14:16, KJV.) What is His job? According to John 14:26, "But the Comforter, the Holy Spirit whom the Father will send in My name, He will teach you all things …" (NKJV).

There's the hidden "C." It's the Comforter. This, my dear Seventh-day Adventist Christian friend, this is the secret of the successful Christian life! This is the hidden prize in the Commandment Cracker Jack! Congratulations! You found it! This makes getting through all that Commandment Cracker Jack worth it. In fact, this prize, the Holy Spirit, is what makes getting through the Commandment Cracker Jack even possible.

---

*This prize,
the Holy Spirit,
is what makes getting through
the Commandment
Cracker Jack
even possible.*

Now turn to 2 Peter 1:3, 4: "… seeing that His Divine Power [Holy Spirit] has granted us everything pertaining to life and godliness, through the true knowledge of Him who called us by His own glory and excellence. For by these He has granted to us His precious and magnificent promises, in order that by them you might become partakers of the divine nature."

The Holy Spirit is the Person who makes this promise of God possible so that you and I can become partakers of the divine nature. This is the Person who gives us the hope that we can become like our heavenly Father.

Do we as Seventh-day Adventists believe in the Commandments? You bet! Look at Revelation 12:17. This verse describes the anger of "the dragon" at those "who keep the commandments of God and hold to the testimony of Jesus." I'm pretty sure that we think that this is us.

But do Seventh-day Adventist Christians believe in the Commandments in the way you and I have been discussing, as written on the heart by

the Holy Spirit? Yes, Seventh-day Adventists have read about spiritual gifts in Ephesians 4, Romans 12, and 1 Corinthians 12. Yes, we believe in the indwelling of the Spirit, in the gifting and the empowering of the Spirit.

But we still struggle. We are still not sure how to keep the Ten Commandments from the heart. Just like the rich young ruler, we still say, "All these things I have done from my youth up; what do I still lack?" (Matthew 19:20). We still don't realize that without the indwelling of the Holy Spirit, when we *don't* or *won't* give Him permission to change our hearts, we fit the description given in Revelation 3:17. We are wretched and miserable and poor and blind and naked.

As Seventh-day Adventist Christians, you and I aren't alone in this. Most Christians—even mainstream conservative evangelicals—know that the process of becoming perfect or "mature," partaking of the divine nature, becoming like our Father in heaven, is a struggle. It's one of the big reasons why we're still in this world and not in heaven. (What? You want to know more about this process of becoming like the Father? Good. Me too. And I promise to discuss this process in great detail when we get to Chapter 6.)

But don't worry. When the crisis comes, when every worldly support that we now use to help us be mature is taken away, then we—like Jacob at the brook Jabbok—will learn to depend on the Holy Spirit.

But for now, yes, we Seventh-day Adventist Christians believe very much in keeping the Commandments of God—even if we're unsure how that's done, even if we don't always remember that there is a Holy Spirit Comforter prize in every box of Commandment Cracker Jack.

Are you looking up these scriptural references as I mention them? I know I've had quite a few in these first three "Cs." Be sure you check them out for yourself. Hold me, and yourself, accountable.

The fourth "C" stands for the Great Controversy.

I hate to bore you with an old story, but it's so true and so useful as an illustration that I'm going to use it right here.

"There was once a group of five very wise men who were blind. When asked to describe an elephant, they each reached out and touched the elephant at the point that was closest to them. The man who touched the elephant's trunk described the elephant as a large, tough vine. The man who touched the elephant's leg described the elephant as a tree. The man who touched the elephant's tail described the elephant as a rope. The man who touched the elephant's side described the elephant as a wall. The man who touched the elephant's ear described the elephant as a large leaf. All the blind men were right and each of them were incomplete in their description of the elephant."

So it is with our fourth "C."

At the beginning of the Bible, in the Garden of Eden (Genesis 3); in the middle of the Bible, in the wilderness of temptation with Jesus (Matthew 4); and at the end of the Bible, in Revelation 12 and 13, the confrontation of God with Satan is clearly described. In other parts of the Bible, Satan's opposition to God is not so clear-cut as it is being portrayed through Satan's surrogates—through the kingdoms of Egypt, or Assyria, or Babylon.

Only on occasion in the rest of the Scriptures does the real story break through. Ezekiel 28:12 is one of those times. We see the prophet taking the King of Tyre to task for his pride and arrogance. "Son of man, take up a lamentation over the king of Tyre," he begins. Then Ezekiel continues in verse 13: "You were in Eden, the garden of God …" Suddenly we know that God is no longer talking about the King of Tyre. He is talking about the being that inspires pride and arrogance in the King of Tyre. He is describing Satan himself.

All Christians read the Bible, but only some Christians get this perspective—something is going on that is bigger than just us. This is a battle "not against flesh and blood, but against the rulers, against the powers, against the world forces of this darkness, against the spiritual forces of wickedness in the heavenly places" (Ephesians 6:12).

Just as the blind men in our story, some Christians read the story of Job but aren't sure that it's an actual story and that Satan is a real person. They think that he's just a characterization of the evil that is in men's hearts. Some Christians have allowed liberal theology to steal away their understanding that God is the all-powerful, immortal Creator who is in a war with a created heavenly being. And this created being is challenging Him for the very throne of heaven.

In understanding this bigger picture, we have more in common with Evangelicals than with other mainstream Protestant denominations. Many of the Evangelicals understand the Great Controversy. Many of them see the elephant in its entirety. They may not use these same words. They may not call it the Great Controversy. But they know the concept.

What do Seventh-day Adventists believe about the Great Controversy? This is the area where we shine. This is probably our biggest contribution—to date—to Protestant theology. For Seventh-day Adventists know that in this Great Controversy the character of God is being challenged. In this very real war the enemy is attempting to replace God's government with a government of his own devising. In this Great Controversy the problem of Sin and its pollution of the world with suffering and death and the grave will be brought to an end. Seventh-day Adventist Christians understand that when this war is finally settled the problem of Sin and its pollution will be at an end and "sin will not rise up again a second time" (Nahum 1:9).

It's true that some denominations and most Evangelicals think that this struggle will result in a literal war in the Middle East. Seventh-day Adventist Christians do not believe that this is how it will end, but many other Christians understand that the heavenly powers are struggling and we Christians are being enlisted on one side or the other of this great war. Oh, yes, in the area of the Great Controversy, Seventh-day Adventists are definitely Christian.

And finally, the fifth "C"—the Second Coming of Jesus.

Now this one should be a no-brainer, right?

Every Christian knows that Jesus is coming again. Right? More is said about the Second Coming of Jesus in the New Testament than about any other topic. One verse in every twenty-five addresses this event. And most mainstream conservative churches teach that Jesus is coming again. All the Evangelical and Pentecostal Churches teach that Jesus is coming again. But there the similarities end.

Let me illustrate the problem. Let's say you live in Ohio and you're coming to see me. You send me a letter in the mail telling me that you are coming to see me. In the letter you describe how you will arrive *when you come*, what you will be wearing *when you come*, who will be with you *when you come*, that you will have a big brass band with you *when you come* (because you are such an important person). *But* you don't tell me *when* you are coming. Yes, you tell me about other events that will be happening around the same time as *when you come*, but you don't give me a specific date.

A long time passes and I've been watching for you to come. But after a while I get tired of waiting. Finally, I try to figure out what happened. I reason that maybe you aren't coming at all, or you came when I wasn't home and I missed the whole happy event, or actually you came in some other way, through an e-mail or a photograph or … You see, the difficulty is that—you haven't come yet.

There are so many theories about the Second Coming of Jesus because … He hasn't come yet.

Do you understand the problem? There are so many theories about the Second Coming of Jesus because … He hasn't come yet. And theories about His Coming run rampant.

However, this fact remains: Jesus is coming back to earth. To this earth. Our planet. And at His coming a great many changes will take place. The Scriptures record earthquakes, the dead coming to life, the end of deception and temptations, a massive loss of life and a great cleansing fire—all at His coming.

Here Seventh-day Adventist Christians differ from many other Christian groups. Here we begin to separate from other Christian groups. In fact, this is the beginning of another discussion we will have elsewhere in this book about who we are and how Seventh-day Adventist Christians differ from other Christians.

For now, let me say that Seventh-day Adventists believe in 1 Thessalonians 4:16, 17. Seventh-day Adventists believe that the Second Coming of Jesus Christ is literal, is noisy, is seen by everyone, and is going to happen soon.

Do Seventh-day Adventists believe in the Second Coming of Jesus? Look at our name. We are Adventists. We believe in the Second *Advent* of Jesus Christ. And we believe that it is going to happen soon. Very soon indeed!

Okay, I've given you some very heavy material to think on. I'm going to suggest that you go somewhere by yourself now and think about the five "Cs." Commit them firmly to your mind. Know who you are. Understand clearly that you are a Christian and be able to explain this fact to others who may ask you, "Do you know who you are?"

When you are ready, come back and we'll continue our conversation.

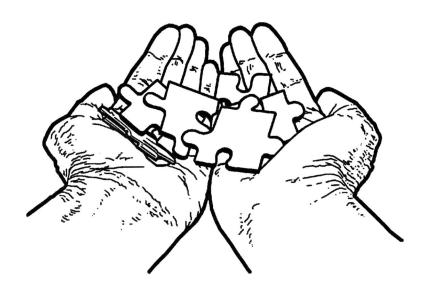

Chapter 4

Do You Know You Are to Live in a Relationship With God?

"Whether, then, you eat or drink or whatever you do, do all to the glory of God."
1 Corinthians 10:30

Welcome again. I was hoping we could speak today. I want to continue my conversation about the question I asked you, "Do you know who you are?"

I'm guessing that by now you've figured out that our first few conversations discussed the characteristics that all Christians have in common. So I want to continue in that same vein by talking about the Christian's relationship with God.

As I get into this conversation, you'll be tempted to say, "Oh, you mean justification" or "I see, you're talking about sanctification." For the sake of this conversation, I don't want to go there. (Let's save that for the next time we get together.) For now I want to address the relationship without

the baggage of theological labels. I know this may be difficult for you to do, but I want to stay clear of splitting the relationship into easily pigeonholed, preconceived ideas. I want to discuss just the relationship, the whole relationship, from start to finish and see it as a single unit. I want to concentrate on the essentials of the relationship itself.

Now as we go along, I need to warn you that this conversation is going to get more intense and more personal. The topic is a large one and a deep one. Therefore, in some areas I'll just be skimming the surface, leaving other areas to be explored more deeply at another of our sessions. I know you will want to ask some questions like, "How does that work exactly?" If I may, please let me put off those questions until the next few conversations. I've been laboring over "how does that work exactly" myself. But let's wait on the specifics until we establish the dynamics of the relationship.

The Scriptural references are many, and I will not read them all with you. We have come far enough in our previous conversations that I think I can suggest some areas of study for you to do on your own. But please, bring your Bible, if at all possible, and use it as we discuss. So, if you're ready, as usual, I need to tell you a story. It helps me get started and hopefully it helps you to focus.

In June 2000 I had a serious illness. I got up on a Tuesday morning and tried to work in my office, but I was cold. I began to urinate more frequently than usual, and it burned slightly. And I was still cold.

I was so consumed with trying to get my work done that I did the usual things people do when they get cold. I put on long pants, a turtleneck, and a sweatshirt. I got a heater from the basement and put it at my feet. I continued trying to work, but my hands were beginning to shake so violently that I could hardly strike the keys of the computer keyboard.

It finally occurred to me (duh!) that this was not normal for the middle of June. I said to myself, "I think I am getting a urinary tract infection." Whereupon I called my urologist friend who agreed with my "astute" diagnosis and said I should get a urine culture and start antibiotics.

My wife had been out shopping in her shorts and T-shirt. When she came home, she wanted to know why I'd put on long pants and heavy shirts and had a heater at my feet. When I told her I was cold, she wasn't impressed.

While talking to her, I suddenly got very hot. The blood began to drain out of my eyes and everything started to go white—not black, but white. Suddenly, I couldn't see very well. I felt faint and said I needed to get my shirt off and lie down before I fell down.

At this point I began to think more seriously about my diagnosis.

"I need to go to the hospital," I told my wife.

Again she wasn't too impressed and started to fix lunch.

But I said, "I mean *now*. I have septicemia and this can kill me in just a few hours. Put down the sandwich. We are going to the hospital." So we did!

While lying on the gurney in the emergency room, I had a very serious talk with the Lord. I said, "This is not the way I thought I would die, Lord." I was crying because I knew that indeed this could kill me in a very few hours. I said, "It's okay if this is the way You want it. You will need to make me strong enough to witness in this. But I would really like to live if that's all right with You. But whatever is Your will is okay with me. Just help me do whatever I need to do to get through this."

Obviously, I didn't die. It was God's will that through the miracles of IVs, antibiotics, and hospital bed rest, my life was preserved.

Four weeks later while I was in Toronto at the General Conference meetings, I e-mailed my friend Steve and told him about my illness. He wrote back and asked, "Why is spiritual salvation by grace, but physical salvation is by works?" In other words (his words), "Why do we get spiritual health by grace but physical health [by following the rules and doing what we know we should do] by works?"

Please think with me now about this question and consider physical health for a moment. Physical health has become part of the secular gospel (the good news) of our present age. People from all walks of life, religious and non-religious, are seeking good physical health. As a Seventh-day Adventist, I'm glad. For one thing, it means that I can find more restaurants with vegetarian options.

But more importantly, you and I—as Seventh-day Adventists—believe that physical health is a part of God's Gospel as well.

In our Seventh-day Adventist Christian theology as it relates to physical health, we understand two things:

1) Our bodies are the temple of the Holy Spirit and should be treated as such. In 1 Corinthians 3:16, 17 Paul says rather pointedly that if we destroy the temple of God, God will destroy us. So we are not to trifle with the health of our bodies. While this is a negative, it is the truth that physical health is important to God.

2) We are whole beings, not just spiritual beings (1 Thessalonians 5:23). The health of each part of our being—spiritual, physical, mental, and social—contributes to the health of the other parts. The health of the physical body directly affects and supports the health of the mind, which is the means by which we reach out to God and to our fellow man. Therefore, here is the positive: Good physical health positively impacts the health of the rest of our being. Physical health is important to us.

And this is where we get into trouble. We try very hard.

Thus, in Seventh-day Adventist theology, physical health is very important. We call it "the health message." You and I try very hard to have a healthy lifestyle. And this is where we get into trouble. We try very hard.

You and I cannot have physical health by *trying very hard*—for the same reason that we cannot have spiritual health by trying very hard. Let me repeat that for emphasis: physical righteousness does not happen by works just as spiritual righteousness does not happen by works.

Now use your sanctified imagination and visualize these three scenarios.

Scenario 1: Imagine two joggers running down a road under a sign that says "Gates of Hell." The first jogger says, "I love this healthy lifestyle—good food, good exercise." The second jogger says, "Yeah, me too. I've never felt so healthy in my whole life."

If we try very hard and are successful, we think we have *earned* good health. We become proud that we have done this great thing and we forget God.

Scenario 2: Imagine an old lady in a wheel chair in a nursing home. A young attendant brings her a bowl of oatmeal. The old lady throws the bowl on the floor and cries out, "Take that stuff away and bring me some eggs right now."

The young attendant says, "But you never eat eggs. You know they aren't good for you and will raise your cholesterol."

The old lady shoots back, "I don't care. I ate healthfully all my life and look at me. I've got cancer. A lot of good that healthful living did me. I always wanted those eggs but never ate them. Now I want my eggs and I'm going to have them."

If we try very hard, follow the rules, but don't get what we think we've *earned*, then we become angry. We become bitter toward God and we turn away from Him.

Scenario 3: Here's one more. Imagine a young man pacing in front of a drug store magazine counter. As he walks back and forth, he is nervously turning a cigarette pack over and over in his hand. With each pass he steals quick glances at the girly magazines, then suddenly shouts,

"What's the use? I can't take this anymore. I give up."

Snatching one of the offensive magazines, he heads for the counter. As he slaps the magazine down on the counter, he shakes a cigarette from the pack and puts it in his mouth.

If we try very hard to follow the rules and *fail*, we get discouraged and quit—and blame God.

The result of *trying very hard* is one of the following: pride, bitterness, or discouragement. Do these three results sound like anything you have experienced? Are they familiar to you? Do you know who you are?

For years I've studied the Scriptures and commentaries on the Scriptures, attempting to understand what many Christians identify as the very core of their Christianity—the Grace-Faith Relationship. For many Christians this is also known as righteousness by faith, but I want to expand that concept, embrace both sides of the equation—both grace and faith, from God's point of view as well as man's point of view. I want to use an incident in the narrative of Jesus' life to illustrate the development of this relationship in the life of one man. Then I want to broaden the application of this concept to our spiritual relationship and our physical relationship with God.

Are you willing to hear me out on this?

I told you at the beginning of this conversation that this would get intense and very personal. When we are asked to examine those ideas that are at the core of our existence, it always gets intense.

Turn in your Bible (which you faithfully brought with you) to Luke 5:18, the story of the crippled man who was lowered through the roof by his friends to obtain physical healing. I'm sure you remember the story, but look at it again and picture it in your mind's eye as it unfolds.

The four friends are in front of the house where Jesus is teaching, but they can't get close to the door because of the crowds of people. Can you see them, frustrated, standing with their friend who is lying on a pallet between the four of them? One of them suggests a different approach, and they all agree. (We could call it a top-down approach, as we might say today.)

Soon the people in the house hear a noise over their heads. They look up as dust and small bits of mortar begin raining down. As sunlight breaks through the ceiling, four sweaty faces peer through at the crowd. More of the roof is removed, and soon the crippled man is being lowered into the very presence of Jesus, right at His feet.

In order to follow the developing relationship between this crippled man and God, I'm going to make some sanctified estimations of what I think are the thought processes going through the minds of the characters, expanding beyond what is actually written in the story. And to reassure you that I'm not superimposing my thoughts and ideas on the story, I'm going to pause from time to time to add some commentary from Paul and some of his friends. In fact, let's get some Pauline help right here by reading my favorite Bible definitions of Grace and of Faith.

Keep your finger in Luke 5 and flip over to Ephesians 2:4–7 for a scriptural definition of Grace. "But God, being rich in mercy, because of His great love with which He loved us, even

> *When we are asked to examine those ideas that are at the core of our existence, it always gets intense.*

when we were dead in our transgressions, made us alive together with Christ … and raised us up with Him, and seated us with Him in the heavenly places, in Christ Jesus, so that in the ages to come He might show the surpassing riches of His grace in kindness toward us in Christ Jesus."

I know that you are reading along in your Bible just as I am reading with you. (At least, that's what you are supposed to be doing.) But if you want to see Grace defined further, you might spend some time on your own comparing this passage with Colossians 2:9–15 or Titus 2:11–14.

But for right now, do you see the hallmarks of Grace in this passage in Ephesians? First, God is full of mercy and great love. Second, however, we are helpless sinners, enemies of God (Romans 5:6, 8, 10), being "dead in our transgressions." Third, because of these characteristics of His, God *gives* us the *gift* of Jesus Christ (read further in Ephesians 2:8, 9 to see the gift) to make us alive, raise us up, and seat us with Jesus. This is God's Grace.

Now, without losing your place in Luke 5, turn to Romans 4 and read verses 18–22: "In hope, against hope, he (Abraham) believed … without becoming weak in faith, he contemplated his own body, now as good as dead … and the deadness of Sarah's womb, yet with respect to the promise of God, he did not waver in unbelief, but grew strong in faith, giving glory to God, and being fully assured that what God had promised, He was able also to perform."

This is my favorite definition of Faith. Abraham believes not in his own abilities, but in the promise and abilities of God. Abraham 1) believes in God and 2) believes that what God has promised, He is able to do. (If you're interested, you can compare this with Hebrews 11:6, then for fun, read Hebrews 11:5 and carry this concept of faith back to the Enoch story in Genesis 5:21–24, which will get you prepared for a later conversation.)

But for now, having gotten these two definitions of Grace and Faith in place, let's return to our story.

Can you see the crippled man lying there on his old, worn pallet? He is looking up hopefully at Jesus just as his friends—still on the roof—are looking down hopefully. What do you see? What happens to initiate this budding Grace-Faith Relationship? Where is the Grace? Where is the Faith?

It's easy to spot the Faith, and what a faith! The crippled man's friends have brought him to Jesus. While they can do nothing more, they're here where *Jesus* can do something. Of course, in the process they've made the crippled man and themselves extremely vulnerable (always the downside of genuine Faith). For starters, they've opened themselves up to the ridicule of the Pharisees and the crowd for disturbing this famous teacher. This is to say nothing, of course, about the anger of the man (Peter, a tradition suggests) who owns the house and who now has a hole in his roof.

But where is the Grace, you ask?

Good question, for it would seem that Jesus and God have played only a passive role so far in this story. But wait. How did Jesus come to be in this house in the first place to be found by the crippled man and his friends? To answer that we need to go back in time, back past Jesus' announcement that "the time is fulfilled and the kingdom of God is at hand" (Mark 1:15), back past the angel's announcement to Joseph that "you shall call His name Jesus, for it is He who will save His

Abraham believes that what God has promised, He is able to do.

people from their sins" (Matthew 1:21), back past the prophecy of Isaiah that "a child will be born to us … and His name will be called Wonderful Counselor, Mighty God, Eternal Father, Prince of Peace" (Isaiah 9:6).

We must go back even past God's promise to the serpent that He would put "enmity between you and the woman, and between your seed and her seed" (Genesis 3:15). We have to go back to that time "before the foundation of the world" when God the Father chose us to be with Him in Christ Jesus (see Ephesians 1:4). This is the beginning of God's Grace to mankind, and this is the Grace that you see here in this first step as the crippled man moves toward a relationship with God.

After all that, let me pause here a moment and summarize to be sure that you caught it. *God always makes the first move toward mankind* before mankind moves toward God. And God's first move in the Grace-Faith Relationship with you and me began a long time ago when He offered the Gift of Jesus Christ "from the foundation of the world" (Ephesians 1:4). And this first move by God and the Gift has continued down to us individually to this very moment. In the same manner, *our* first move in response to God's Grace (in the Grace-Faith Relationship with God) is to *choose* to display Faith and move toward God.

(As I describe it, the Grace-Faith Relationship can sound like it's made up of individual steps. It is not. The moves are connected and run together in a continuous movement, like swimming in deeper and deeper water or like a crescendo of musical sound becoming louder and fuller. The Grace-Faith Relationship does not occur in jerky steps, but flows, becoming deeper and more intense.)

How do you and I display Faith, you ask?

Observe the crippled man. He *chose* to place himself—with a little help from his friends—vulnerably at the feet of and into the will of Jesus. To observe a similar *submission* of self, look at the

publican and his prayer in Luke 18:13: "God, be merciful to me, the sinner!" We have many fancy theological words for this initial phase of the relationship, but it really comes down to making yourself completely vulnerable to the will of God.

While this is a *choice* that we must first make in our hearts, God says that He wants us to do what the crippled man did. He wants us to make a public declaration of our decision to submit to His will, to "confess with your mouth Jesus as Lord, and believe in your heart that God raised Him from the dead, you will be saved" (Romans 10:9).

More than that, Paul graphically describes how we seal this first step publically and in our own hearts in Romans 6:4, 6, 11. Turn there in your Bible and let's read. "Therefore we have been buried with Him through baptism into death, in order that as Christ was raised from the dead through the glory of the Father, so we too might walk in newness of life … knowing this, that our old body of sin might be done away with, that we should no longer be slaves to sin … even so, consider yourselves to be dead to sin, but alive to God in Christ Jesus."

When you *choose* to place yourself in God's hands, when you display Faith like this, you become "dead to sin but alive to God …" You aren't really *dead*, but you are metaphorically insensate to the hostile control of Sin and no longer living under the fear of the fatal penalty of Sin. This is the same transaction that Jesus calls "being born again" (John 3:3). Again, the metaphor says that you do not come out of a physical womb, but you do enter into such a startlingly new relationship with God that it's like starting over as a newborn. Paul describes this by saying that we're "becoming a new creature" (2 Corinthians 5:17). Much like the metamorphosis of a caterpillar into a butterfly, Paul emphasizes that you are still you, but so remarkably different as to be described as new.

In this "born again, new creature" state, you are no longer whatever it was that you were before, whatever it was that created a barrier between you and God—and other humans: Greek or Jew; Black, Hispanic, or Caucasian; male or female. You are no longer a child molester, a philanderer, a murderer, or a thief. You are no longer a gossip, a busybody, or a pew warmer. Do you think I've included everyone? Did I include you? Do you know who you are?

When you and I display this Faith, we are now Christians; that is, we now belong to Christ. We are new creatures in Jesus. We are clean, without spot or blemish (Ephesians 5:27; 1 John 1:9). To initiate the Grace-Faith Relationship with us, God, in His grace and mercy, gives us the Gift and we respond by choosing to submit to Him in Faith.

If I wrote this as an equation, it would look like this:

Grace		**Faith**
God Gives the Gift	⇄	Man Accepts and Submits
(Cross)	(Choice)	(Baptism)

Now that we have entered into this Grace-Faith Relationship with God, how do we maintain this new relationship, this new faith experience, this *new creature-ness* day by day?

Jesus suggests the answer in John 15:5. (Are you still following along in your Bible?) "I am the vine," Jesus says, "you are the branches; he who abides in me, and I in him, he bears much fruit; for apart from me you can do nothing." In John 14:16, 17, Jesus says that He will request the Father to send the Holy Spirit who will abide in us, and in verse 23 He says that both the Father and the Son are abiding in the believer who loves Jesus and keeps His word. Jesus says that the secret to remaining in the relationship is *abiding*.

Look at our crippled man on the pallet. What do you think is going through his mind? He knows that whatever happens to him next will be up to Jesus. In other words, the crippled man has *chosen* to place himself in the hands of and under the control of Jesus and to *abide* there until Jesus does whatever Jesus decides to do.

But what if Jesus ignores him, makes fun of his unusual entry into the room, or orders him out of His sight? The crippled man has made a second choice (he made his first choice when he entered the room); he trusts that Jesus will do something for him. This is the Job choice (see Job 13:15). Whatever the risk, he has chosen *to abide* in Jesus.

To get some perspective as to what might be happening in the mind of the crippled man, let's continue to read our Pauline commentary in Romans 6:12–14. "Therefore, do not let sin reign in your mortal body that you should obey its lusts, and do not go on presenting the members of your body to sin as instruments of unrighteousness, but *present yourselves* to God as those alive from the dead, and your members as instruments of righteousness to God" (italics supplied).

Paul describes our continuation in the Grace-Faith Relationship with God by telling us to "present" ourselves.

The crippled man certainly has presented himself to Jesus. But now what does he *do*? Have you ever been in this predicament? You now have a Grace-Faith Relationship with Jesus but you don't know what else to *do*. You've tried to *do* all the right things in your life but you know you have failed, miserably, in some cases. You know you haven't *done* enough, will never be able to *do* enough.

Do you know who you are?

I've found myself in this same situation many times. Haven't you? I know that theologians still don't agree about the meaning of Romans 7:18, 19, but here are my thoughts: "For I know that nothing good dwells in me, that is, in my flesh; for the *willing* [or choosing] is present in me, but the *doing* of the good is not. For the good that I want [choose], I do not do; but I practice the very evil that I do not want [choose]."

Theologians may not know, but I know *exactly* what Paul is saying and what he is feeling. I have been in this same predicament a thousand times. I know what is *right*. I can even *choose* to do right. But I don't have *the power* to actually *do* right. Instead, I find myself doing wrong.

Have you been here?

Do you know who you are?

Okay, then, we're in this together.

So let's see if Paul can explain this. Let's go back to where we left off in Romans 6 at verses 16, 17, and 19. "Do you not know that when you *present yourselves* to someone as slaves for obedience, you are slaves of the one you obey, either of sin resulting in death, or of obedience resulting in righteousness. But thanks be to God that though you were slaves of sin, you became *obedient from the heart* to that form of teaching to which you were committed … so now *present your members* as slaves to righteousness, resulting in *sanctification*" (italics supplied).

Whoa! Time out! We're into some heavy words—abide, present, obedience, sanctification. Let's back off and try to understand what's happening here in terms of our Grace-Faith Relationship. I've personally tried to do this on my own: to obey. I suspect that you have, too. This is the hard part of Christianity. And besides, we haven't seen clearly the two sides of our Grace-Faith equation.

Where is the Grace of God?

How do we display Faith?

So, let me ask this question about what we've just read. Where is the *do* in *present yourselves?* Where does it say that you *do* anything? It says *choose* to become a slave of righteousness, and the result is sanctification.

But you ask, if I wanted to stop smoking or to begin paying tithe, wouldn't I need to change something in my life, *do* something in order to qualify for sanctification? Don't I need to obey?

What's the connection between *present yourselves* and *obedience from the heart*?

Read Philippians 2:12, 13: "So then, my beloved, just as you have always obeyed, not as in my presence only, but now much more in my absence, work out your salvation with fear and trembling; for *it is God who is at work* in you, both to will and to work for His good pleasure" (italics supplied).

To "present yourselves."
To "obey."
To "abide."
All of these expressions are actually the same concept.

According to Philippians 2:13, God does the *work* and God's *will* is the one being followed. Then what's our part? Romans 6:16 said to "present yourselves." Philippians 2:12 said to "obey." John 15:5 said to "abide." Do you understand what Paul and his friends are telling us? All of these expressions are actually the same concept.

How do you "present your members as slaves to righteousness"?

You give up control of yourself. In "confident expectancy" (the biblical concept of *Hope*) you *choose* to trust Someone else to become your master. You are no longer making all of your own choices based on your own thoughts and ideas except as you choose which one will be your master, sin or righteousness. To "present for obedience" is the same thing as the old-fashioned word trust. It means "confident expectancy," placing yourself under the guidance of God and permitting His Will to power you when you have no willpower of your own. In other words, choosing to let Him *do*. At this point, just like the crippled man's friends when they set him down in front of Jesus, what *you do* comes to an end. According to Philippians 2:13, now it is for Him to will and to work according to His good pleasure.

(If it interests you, at some other time do a concordance search of the theological concept of *hope*, especially in Job, the Psalms, Lamentations, Acts, and the letters of Paul.)

Thus, Paul concludes in Romans 6:20, 21 (turn there and check me out) that if you *choose* to be a slave to sin you will do those things of which you are ashamed, and that leads to death. But if you *choose* to be a slave to righteousness, you will be sanctified, resulting in eternal life.

Do you see the difference? Slavery to sin is a choice followed by an active process: "you will do …" Slavery to righteousness is a choice followed by a passive process: "you will be …" Slavery to sin is a choice which causes you *to do* things that result in death. Slavery to righteousness is a choice which causes *righteousness to be done to you* that results in eternal life. Death is *earned*, like wages. Righteousness—and its result, eternal life—is *given* to you; it's a gift. And I'm hoping that—like the prize in the box of Commandment Cracker Jack—you noticed the other free gift that Jesus included here and what this Free Gift is to do *in you*. If you aren't sure what I'm talking about, see John 14–16 and check your notes from our last conversation. If you still aren't sure, please bear with me until we have a chance to talk about that topic in a later session (Chapter 6).

Our crippled man on his pallet has chosen to abide in Jesus, to place himself in full hope in the hands of Jesus. He is under no illusion as to his own abilities. This is all he *can* do. The change that will take place now will be the will and the work of Jesus. And the crippled man is about to receive eternal life.

"And seeing their faith, He [Jesus] said, 'Friend, your sins are forgiven you'" (Luke 5:20).

"Obedience from the heart" (Romans 6:17) means deliberately choosing to remain (to abide) under God's control. To say it more precisely: By *choosing* to abide in God, we receive from God our second Gift of the Holy Spirit. In the Spirit, we can confidently expect (hope for) an internal change that will enable us to obey by His guidance and through His power when we were unable to obey on our own. To remain in the Grace-Faith Relationship with God, you and I must Abide in Hope.

How does the Holy Spirit make this internal change? How does this actually work?

Turn to Ezekiel 36:26, 27: "Moreover I will give you a new heart and put a new spirit within you; and I will remove the heart of stone from your flesh and give you a heart of flesh. And I will put My Spirit within you and cause you to walk in My statues, and you will be careful to observe My ordinances."

This just barely gets us started as to "how this actually works." To follow it further will require a conversation devoted entirely to this topic. So let's leave it for now but return to it in a later conversation in Chapter 6. (Have you noticed how much I am anticipating Chapter 6?) But be sure that you notice in Ezekiel 36:27 the prize from the Commandment Cracker Jack box without which we can't continue in this relationship at all.

If I wrote this continuation of the Grace-Faith Relationship as an equation, it would look like this:

Grace		**Faith**
God Gives the Gift	⇄	Man Abides and Trusts
(Holy Spirit)	(Choice)	(Internal Change of Heart)

Does the man on the pallet trust in what Jesus has just said? The scribes and the Pharisees who are present certainly don't believe. Look in the man's eyes. What do you see? There's a shining light in his eyes that suggests "peace with God through our Lord Jesus Christ" (Romans 5:1). The man knows that he is forgiven, that his relationship with God has changed, that he has begun to internally change—and it is enough. Like Shadrach, Meshach, and Abednego who were threatened with the fiery furnace, whether he is physically healed or not is no longer the point. He is forgiven. He is in a Grace-Faith Relationship with God, and this is enough.

Is this enough for you? Are you prepared to give up on *trying very hard*? Are you ready to let the Holy Spirit *work* and *will* in your life?

Can you see yourself as the crippled man?

Do you know who you are?

O kay, back to Luke 5. I know your finger is getting tired being stuck in Doctor Luke's gospel, so let's return to our story and see how the crippled man's new Grace-Faith Relationship with God is about to be tested. For now Jesus tells him, "Get up, and take up your stretcher and go home" (Luke 5:24).

What will the crippled man *do*? Why will he even try? What would you do?

It's such a foolish thing to attempt. He has not gotten up in years. That's the reason his friends lowered him into the room on his pallet in the first place—because he couldn't walk. What does the crippled man know that you and I don't know?

Please understand that this man must now *do* what he is being asked to do. He must obey. This Grace-Faith Relationship is no free-and-easy, do-nothing relationship. In the face of peer, cultural, and worldly pressures to do otherwise, we must make very difficult choices to accept and abide in Jesus. And we must now *do* what we are instructed to do. As Paul describes it: "If we live by the Spirit, let us also *walk* by the Spirit" (Galatians 5:25), or as John describes it: "the one who says he abides in Him [Jesus]; ought himself to *walk* in the same manner as He walked" (1 John 2:6).

Because it's not about getting the work done. It's about entering into the Grace-Faith Relationship

(Verify this in your Bible, and look at Ephesians 5:2 and Colossians 2:6 for further study.)

Now read Galatians 5:5, 6 with me. "For we through the Spirit, by faith, are waiting for the *hope* of *righteousness*. For in Christ Jesus neither circumcision nor uncircumcision means anything, but faith [beginning the relationship] working [continuing the relationship] through love [consummation of the relationship]" (italics supplied). This is the "obedience from the heart" that Paul described in Romans 6:17.

The man knows that he is forgiven, that his relationship with God has changed, that he has begun to internally change—and it is enough.

But what's the difference, you say, between doing the work within the Grace-Faith Relationship and doing the same work because I'm able to do it on my own? The work gets done either way, right?

No, it does not, *because it's not about getting the work done*. It's about entering into the Grace-Faith Relationship; it's about Faith, abiding Hope, and Love. It's about motive. And motive is everything.

This is the meaning of Jesus' teaching in Matthew 7 about those who say "Lord, Lord" but who never really knew Him, or He them. This is the difference between not stealing the cookies from the cookie jar because you think you will get a reward and not stealing the cookies because you love your mama. On the one side—the side of doing it yourself—this is the "filthy rags" righteousness of Isaiah 64:6. On the other side—the Grace-Faith Relationship side—this is why Paul is so exultantly joyful in Romans 8:1–4: "There is now therefore no condemnation for those who are in Christ Jesus. For the law of the Spirit of life in Christ Jesus has set you free from the law of sin and death … in order that the requirement of the law might be fulfilled in us who do not walk according to the flesh, but according to the Spirit."

This is a matter of "obedience from the heart."

Until the heart is changed, doing the right thing is just a cover up for the unrepentant, unchanged heart, a condition you and I cannot change on our own.

The crippled man knows that he is accepted and loved (Grace), and in love he wants to respond (Faith). Anything that Jesus asks of him, he will try to *do*. So Jesus says, "Get up and walk." And because the crippled man is loved and loves in return, he tries to get up. And Jesus, who has already changed the man's heart, changes his body. And he gets up and he walks! In fact, I imagine that he leaped up. The result of faith and abiding hope and love is healing and wholeness.

After these several conversations, I feel free to address you as a friend. So, my friend, what is it that you have been trying for years to *do* and have

not been able to *do*? You can do just like the crippled man did. Place your faith in Jesus. Abide in Him, hope in Him, and give Him complete reign. And be prepared to do whatever He asks of you, because you love Him. Because when you try, He will change you.

Now—do you know who you are?

The final consummation of this Grace-Faith Relationship with God is Love, His love for you and your answering love for Him.

And the Gift?

There have been gifts all along the way. Did you miss the fact that there is also a gift to be offered here in the third step?

The first Gift was Jesus and His life, death, and resurrection for you. The second Gift was the Holy Spirit and that confidently expected internal change which is the will and the work of the Holy Spirit (a topic we will take up in a future

Until the heart is changed, doing the right thing is just a cover up for the unrepentant, unchanged heart

conversation). And the third Gift. It is the external change and the power to *do* that comes as a result of the internal change, including the promised eternal life that involves some extraordinary external changes. (Another Gift comes here also, but I want to save this surprise for a later conversation. If your curiosity is insatiable, look at Galatians 5:22, 23 and 2 Peter 1:4 for clues as to what conversation we will be having in the future. For completeness I have added this Gift to the following diagram.)

If I wrote the consummation of the Grace-Faith Relationship as an equation and added it to the establishment and the continuation of the relationship, it would look like this:

Grace		Faith
God Gives the Gift	⇄	Man Accepts and Submits
(Cross)	(Choice)	(Baptism)
God Gives the Gift	⇄	Man Abides and Trusts
(Holy Spirit)	(Choice)	(Internal Change of Heart)
God Gives the Gift	⇄	Man Loves and Acts
(Motive and Power to Do)	(Choice)	(External Change— Empowered to Obey)
(Character of the Father)		(Change of Character and Personality)

This is the Grace-Faith Relationship—the Gifts that God chooses to give to us and the response of Faith that we choose to give Him. The entire relationship is based on God's Grace, our Faith response, and our choice. To take a quick peek at a future conversation, this is the Covenant of Faith, abiding Hope, and Love that God wants to establish with all His children and is the central core of all Christian experience. And this interactive experience with God we hold in common with all Christians.

Now I have to tell you that as I have worked through this understanding of the Covenant Grace-Faith Relationship, I just had to stop and ask: Why does God's salvation system work like this? What's the purpose of all this Faith, abiding Hope, and Love? What goal is so important that God asks us to work within a relational system that is a stumbling block to religious people and is foolishness to the secular mind (1 Corinthians 1:21,22)?

I want to share with you in a simple, elementary fashion a biblical summary of what I think God is doing, and some of my own personal reactions to these summary points. I realize that the comments are going to come fast and furiously, so I'll go slow and allow you time to think on each one.

1) Romans 1:16, 17: "For I am not ashamed of the gospel, for it is *the power of God for salvation* to everyone who believes …"
    (Aren't you glad for salvation? I know that I'm all for salvation!)

2) Romans 1:17: "For in it the *righteousness of God* is revealed."
    (Hmm. Didn't we already know that God is righteous? Or is there some kind of controversy over whether God is righteous? Are there bigger things happening here than just our salvation?)

3) Two verses here—one from Paul and one from Peter: Ephesians 2:10, "For we are *His workmanship*, created in Christ Jesus for good works …" 2 Peter 1:4, "… that you might become *partakers of the divine nature.*"
    (Stop and think about this for a moment. There's more involved here than just our salvation or our sanctification. Something bigger is happening here. Why this restoration of the image of God in man? What's that all about?)

4) Two more verses from Paul: Philippians 2:15, "… that you may prove yourselves to be … children of God … in the midst of a crooked and perverse generation, among whom you appear as *lights in the world*." Ephesians 3:10, "… in order that the manifold wisdom of God might now be made known through the church to *the rulers and the authorities in the heavenly places*."

5) And the last comment from Jesus Christ Himself, Matthew 5:16—"Let your light shine before men in such a way that they may see your good works, and *glorify your Father* who is in heaven."

(In points 1 through 4, italics are supplied.)

In a nutshell, besides our salvation, God is putting in place 1) His righteousness 2) by restoring in His people His own image 3) so they can be as shining lights before men and heavenly beings 4) to glorify the Father who is in heaven. By developing in His people Faith, abiding Hope, and Love, God is creating His Witnesses (Isaiah 44:8). Yes, that's you and me; actually, that's all of God's people. In Scripture these people are also called the Remnant (Genesis 45:7; Isaiah 37:31, 32; Romans 11:1–5), a concept that we'll return to in Chapter 11.

But for now, before we discuss this in more detail, please consider that this is the role of the Remnant (God's People) before the world. By their Faith, abiding Hope, and Love in their Covenant Grace-Faith Relationship with God, the Remnant are to testify that God can do what He says He *will* do (Isaiah 43:10–12; Acts 1:8). As Revelation 14:12 tells us, "These are they who keep the commandments of God and their faith in Jesus." The witness of the Remnant is essential to the vindication of God.

Is the answer to my original question beginning to come into focus for you?

Seventh-day Adventist Christian: Do you know who you are?

Not to lose sight of where our discussion began—physical health—do you know what the two texts are that we always use to talk about the Christian's reason for healthful living?

- "Or do you not know that your body is the temple of the Holy Spirit who is in you, whom you have from God, and that you are not your own? For you have been bought with a price; therefore *glorify* God in your body" (1 Corinthians 6:19, 20).

- "Whether, then, you eat or drink or whatever you do, do all to the *glory of God*" (1 Corinthians 10:31). (Italics supplied.)

Notice what both of these scriptures give as the reason for doing these *physical* things: to bring glory to God.

Now be careful. Let me sound a note of warning to you. Frequently we *bring glory to God* by following the laws of healthful living and by reaping a healthy, long life as a result. But sometimes we *bring glory to God* by *not* being healed. Just as in our spiritual life, sometimes in our physical life we are asked to go through trials by His power and not be healed. As God told Paul concerning his own physical issues, "My grace is sufficient for you, for My power is perfected in weakness" (2 Corinthians 12:9). In other words, God says to Paul, "I can be more honored by your enduring this physical problem than by My taking it away."

Tradition says that Elisha the prophet died of a slow, malignant disease even though he had asked for, and received, a double portion of the Spirit of Elijah. Which took more of God's Spirit, do you think, to be carried off in a fiery chariot or to die a slow death from a malignant disease?

The point is—if you place God in control of your life because you love and trust Him, you must be prepared to follow His agenda. He will probably ask you to witness for Him by observing the health laws that you know and by reaping the physical benefits. But He might ask you to witness for Him and bring glory to Him in some way other than through a miraculous healing. Your part is to submit (accept, abide, and be empowered). His part is to will and to do. (I warned you at the beginning of this discussion that it would get intense.)

Now to answer Steve's question, which opened our discussion, by applying our understanding of spiritual health to our physical health—all righteousness, all wholeness, all health is by Grace-Faith and not by works. We—you and I—*do not* keep the laws of health because we want to be healthy. We keep them because we have a Covenant Grace-Faith Relationship with God. Just as Jesus noted in the Sermon on the Mount (Matthew 5:21–32) concerning God's Ten Commandment Law about murder and adultery, the committing of the act itself is important but the motive behind the action is more important.

When we commit to the Covenant Grace-Faith Relationship, we choose to place God in control of our lives (Romans 6:17). We choose to love Him, wanting to respond positively to what He asks us to do (Galatians 2:20). We seek the Holy Spirit to will and to do in us so that by His power we can do what we ourselves know we, on our own, are incapable of doing consistently (Romans 8:11).

Yes, the result of obeying the laws of health is having good health (Exodus 15:26). But that is *not* the underlying reason *why* we obey the laws of health nor is it how we obey the laws of health. We obey because we love God and we want to abide in Jesus our Lord (3 John 3). And since we know that we—on our own—are incapable of consistently

Your part is to submit. His part is to will and to do.

obeying even the laws of health (just those that we happen to like, and then not consistently), we ask for the Holy Spirit's power to enable us to obey Him, even in the laws of health (Ephesians 3:16). We want to witness to the whole world as "shining lights" (Matthew 5:16) to our faith that He is not only our Savior, He is our Lord. We want to follow Him wherever He might lead us (Revelation 14:4).

When I was lying on that gurney in the emergency room, I didn't know where the Lord was leading me except that I knew I was expected to witness for Him and bring glory to Him. Even now I don't know what else might be asked of me. About a month after that trip to the emergency room, I was diagnosed with lymphoma. If I thought dying of an infection very quickly was going to be hard, now I had to think about dying slowly from cancer.

But I know this: Jesus loves me. Jesus died for me. Not just an ordinary death, but a slow death on a cross of shame. The second death! The death of separation from God, His Father. And He did it for me. That is love that I cannot ignore. I have to respond, like Job, "Though He slays me, yet I will hope in Him" (Job 13:15). Or like the Three Worthies facing the fiery inferno, "Even if He does not [save us] … we are not going to serve your gods or worship the golden image" (Daniel 3:18).

For me, God is in charge.

This is my effort to work out my own salvation: By my choice, I let Him have His will and His doing for His good pleasure in my life. In my Covenant Grace-Faith Relationship with Him, my choice is to let Him be in charge and to glorify Him by obeying as He empowers me to do—because He loves me so.

Because He loves *you* so, my friend, I am praying that this is also your choice.

Wow, that was much longer than I intended, and you were very patient and hopefully blessed. Even so, we were able to discuss just an overview of the Covenant Grace-Faith Relationship. As I suggested, some areas we can explore in more detail in a later session. But now, it's time for a little break. When you come back, I want to expand on the idea that there are three—count them, three—parts in the Grace-Faith Relationship.

Why three? We'll talk about it at our next session.

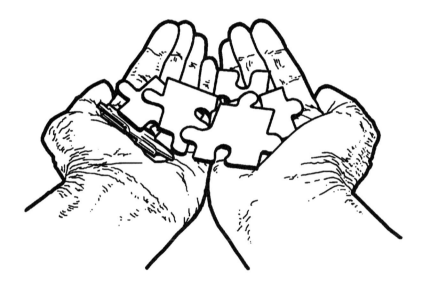

Chapter 5

Do You Know You Live by the Gospel of RGB?

"But now abide faith, hope, and love, these three; but the greatest of these is love."
1 Corinthians 13:13

Well, here we are again, comfy chairs and all. (I pray that you are in a comfortable position wherever you are.) I hope you had a good rest and took a little time to think about what we discussed last time. Even as an overview, I know it was a lot to absorb in one sitting. But I'm trying to limit my discussion to only a review of the characteristics that you and I—as Seventh-day Adventists—share with Christians in general. I am praying that you'll take some time when you are alone to think about and to solidify in your own mind these basic concepts.

And I'm going to trust that you and I don't need to read all of our Bible texts together. We'll read some because the words speak directly to a concept I will share. But please don't let me get away with dropping in Bible texts that you've not checked out for yourself. This is not about my opinion of what the Bible says. Be a good Berean (Acts 17:10, 11). Study "to see whether these things were so."

Having said that, let's look at Genesis 3:1.

It's a beautiful day in the garden where Eve is wandering by herself. She finds herself near the tree—the tree that Adam and Eve were told to avoid. She wonders to herself why they should have to avoid it. She comes closer. She remembers that she and Adam were told often enough to stay away. Something called "death" will happen if they touch it or eat it.

She is standing right under it. It certainly looks harmless enough.

A voice speaks. Eve is startled. She has never heard any voice but the voice of Adam and the voice of God. It's a pleasant voice. Where is the voice coming from?

"Has God said you shall not eat from every tree of the garden?"

Of course not, she thinks. "From the trees of the garden we may eat," she says. *To whom am I talking?* she wonders. Then she recites from memory, "But from the fruit of the tree in the middle of the garden, God has said, 'You shall not eat from it or touch it, for then you will die.'"

She's not sure what "die" means. She has never seen anything dead. She has heard the story of the war in heaven. She knows about the unhappiness and the loss of contact with God. But did anyone die? She has never seen anything stop living.

"You will not surely die," the voice says.

Now Eve can see that it's a serpent which is talking to her, a serpent in the tree, a serpent that is obviously eating the forbidden fruit. And he isn't dead. He's very much alive—and talking!

"For God knows that in the day you eat from it—your eyes will be opened and you will be like God, knowing good and evil," the serpent says.

"And when Eve saw that

1. The tree was good for food
2. That it was a delight to the eyes
3. And that the tree was desirable to make one wise,

she took from its fruit and ate" (Genesis 3:1–6).

Let's stop right here. Did you see those three go by? Good for food; delight to the eyes; desirable to make one wise. Let's see the same three in 1 John 2:16. Turn there with me. "For all that is in the world, [1] the lust of the flesh and [2] the lust of the eyes and [3] the boastful pride of life." Here are the same three in a slightly different form.

Please note: it's a set of three. Sin came into the world in a set of three. And the solution to the Sin problem came in a set of three. If we were to turn to Matthew 4 (you can turn there if you like and see it for yourself), we would see that Jesus overcame the temptations of the evil one in a set of three. I want you to consider this concept—a set of three. The Gospel is always presented in a set of three. The plan of salvation is always presented in a set of three. And I call this set of three—R-G-B.

Maybe you have a DVD player or a fancy television at home; most everyone does. Have you ever looked at the variety of ways to hook up things to it? If you looked on the back of your DVD player or television, you would find that one of the plug-in options is a section with three colors—red, green, blue—R-G-B. I want to plant this in your brain so that every time you see R-G-B you will think of God, the plan of salvation, and the gospel.

As I have studied my Bible over the years, I have found a great many instances of a set of three. Ephesians 2:5, 6, Titus 2:11–13, and 2 Peter 1:1–4, 5–9, 10, 11 would be three quick examples as well as multiple instances in Revelation 1, but I will not attempt to mention them all. Instead I want to introduce the concept of R-G-B to you through one of Paul's famous scriptures. "But now abide Faith, Hope and Love, these three; but the greatest of these is Love" (1 Corinthians 13:13, NKJV).

In our last conversation we talked about the Covenant Grace-Faith Relationship as a single concept. Today I want to break that concept down into its three parts and look at the contribution each one makes to the whole.

The Gospel is always presented in a set of three.

The first part of R-G-B involves Faith and a Gift, the Son.

Come with me and let's explore a very familiar story—the story of the prodigal son as found in Luke 15. We aren't going to read it because I think you already know it. But in case you want to follow along (and I hope you do), the story starts in verse 11. For my purposes I want you to see some aspects of this story that we don't normally notice.

You know the story. It tells how the boy demanded his inheritance, took it, and wasted it in a far country in riotous living. You know how he ended up taking care of pigs and eventually was so hungry that he wanted to eat the pigs' food. And when he came to himself, he decided to return to his home and to his father.

As he came within sight of his home, he saw his father running toward him. The boy had already decided to return home as a servant and not as a son. But the father would not hear of such a thing. Despite the boy's protests, the father gave him the best robe, and a ring for his hand, and sandals for his feet.

The "R" stands for—Received From.

I want to zero in on the gifts that the father gave. Gifts are exactly what they were—gifts that the son did not deserve. He had given away every right to any of these symbols of a son: the best robe, the family ring, and sandals. Only family members wore the fancy robes; servants wore plain pullover smocks. The family ring certainly was only for family members. Servants went barefoot; only sons wore sandals. He deserved nothing, nothing that pertained to being a son. And yet he received from the father—gifts.

Although I suspect you know this, let me just make sure you understand whom we are talking about. You and I are the prodigal son. Our Seventh-day Adventist Church is the prodigal church. This world is the prodigal world.

Romans 3:10–12 tells us that "there is none who are righteous, not even one. There is none who understands, there is none who seeks for God: All have turned aside, together they have become useless; there is none who does good, there is not even one."

These are harsh words. But they are true words that pertain to you and me.

Do you know who you are?

Daniel—precious, blessed Daniel, who was highly esteemed (greatly beloved) by God Himself—in his prayer recorded in Daniel 9, placed himself in this category. If he was in this category, then we must include ourselves in this confession. None of us are righteous; that is, none of us do the right thing all the time. Not one of us *consistently* seeks after God. Not one of us deserves the Gift. But God in His Grace gives the Gift to us. The most precious Gift in all of heaven is given to us. And what is that gift? Jesus Christ, yes? I know that you know that.

But keep going; stretch it out. Jesus Christ, the second member of the Godhead, takes on the physical, mental, emotional limitations of humanity and becomes one of us (see John 1:14) in order to save us (see Luke 19:10). There is so much more to say about the Gift, but right now just concentrate on the fact that the Grace of God gave us the Gift. We did not deserve it. We did not earn it. In fact, we were not consulted about whether the Gift would be offered to us.

John 3:16 says, "For God so loved the world that He gave His only begotten Son that whosoever believes in Him should not perish but have everlasting life."

God gave the Gift. It is ours—if we will receive it.

The "R" stands for—Received From.

And notice how we receive it. Ephesians 2:8: "For by grace you have been saved through faith

…" This is the Covenant Grace-Faith relationship. God's Grace reaches out to us, and we respond in Faith by reaching out to Him by accepting His Grace—a never-ending relationship that we discussed in our last conversation. For now, just concentrate on the Gift of Jesus Christ that is accepted by Faith. Received from.

Can you see yourself in the first part of the Grace-Faith Relationship?

Do you know who you are?

The second part of R-G-B involves abiding in Hope and a second Gift, the Holy Spirit.

Let's return to our story of the prodigal son (yes, *our* story). And let's turn back the clock to the time before the Prodigal decided to come home. Can you see him there in the pigsty, holding the pigs' food—the locust pods—in his hand, considering the possibility of eating them himself? And then, Luke 15:17 says, "And when he came to his senses …" or as the KJV says, "And when he came to himself …"

Here is a young man who has been led by the devil into so much sin, who has so steeped himself in sin, who has become so enslaved to sin, that he has been reduced to the level of a pig. Suddenly this young man develops amazing insight into his own situation. Really?

Let me remind you of another scripture, John 16:8: "And when He comes, He will convict the world concerning sin, and righteousness, and judgment."

This young man was not alone. Someone was watching over him, tending to him, nudging him into an awareness of his situation. Call it conscience, call it a still, small voice, call it what you will. The Holy Spirit has a job to do and He does it—sometimes with all the force of a hurricane and sometimes with such a gentle breeze that you would not know the air had moved except you feel it deep within your soul.

John 3:8 says, "The wind blows where it wishes and you hear the sound of it, but do not know where it comes from and where it goes: so is everyone who is born of the Spirit."

Jesus was describing the work of the Holy Spirit. Now watch the young man begin to *grow in* the Spirit.

The "G" stands for—Growing In.

"And when he had come to his senses" could be translated in my own very free translation (MOVFT) as "and when the Holy Spirit had prompted him once again with the memory of the love of his father."

This young man did not come to his senses all by himself. He didn't know how. He had forgotten how. But the Holy Spirit knew how. The Holy Spirit knew that the Father still loved him. And the Holy Spirit knew how to raise up that wonderful working of the mind called—Hope.

Watch this Hope *growing in* this young man.

The Holy Spirit brings to the young man's mind scenes that he needs to remember. Let's read these particular passages together. (I pray that, wherever you are, you have your Bible open. I want you to see for yourself the impact of these verses.)

In Luke 15:17, he remembers the generosity of his father toward the hired servants—"How many of my father's hired men *have* …"

And in verse 18, he remembers the constant love of his father in the face of all his young foolishness—"I will get up and go to my father …"

And in verse 19, this young man knows that he has thrown away his inheritance and that all his own righteousness is worthless—"I no longer deserved to be called your son …"

The Holy Spirit helps him remember, convicts him of his helpless situation, and convinces him of the goodness of his father. And this gives him

Hope, not in himself, but in the goodness of his father.

Remember: You and I are the Prodigal. We're wallowing in the pigsty of our own sins. Are you with me here? You have to see yourself in the pigsty. You have to be convinced of your Sin or you can't *grow in* this kind of hope.

Do you know this kind of Hope?

Do you know who you are?

This is not the "I hope the airplane lands safely" or the "I hope my favorite baseball team has a winning season" kind of hope. This is not wishful thinking. Neither is this kind of Hope, this biblical Hope, based on "I hope someday my goodness will be good enough." This Hope is not based on my being good enough.

This kind of Hope is expectant certainty—the certainty of the faithfulness of God.

Hebrews 10:23 says, "Let us hold fast the *confession of our hope* without wavering, for He who promised is *faithful*." (Italics supplied.)

Now watch what this Hope does to our young prodigal. Read Luke 15:20: "And he got up and came to his father."

The Holy Spirit was abiding with this young man. And the young man decided to take an action based on the promptings of the Holy Spirit. "And the Spirit of truth … He abides with you, and will be in you" (John 14:17). "But when He, the Spirit of truth comes, He will guide you into all the truth" (John 16:13).

The "G" stands for—Growing In.

Do you see the young man *growing in* the Spirit? The young man has decided to "abide" with the Spirit; that is, he has decided to give the Spirit permission to do what the Spirit does—change us. "But we all … beholding in a mirror the glory of the Lord … are being transformed into the same image … from the Lord, the Spirit" (2 Corinthians 3:18).

The Holy Spirit has a whole range of tools to help us grow. The Spirit uses the tool of the

enlightened Word to teach us (see John 16:13–15). He uses the tool called the gifts of the Spirit

You have to see yourself in the pigsty.

to guide us and empower us in experiential ministry (see 1 Corinthians 12:7, 11; Ephesians 4:12, 13). And He uses the tool of intercessory prayer to lead us to compassionately help others (see Mark 6:31–34; 1 John 5:14–16). And while these tools are leading us externally to help others, these tools internally are growing our character (Ephesians 4:13, 15, 16). We call the results of this process "character." Paul calls these results the "Fruit of the Spirit," which develop from being "led by the Spirit" (Galatians 5:18). Peter calls these results "becom[ing] partakers of the divine nature" (see 2 Peter 1:4) which flows directly from the "precious and magnificent promises" of God (including the Holy Spirit, kinship, and Covenant.) We've already talked about some of these previously and some we will cover later.

But for now just concentrate on abiding. Concentrate on the *growth* of character that the Holy Spirit does *in* us by abiding in us.

Can you see yourself abiding in the confident Hope that we have in the love and faithfulness of God—to transform us?

Do you know who you are?

The third part of R-G-B involves Love, Covenant, and the Father.

Now, once again, let's return to Luke 15:20 to our young man who is on the road toward home. He is weary for he has walked a long way. While he is returning in the certain hope of his father's goodness of character, nevertheless, as he approaches the point where the road to his house leaves the main road, he is a bit hesitant. What if … ?

Now I'll let you in on a little secret, a secret that the Prodigal doesn't know about himself, something that you might not notice, if you don't look closely. On the outside he is still the same filthy boy in ragged clothes, walking barefoot like a servant. But inside, he is being changed. He is *becoming like* his father.

Did you see it there in Luke 15:19—"I am no longer worthy to be called your son; make me as one of your hired men."

This is the young man who could think only of himself, when he demanded his share of the inheritance, when he wasted it on himself in riotous living, when he was wallowing in self-pity in the pigsty. Now he is thinking of someone else. He is thinking of what his return will do to his father's reputation. He is concerned about someone else, just like his father who has been concerned about him all along. He is *becoming like* his father.

The "B" stands for—Becoming Like.

Becoming like his father: the father who has been watching for him, the father who has been longing for his return, the father who has been wanting to be with his son, the father whose one consuming thought has been: "I love my son. I want to be with my son."

Are you with me here? Do you remember the one consuming desire of God the Father?

Ever since the Garden of Eden one thought and one project alone has been driving Him. The same statement is in Exodus, Ezekiel, and Revelation.

And it's in Jeremiah. Turn in your Bible and read this one with me. Jeremiah 31:33 says, "'But this is the covenant which I will make with the house of Israel after those days,' declares the Lord. 'I will put My law within them, and on their hearts I will write it; and I will be their God, and they shall be my people.'"

All the words are there in that scripture. This is Covenant—the gift of Faith and the promise of Grace in a binding contract. This is God's promise of Hope—to us—the house of Israel. (Remember: You and I are the Prodigal. As Christians, we are also the New Testament house of Israel.) This is the Loving change of heart, the internal change that makes us like Him externally. This is the final resolution of the Great Controversy: "I will be their God, and they shall be My people."

The "B" stands for—Becoming Like.

We don't have the space to write it all out. But turn to Ephesians 1:1–14 and I'll wait while you feast your eyes on what the Father has desired for us from the beginning of human history. I beg of you: stop and read it right now. Read it through slowly and absorb what has been promised in each phrase. I'm waiting; please go ahead and read it.

I'm serious as a heart attack. Did you read it?

Good. Now let those promises sink into your very being—because this is what the Father has planned for you. Yes, you.

This is the Covenant He wants to make with you.

Do you know who you are?

I know we've talked about this in previous conversations. But we can't say it enough since we always seem to forget it. Why does God do this? First John 4:16 tells us, "We have come to know and have believed the love which God has for us. God is love, and the one who abides in love abides in God, and God abides in him." God loves YOU. God wants to be with YOU and wants YOU to be with Him. (And me, too—praise God!)

That's why God is running. Did you see that in Luke 15:20—"But while he was a long way off, his father saw him, and felt compassion for him, and *ran* and embraced him, and kissed him." One of the most awesome images in the whole Bible is of God running to embrace *you*.

Do you know you are loved that much?

Do you know who you are?

Through God's promises of 1) the Gift of Faith *received from* Jesus and 2) the abiding Hope in the Gift of the Holy Spirit to empower us for our *growing in* Jesus, 3) God in His Love wants YOU to *become like* Jesus.

2 Peter 1:4 says, "For by these [actions of God] He has granted to us His precious and magnificent promises in order that by them you might become partakers of the divine nature, having escaped the corruption that is in the world by lust."

There you have it. The Plan of Salvation. Righteousness by Faith. R-G-B.

Received From—the beginning point

Growing In—the process

Becoming Like—the end product

Received From—Redemption and Salvation

Growing In—Character Growth and Development

Becoming Like—Restoration, Reconciliation, and Judgment

Received From—Repentance

Growing In—Revival

Becoming Like—Reformation

If you are theologically and etymologically inclined:

Received From—Justification

Growing In—Sanctification

Becoming Like—Glorification

And just to press it home, just as an extra added bonus to get you thinking:

Received From—First Angel

Growing In—Second Angel

Becoming Like—Third Angel

---

*This is the Gospel—
the full Gospel—
the three part Gospel.
It's all here in R-G-B.*

There's more. But you get the idea. This is the Gospel—the full Gospel—the three part Gospel. It's all here in R-G-B. "But now abide Faith, Hope, Love, these three: but the greatest of these is Love" (1 Corinthians 13:13).

And so I have come to the end of the conversations where I am comparing you and me—Seventh-day Adventist Christians—to our Christian brothers and sisters. In our coming conversations we will move on to a discussion of the deeper, more intense, and more intimate relationship that God is calling us to have with Him. We will also explore some of the metaphors we use as Christians in referring to ourselves in this relationship with God. These discussions are not parenthetical. They are very much a part of the answer to the question: Do you know who you are? And the concepts we discuss will be very important to the last section of our discussions: Who we are in the Time of the End.

For now, take a break. Think about what we have discussed so far. When you are ready, come back and take a seat across from me (or wherever you might be). I'll be waiting here for you.

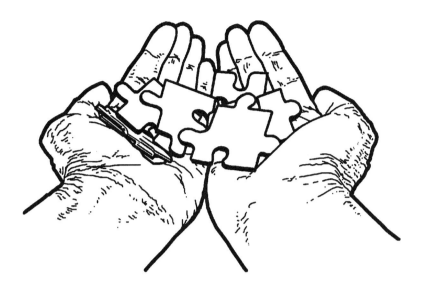

Chapter 6

Do You Know You Are to Walk With God?

"By faith Enoch was taken up so that he should not see death:
and he was not found because God took him up; for he obtained the witness that before his
being taken up he was pleasing to God." Hebrews 11:5

"And Enoch walked with God; and he was not, for God took him." Genesis 5:24

Welcome back. Make yourself comfortable while I explain what I want to do during our next few discussions (chapters, for those of you whose circumstances do not allow an imagined personal conversation). If you're keeping track, this is the "middle section" in our series of conversations that I mentioned in our very first session together. This is the point where I want to transition to a discussion about having a deeper, more intimate, more intense relationship with God.

I know I'm setting aside the opportunity to have any further, fruitful discussion of the basics of a Covenant Grace-Faith Relationship with God. I'm quickly brushing past several crucial areas that we would explore—if that was our purpose. Instead, I'm trying to stay on task, to "leav[e] behind the elemental teachings about the Christ, [to] let us press on to maturity, not laying again a foundation" of the plan of salvation (Hebrews 2:1).

Understand that this "middle section" discussion is not just for Seventh-day Adventists, although it's my self-assigned task to speak to you as a Seventh-day Adventist Christian. Please be aware that many Christians of other denominations also desire a deeper relationship with God. These people are also God's people; He is drawing them, as well as drawing you, closer to Himself.

Most importantly, this conversation is not parenthetical, but absolutely essential. We—you and I—cannot mature in our relationship with God unless we have this particular conversation, receive this particular understanding, and act on the conclusions that we will discover. We cannot go on in our conversations—until we have this one. To be perfectly honest with you, twice I've moved this conversation from later on in our series to this crucial spot. Quite frankly, if what we are about to discuss *does not happen* in the Christian life, the rest of what we have to discuss *will not happen* in the Christian life.

This is especially true for Seventh-day Adventists. Unless and until Seventh-day Adventist Christians allow God (pay particular attention to how I say this)—*unless and until* Seventh-day Adventist Christians *allow God* to make this concept operative in their lives, individually and corporately, they will not be able to participate in and carry out the special assignment given them by God. It won't happen. It's just that crucial.

Now that I have your attention, stay with me for just a little more introduction.

As Seventh-day Adventists we've adopted several metaphors and code words to refer to ourselves—and to Christians in general—without really knowing what they mean. At times, because we don't truly understand them, our use of the metaphors only serves to add another layer of murkiness to our understanding of who we are. Remember the curiously hard question that we are attempting to answer: "Seventh-day Adventist Christian, do you know who you are?"

The code words or metaphors, among others, include: Witness, Remnant, Laodicea, and Priest. I want to explore these concepts and clarify them so

that you and I, as Seventh-day Adventists, will have a clearer idea of their contextual meaning. To say it another way, the discussions we are about to have

---

If what we are about to discuss does not happen *in the Christian life, the rest of what we have to discuss* will not happen *in the Christian life.*

---

concerning these concepts is critically important in preparing us to discuss the unique role and work that God's People, and Seventh-day Adventists in particular, are to carry out during the Time of the End.

But before we can consider these metaphorical concepts, we must have the conversation that I had asked you to allow me to put off until later: "How does it actually work?" Later has now come. So if you're settled in and comfortable, let's begin.

My grandson Braeden had continuing difficulties at his Seventh-day Adventist grade school, the Gulf Coast School in St. Petersburg, Florida. He was a "boy," enthusiastically and totally committed to whatever he was doing, including little pranks and play. Grabbing, pushing, tackling, hugging—they were all the same to him—a display of genuine affection. So it was with great difficulty that he was learning socially appropriate behavior. In the process he was getting into trouble.

His teacher adopted a clever mechanism for letting each student know—on an hourly basis—where they were in this process. Excessively inappropriate behavior earned you a "red card" (yes, just like in soccer). In similar fashion as behavior improved the child moved up through a "yellow card" to an "orange card" to a "green card." A green card with a sticker was for the most excellent behavior. Braeden resided mostly at "orange," occasionally slipped into "yellow," and once in a while into "red." A "yellow" three days in a row or a "red card" resulted in some dire consequences from his father, which he desperately wanted to avoid. Staying out of the "yellow" zone for five days in a row resulted in a reward from his father. He was making progress.

Braeden and I had several conversations about his difficulties. He knew what he should do and truly wanted to do it, but sometimes he found himself unable to do it. "Papa (my code name to differentiate me from his other grandfather), what am I going to do?"

I explained to him that he was not able to do the things he truly wanted to do. He could not make the changes in his behavior on his own. He needed God's help, and specifically, he needed the Holy Spirit as his coach and helper. I told him that he needed to pray for the gift of the Holy Spirit each morning when he first woke up.

One day when he got a "yellow card," I asked him what happened. "I forgot to pray this morning." On another "yellow card" day he said, "I prayed two times today, but it didn't seem to help."

I can imagine Enoch (yes, the Enoch from Genesis 5), growing up in a world going radically anti-God and struggling, in the same way as Braeden struggled, to maintain a Covenant Grace-Faith Relationship with God. Can you see him sitting quietly in his private meditation place as he asks, "How do I do this? More prayer? More evangelism efforts? More church time?" He is really struggling. In tears, he pleads, "What can I do so that I will be more pleasing to You, O God? So that I can truly walk with You?"

(This is your opportunity for a self-Bible study. Compare Hebrews 11:5 with Genesis 6:22.

Then ask yourself this question: do these two words—"walk" and "pleasing"—belong together? You can get a head start on our conversation and the beginnings of an answer by looking at 1 Thessalonians 4:1 and Colossians 1:10).

How does this actually work? How do we become "pleasing to" and "walk with" God?

As I pointed out in our two previous conversations, the Gospel comes in three parts. Every Christian prays to be included in the final third part of the Gospel: "And the dead in Christ shall rise first. Then we who are alive and remain shall be caught up together with them in the clouds to meet the Lord in the air, and thus we shall always be with the Lord" (1 Thessalonians 4:17, NKJV). And all Christians know the first part of the Gospel: "Believe in the Lord Jesus Christ, and thou shalt be saved" (Acts 16:31, KJV)

However, for most people, this is all there is to their Christianity. They feel convicted by the Spirit. They express sorrow for their sins and repent of their past life. They go through a major struggle to make a choice for Jesus, and they make that choice. They know they want to go to heaven at Jesus' Second Coming. But they wonder, what happens until then?

The thief on the cross made the transition from the first part to the third part in a few short hours. But for most of us the time lapse between our choice to follow Jesus and our elation at His Second Coming involves years, not hours. We have to live in a real world that does not follow the Ten Commandments. We have to maintain our Christianity in the midst of people who do not. We know that if we are to follow Christ's Great Commission we must grow our Christian witness. And in the back of our minds is this gnawing uneasiness: something is supposed to happen between the first part, our personal acceptance of the Gospel, and the third part, the culmination of the Gospel. What's the second part? What should Braeden do? How does Enoch "walk" with God?

How does this actually work? Does this sound like a question you have asked?

Do you know who you are?

Do you remember the diagram that I presented to you two conversations ago? Good, I was hoping you would. (If you don't remember, welcome to the human race. Review Chapter 4 for an in-depth review, or scan it for the chart and a quick explanation.)

Grace		Faith
God Gives the Gift	⇌	Man Accepts and Submits
(Cross)	(Choice)	(Baptism)
God Gives the Gift	⇌	Man Abides and Submits
(Holy Spirit)	(Choice)	(Internal Change of Heart)
God Gives the Gift	⇌	Man Loves and Acts
(Motive and Power to Do)	(Choice)	(External Change— Empowered to Obey)
(Character of the Father)		(Change of Character and Personality)

This diagram outlines the Covenant Grace-Faith Relationship—the Gifts that God chooses to give to us and the response of Faith that we choose to give Him. The entire relationship is based on God's Grace, our Faith response, and choice.

Notice three things:

1) The Covenant Grace-Faith Relationship is always initiated by God, never by us (Romans 5:10).

2) While one member of the Godhead is especially emphasized at each level, all three members of the Godhead are involved at all three levels. For example, although the offering of Jesus on the cross is the emphasis of Level 1, in reality the Father loves (John 3:16), the Son sacrifices (Matthew 20:28), and the Holy Spirit convicts (John 16:8). All Three are wooing us to accept the Gift of the Cross.

3) Each level is more complex than it appears in the diagram. For example, Level 1 shows the Cross as the First Gift being offered by God. What it doesn't show in its simplicity is that there are multiple gifts inherently present in the Gift of the Cross: the gift of cleansing (1 John 1:9), the gift of righteousness (2 Corinthians 5:21), the gift of adoption (Galatians 3:29), and the gift of reconciliation (2 Corinthians 5:18).

Again, I'm not pressing you to look up every scriptural reference, especially if you know it. But I am asking you to check me out. Make sure I am using the Scriptures correctly. Find out, like the Bereans, by looking in the Scriptures to see if these things are so.

Now focus with me on Level 2 of the diagram. This is Braeden's second part, and I want to unpack it in its complexity—to see how it actually works.

This Level 2, this second part is the same as the "G" of Growing In of R-G-B, which I presented to you in our last conversation. Two conversations ago I also introduced the concept of "obedience from the heart." (As a reminder, look in your Bible at Romans 6:17.) If you remember that conversation, you will recall that "obedience from the heart" means the same thing as "present yourselves" (Romans 6:16), "abiding" (John 15:5), and "obey" (Philippians 2:12). So let's look at the connection between Growing In and obedience from the heart. If obedience comes from the heart, then let's talk about the heart—the human heart of the Scriptures. Let's see what growth takes place there.

I hope you have learned by now that I don't do anything half-heartedly (pun intended). We are going to dig deeper than most Christians ever go. Open your Bible to Romans 10:8–10. Yes, let's look at this one together. (It's what Paul says to do, so let's do it.)

"But what does it say? 'The word is near you, in your mouth and in your heart' [Paul is quoting Deuteronomy 30:14]—that is, the word of faith which we are preaching, that if you confess with your mouth Jesus as Lord, and believe in your heart that God raised Him from the dead, you shall be saved; for with the heart man believes and with the mouth he confesses, resulting in salvation."

The mouth and the heart—Paul reverses the two words in his explanation, but let's keep them in the same order. To confess with the mouth, to make a biblical confession, is to speak a public declaration of faith in Jesus Christ as Savior and Lord. This is what Simon Peter did when he declared that Jesus was "the Christ, the Son of the living God" (Matthew 16:16). This is the choice a Christian makes in Level 1 in our diagram, the choice we discussed previously, the choice we confirm at baptism.

As the Covenant Grace-Faith Relationship deepens, this choice will become more than an intellectual declaration; it will become a declaration of love. "You shall love the Lord your God with all your heart, and with all your soul, and with all your mind" (Matthew 22:37). It will become worship. This choice to love and to worship becomes the motivation for all the other choices in our diagram. This is why Jesus pressed Simon Peter at the breakfast by the lake (John 21:12–17). Jesus wanted Peter to carry his Messianic declaration beyond an intellectual confession of the mind to a confession of love and worship of the heart. But I am digressing—quite a bit, actually—from my intended goal for this conversation. You see, I love the story of Peter so much. But let's return to the conversation at hand.

In response to our confession of the mouth and belief in the heart, Jesus promises: "I will ask the Father and He will give you another Helper, that He may be with you [abide] forever" (John 14:16). According to one of the first scriptures I learned as a Seventh-day Adventist, this same promise is described as "I will give you a new heart and put a new spirit within you; and I will remove the heart of stone from your flesh and give you a heart of flesh. And I will put my Spirit within you and cause you to walk in My statutes, and you will be careful to observe My ordinances" (Ezekiel 36:26, 27). It would appear that when the Holy Spirit comes, He has something to do with obedience—and with the heart.

What does it mean to "believe in the heart"? What is the "heart"? Where is the human "heart"?

Let me draw for you my simplified model of the functions of the human mind and the location of the "heart." After you have looked it over, I will try to give you a simplified explanation of its contents.

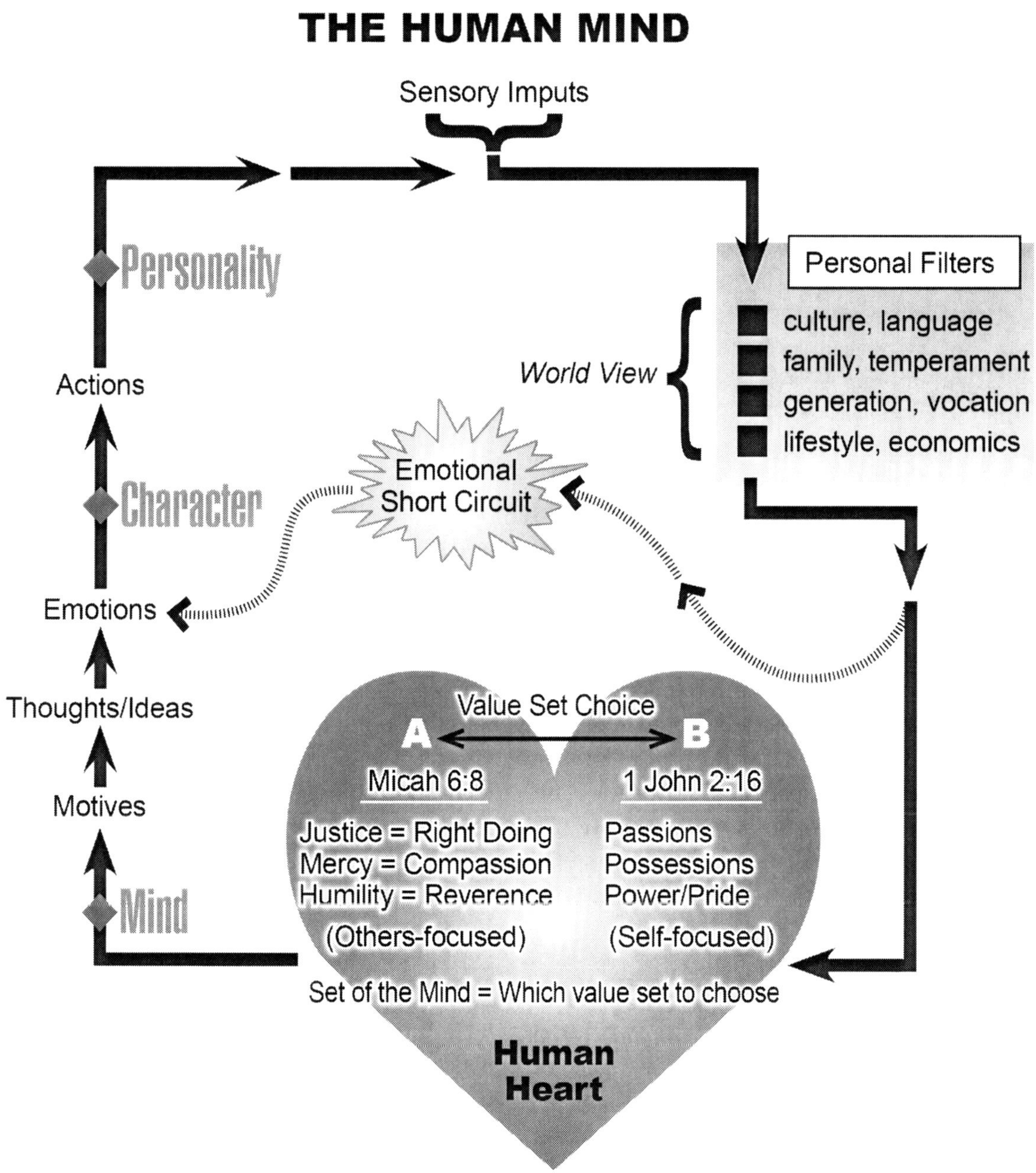

THE HUMAN MIND

Sensory Imputs

Personality

Actions

Character

Emotions

Thoughts/Ideas

Motives

Mind

Personal Filters

World View

- culture, language
- family, temperament
- generation, vocation
- lifestyle, economics

Emotional Short Circuit

Value Set Choice

A ↔ B

Micah 6:8 | 1 John 2:16

Justice = Right Doing | Passions
Mercy = Compassion | Possessions
Humility = Reverence | Power/Pride

(Others-focused) | (Self-focused)

Set of the Mind = Which value set to choose

Human Heart

I know, it seems a bit complex. So let me walk you through the diagram, especially my description of the human "heart," where it fits and how it functions.

We receive and process sensory inputs of all kinds. As humans with past experiences, we perceive these inputs through our interpretation screens, including, specifically, our cultural norms and taboos, our language and communication skills, our core family, our temperament, our vocation (and its accompanying culture), our generational cohort, our economic situation (have vs. have-not, extravagant vs. penurious, generous vs. miserly), and our lifestyle choices and assumptions. This is the way we "see" the world, our worldview. Therefore, we each perceive these inputs differently, which is why witnessing and evangelism must be contextualized. But in each of us these inputs and their perception and interpretation will reach our central core—the place where the choice is made as to what these inputs mean, what decisions we should make with regard to them, and how we should act in response to them.

We make these choices by comparing these inputs to *a set of values* that we hold as humans. We value one motive over another; we hold one object as of more worth than another; we consider one idea to be more beneficial than another; we judge one action to be more productive than another.

We use this currently held set of values to make "value" judgments about the sensory inputs that we interpreted through our worldview screens. From these value judgments we make our decisions—why, what, and how we will function. From these decisions we take a course of action. Based on the results of these actions, we modify the reception of our next set of inputs. That is, based on the previous pattern of response and its result, we modify the perceiving screens—our worldview—that we use to interpret the next set of inputs that we receive.

As you can see in the diagram, the set of values you choose to use will make the difference as to what thoughts, ideas, decisions, emotions, and actions will come from your heart. "But the things that proceed out of the mouth come from the heart" (Matthew 15:18; Luke 6:45). For an incredibly interesting study, look up the phrase "out of the heart" in a Bible search program. Especially note in Deuteronomy (8:14; 9:3, 4; 13:3), in the story of David (2 Samuel 13:39; 1 Kings 2:4), and in the story of Josiah (2 King 23:3 and onward), and others.

This place of selecting a value system, of

> *This place of selecting a value system, of selecting a "mindset," is the human "heart."*

selecting a "mindset," is the human "heart." When we accept Jesus as Savior and Lord, He sends the Holy Spirit to suggest and—if we allow Him—to replace our old set of values, which were based on natural human inclinations, with a new set of values based on the choices and actions of Christ. He comes to give us a new heart (Ezekiel 36:26, 27) and to write on our heart (Jeremiah 31:33) the "Law of the Spirit of life in Christ Jesus" (Romans 8:2). This selection of a "mindset" is a choice of which values we will use—to choose "the mind set on the flesh [which] is death" or "the mind set on the Spirit [which] is life and peace" (Romans 8:6).

By Faith we use our will (our choice of value set) to accept God's offer of *continuing* the Covenant Grace-Faith Relationship. "If we live by the Spirit [Level 1], let us also walk by the Spirit [Level 2]" (Galatians 5:25). If Level 1 is a Faith choice to receive the first Gift of God (the Cross), Level 2 is also a Faith choice to receive the second Gift of God (the Holy Spirit), which is "not as a result of works, that no one should boast" (Ephesians 2:9).

What I've just said in the two preceding paragraphs is the "Cliff's Notes" version of the core idea of this conversation. I could quit now, but you would say, "Yeah, okay. But how does it actually work?" So come with me while we dig deeper.

As I warned you in the beginning of our conversation, Level 2, the second part of our Covenant Grace-Faith Relationship—just like Level 1—is a bit more complex. The Gift of the Holy Spirit comes in two phases: phase A, the "choosing" of the value set, and phase B, the "acting on" the choice. The "choosing" is what I really want to focus on, for it is the essence of Level 2. But the "acting on" (it actually belongs in Level 3, which we will take up in a later conversation) is so closely tied to the choice of the value set that I have to begin to talk about it here as well. I know. It's messy. And we'll talk about that in just a bit, too.

So let's begin with phase A—the choosing of the value set in the human "heart."

If we are normally functioning humans, our current set of values will resemble 1 John 2:16—the lust of the eyes, the lust of the flesh, and the pride of life. This set of values is based on what we most desire to have (possessions), what we most desire to experience (passions), and what we think will most enhance our personal power base (pride and power). This value set is what Romans 8:6 calls "the mind set on the flesh" and what Romans 8:2 calls "the law of sin and death." This value set is self-focused.

Does this sound familiar?

Do you know who you are?

However, when we accept Jesus Christ as our Savior and Lord, we also accept His Gift of the Holy Spirit. When He comes, He introduces to our mind a new set of values (the mind of Christ—Philippians 2:5), which resembles Micah 6:8—to do justly, to love mercy, and to walk humbly with our God. This set of values is based on

- what God most wants us to choose (do justly—Christ's choices and Christ's actions),

- what God most wants us to feel (love mercy—Christ's compassion for others),

- and what God most wants us to "know" (walk humbly—Christ's intimate experience with the Father)

in our relationship with Him (His Grace as our God and our responding Faith to Him as His people—just as Jesus did). This is what Romans 8:6 calls "the mind set on the Spirit" and what Romans 8:2 calls the "law of the Spirit of life." This value set is others-focused. (Did you notice that each value set comes in three parts? I will leave it to your "pure mind" to decipher the significance of this idea. If you are struggling to understand, review Chapter 5.)

The struggle in the human heart—as to which value set to choose—is a constant one for the natural human inclinations are powerful and are constantly being exploited by the enemy. Besides, the choice to follow God's "mindset" of Micah 6:8 is completely outside the human experience. Almost all of us are born naturally inclined (the Greek word for *iniquity* means "bent") to choose like 1 John 2:16. From birth most of us are trained by our parents and pressured by our peers to function like 1 John 2:16. As we mature we are surrounded by a world that functions like 1 John 2:16. This is the natural human experience.

However, in neurophysiology we learn that the brain can be rewired, new pathways of thinking can be learned. However, it takes repeated uses of the new pathway (repeated cycles of choosing Micah 6:8 under the guidance of the Holy Spirit) to make it the default response. It takes daily, repeated conscious choices to use the new pathway for it to become the natural direction, the default choice. It takes a lifetime of training to make this possible. (Personal Bible Study Alert: For one of Paul's explanations of what this looks like as it plays out in the Christian life look up Galatians 2:20.)

Following directly on the heels of phase A (so closely that it seems but an extension of phase A) is phase B—the power to actuate the choices we make.

The Apostle Paul knew about Level 1 of our diagram (Romans 3:21–26)—that God's quick intervention on behalf of Adam and Eve (Genesis 3:15, 21) in the Garden of Eden (later ratified by the life and death of the Lamb of God (Romans 5:17–19)) saved them from utter slavery and preserved for Adam and the human race the power to choose by Faith (Romans 1:17). However, a startling discovery for Paul (Romans 7:18–20) was that while we as humans have the ability to consider the two values systems, to know which choice to make and to actually make the choice, we don't have the power to take an action on our choice. We can choose (will) but we can't make it happen (do).

Have you ever faced this frustrating—and occasionally terrifying—situation?

Do you know who you are?

What action do we take; what action *can* we take at this critical juncture? We can believe in our "heart" that what He has asked us to do (because He is) He will empower us to do (His reward) (see Hebrews 11:6). Because in His love "what He had promised, He was able also to perform" (Romans 4:21). We can act as if we expect Him to supply

that which He has promised, "for it is God who is at work in you, both to will and to do for His good pleasure" (Philippians 2:13). This is what we talked about before—"confident expectancy"; this is Hope (Galatians 5:5). Faith that takes an action is Hope. This is "faith that works by love" (Galatians 5:6).

Phase B of Level 2 is also completely outside the human experience. The natural drive of the human heart is to "do it myself." And we try. Oh boy, do we try—until we come up against that which we cannot do, up against the terrifying reality of John 15:5 and haven't been in the practice (yes, I said practice) of choosing to live by faith in what He can do. But I am digressing into Level 3 again. So let me return to our present conversation and save this for a later time.

Although we are unable to *do*, the presence of the Holy Spirit now brings the power to do. "But if the Spirit of Him which raised Jesus from the dead dwells in you, He who raised Christ Jesus from the dead will also give life to your mortal bodies through His Spirit who indwells you" (Romans 8:11); "… the Spirit gives life" (2 Corinthians 3:6). That which we in our humanness are unable to do, the Spirit by His power enables us to do.

This is the most amazing, the most glorious, the most important miracle of all—the transformation of the human heart.

Like the crippled man on his pallet, lying at the feet of Jesus in our previous conversation, we are unable to "walk," we are unable to be "pleasing" to God. But at the command of Jesus, by the power of the Spirit, in Faith in God's promises, we attempt "to walk." And to our utter amazement, we do. If you do not believe in a God of miracles, this interaction of Grace and Faith will not make any sense to you. But if you do believe in the God of miracles, then this is the most amazing, the most glorious, the most important miracle of all—the transformation of the human heart.

"For this reason I bow my knees before the Father …that He would *grant you*, according to the riches of His glory, *to be strengthened* with power through His Spirit *in the inner man*, so that Christ may *dwell in your hearts* through faith, and that *you being rooted and grounded* in love may be *able to comprehend* with all the saints what is the breadth and length and height and depth and *to know the love* of Christ which surpasses knowledge, that *you may be filled up* to all the fullness of God" (Ephesians 3:14–19, italics supplied). Look at the action verbs in this passage. Look at Who does the actions and who the recipient of those actions are (marked with my italics). To my knowledge, this is the most compact, yet complete description of the Gospel, how God activates it in the life of a Christian, and how God causes the Christian to grow into all the fullness of God.

This growth—our Growing In—is very "pleasing" to God. Like a parent watching his child take its first steps, God lovingly guides us, holding our hands as we take our first steps in Faith, picking us up if we fall down, encouraging us to try again. God is exceedingly "pleased" when we allow Him to lead us deeper and deeper into an intimate experience of the Grace-Faith Relationship with Him. Through it all we are motivated and empowered by His love for us and our love for Him "with all your heart and all your soul and all your mind" (Matthew 22:37).

This is the essence of how we function in the second part—between the first part, acceptance of our Savior and the third part, living forever with our Savior. We exercise our choice (our will) to use the Faith He gives us—to grasp the Gifts He gives us. To accept—as our own—that value set which the Holy Spirit is willing to transplant into us for guiding our lives *and* to accept the power of the Holy Spirit to actuate the choices we make according to the new value set. To think like Abraham, that when he realized his body was not capable of carrying out "the promise of God, he did not waver in unbelief, but grew strong in faith, giving glory to God, and being fully assured that what He had promised, He was able also to perform" (Romans 4:20, 21). To choose like Enoch what was most "pleasing to God. For without faith it is impossible to please Him, for he who comes to God must believe that he is, and that He is a rewarder of those who seek Him" (Hebrews 11:5, 6).

This is how Abraham, Isaac, and Jacob "walked" before the Lord (Genesis 48:15). This is how Enoch "walked with God" (Genesis 5:22, 23). This is the "walk" that Paul prescribes for the Ephesians when he tells them to "walk no longer just as the Gentiles also walk, in the futility of their mind … but you did not learn Christ in this way … you be renewed in the spirit of your mind" (Ephesians 4:17–23).

This is being "born … of the Spirit" that Jesus described to Nicodemus (see John 3:5). This is what John the Baptist said Jesus would do: "He will baptize you with the Holy Spirit and fire" (Luke 3:16). The Growing In starts here.

As I review what I just said to you, it sounds very calm, benign, and blasé—like an intellectual exercise worked through in the comfort of your living room while having your morning hot drink. I have said it before, and I must repeat it again for emphasis. This is not a calm and benign intellectual exercise. This is the critical juncture; this is the constant, daily struggle of the human heart—to choose to follow the value set of the world or to submit to the value set of God.

This is extremely difficult and extremely painful on two counts. First, it means recognizing that your usual human value set will not help you achieve what you would like to achieve—life more abundantly. (Everybody wants life more abundantly.) You must *give up* your default human value set and choose to let the Holy Spirit do His radical surgery in your "heart" (remember Ezekiel 36:26, 27); that is, implant God's value set.

> *Your usual human value set will not help you achieve what you would like to achieve—life more abundantly.*

Second, it means recognizing that once you've received the "heart" transplant and you begin to make choices based on the new value set, you don't have the power to act on your choices. You don't have the power to *do* it yourself and you must recognize that you can't. It means comparing yourself to Christ and knowing that you fall so far short that you will never, ever come close to "growing up into" (Ephesians 4:12, 13) righteousness on your own.

To grasp the agony of this moment, imagine the fear and trepidation that Jacob felt at the River Jabbok, wrestling with the Angel, knowing he could not win (Genesis 32:24–29). Imagine the fear and hopeless anguish Peter experienced when Jesus turned and looked at him as the cock crowed, knowing that he'd just done that which he'd said he would never do (Luke 22:62). Imagine the fear and utter self-loathing David felt when he heard "thou art the man!" from the lips of Nathan, knowing that his own righteousness was worthless (2 Samuel 12:7). These people were desperate. They needed to be changed and they knew it. The choice was critical. Without the intervention of

the Holy Spirit the outcome was only darkness (see Psalm 107:10, 11; Isaiah 60:2). So dark that David prayed: "Create in me a clean heart, O God, and renew a steadfast spirit within me. Do not cast me away from Thy presence, and do not take Thy Holy Spirit from me" (Psalm 51:10).

> *How desperate are you? How critical is it for you to allow the Holy Spirit to change your heart and to empower your choices?*

How desperate are you? How critical is it for you to allow the Holy Spirit to change your heart and to empower your choices?

Do you know who you are?

Yes, I agree. This is pretty exciting stuff, but this is only the beginning. These are only the internal changes we have discussed so far. There is so much more yet to tell you of the external results of the Spirit's work *in* and *through* the life of the Christian: belonging to a family (see Romans 8:15), developing in spiritual gifts (see Ephesians 4:11, 12), partaking of the divine nature (see 2 Peter 1:4), developing proven character (see Romans 5:1–5), becoming (actually acting like) the sons and daughters of God (see Romans 8:14).

We will speak of external changes and their consequences in more detail in a later conversation (Chapter 12). I have more particulars, a few more delightful surprises, and some startling conclusions to share then. For now, I'll let this enticement suffice to draw you into a later conversation on this topic. For now, just know that we are not perfect at it; we continue to struggle daily; we keep choosing—Growing In. For now, just understand that this is how it actually works.

In Level 1 the Gift of the Cross sets us free from the *penalty* of sin which is death. By His death, resurrection, and life, Jesus Christ ratified our ability to choose Him as Savior and Lord (see Romans 6:6–11). But to continue to make choices—righteous choices—in our newfound freedom requires a righteous heart.

In Level 2 the Gift of the Holy Spirit, which we are given when we accept Jesus as Savior and Lord (Acts 2:38), brings the *power* of God to endure through and to overcome the *power* of Sin—its temptation, deception, and persecution. (Read 1 Peter 1:5, then do a Scripture word search of the phrase "power of God." Awesome, but we'll save it for later.) The Gift of the Spirit brings the *power* to make radical changes internally—in the human heart, that place where the choice is made between Christ's value set or the world's value set. In the wake of that choice comes the new mindset, the new motives, thoughts, ideas, and emotions. Following immediately comes the *power* of the Spirit to actually do that which we have chosen to do—"… not by might, nor by power, but by my Spirit says the Lord of Hosts" (Zechariah 4:6).

This is the promise of Romans 12:2. "And do not be conformed to this world, but be transformed by the *renewing of your mind* that you may prove what the will of God is, that which is good and acceptable and perfect" (italics supplied).

This is how it actually works. This is how the heart is changed and character is developed. It is a lifelong experience, daily repeated over and over until it becomes the default choice.

Do you think that this process of growth always follows this tidy, carefully delineated, step-by-step process? No? Neither do I.

In medical school I was taught that the blood clotting mechanism in our bodies is a double-branched system, an external system that is activated when the body receives an open wound and an internal system that is activated by some critical stimulus within the blood stream. I was taught that each of these two systems follows a step-by-step process of one protein activating the next protein in line, a linear process in each system. Both of these systems end at a final common pathway that interacts with platelets in the blood stream, leading to blood clot formation. It is all nicely delineated in two straight lines, leading to a final, neatly defined outcome.

In actuality, we now know that blood clotting doesn't happen like that at all. The process takes place on the surface of blood platelets in a mass action process—many steps happening simultaneously, sometimes these coming before those—other times those coming before these—but always the combination coming together to the final conclusion of a blood clot. It's a confusing, messy business.

So is Growing In.

When we believe in Jesus as our Savior and our Lord, He gives the Gift of the Holy Spirit who brings the new heart—this mass action of internal changes and external changes—that results in the outcome of a new value set, a new world view, a new way of thinking and deciding, a new paradigm of actions.

This is the working out of our own salvation (Philippians 2:13). This is Enoch "walking with God" (see Genesis 5) and being "pleasing to God" (see Hebrews 11). Both texts are describing the same interaction. This is my grandson, Braeden, remembering to pray sometimes, not always certain of the outcome of his prayers at other times, choosing to follow the urgings of the Spirit sometimes, not recognizing the promptings of the Spirit at other times. It's a confusing, messy business, but it's God's business, always propelled forward by Faith in the promises of God, encouraged by the "confident expectancy" of Hope in God, and supported by the everlasting Love of God (1 Corinthians 13:13 among others. And yes, it's R-G-B, just in case you were wondering).

I would be remiss if I didn't remind you that Level 1 must come before Level 2, "that is the Spirit of Truth, whom the world cannot receive, because it does not behold Him or know Him" (John 14:17). Unlike the first Gift of the Cross (see 1 John 2:2) this second Gift of the Spirit is not available to everyone in the world. Do not try to cut in line; do not try to jump ahead. This second Gift is only available to those who have accepted the first Gift of the Cross, to "the one who believes in the Son of God" (see 1 John 5:10–12). Peter promised the new believers in Jerusalem at Pentecost that if they repented and were "baptized in the name of Jesus Christ for the forgiveness of [their] sins," they would "receive the gift of the Holy Spirit" (Acts 2:38). Level 1 must come before Level 2.

Another quick warning. Are you confused by the metaphors of Level 1 and Level 2? Jesus told Nicodemus that "unless one is born of the water and the Spirit, he cannot enter the kingdom of God" (John 3:5). The metaphor for Level 1 is death, burial, and resurrection to new life as described in Romans 6:4–11, symbolized in baptism; that is, "born of the water." The metaphor for Level 2 is "abiding," "walking," and "growing" as described in 1 Thessalonians 4:1 and Colossians 1:10, 11—Did you look these up as I suggested?—as described for the individual in John 15:4–8 and for the corporate entity in Ephesians 4:12–16; that is, "born of the Spirit." Don't confuse the two metaphors. Level 1 is an action at a moment in time (but sometimes has to be repeated). Level 2 is a continuous action, a learning process, as Ephesians 4:12, 13 says: "to the *building up* of the body of Christ; until we all attain …" (italics supplied).

I know I'm repeating myself, but this is critical. Although it might be confusing and messy, like the vision of Ezekiel's valley of the dry bones (Ezekiel 37:13, 14), Level 2 must happen in order for a Christian to *come to life*!

The Holy Spirit gives life (2 Corinthians 3:6).

The Holy Spirit gives a new heart (see Ezekiel 36:26, 27).

The Holy Spirit transforms the mind (see Romans 12:1, 2).

By presenting to us the new set of values—the mindset of Christ, by leading us to behold Him, we become changed (see 2 Corinthians 3:18).

The choice of mindset—Romans 8:5, 6—leads us to death, or to life and peace.

The result of the presence of the Spirit gives life (see Romans 8:11), changes life patterns (see Romans 8:13), and arranges our adoption—and our behavior—as the children of God (see Romans 8:14–16).

The Holy Spirit empowers the promises of God to make us "to be strengthened with power through His Spirit in the inner man" (Ephesians 3:16), causing not only the individual to come to life, but also causing the People of God to come to life (Ezekiel 37:13, 14) and do the specific task that God has assigned to them (1 Peter 2:9). This is why I said that this discussion is so critical to the completion of the assigned task of the Seventh-day Adventist Church.

This is the Covenant Grace-Faith Relationship in its dynamic second level. This is Growing In. Are you familiar with the messy internal struggles of this deeper level? Are you aware of the fantastic results of this struggle?

Do you know who you are?

As I suggested at the beginning of this conversation, we have reached a transition point, a critical juncture in developing a deeper, more intimate Grace-Faith Relationship with God. In fact, I'm going to suggest that wherever you are (mountain camping, traveling in an airplane, or actually sitting in an easy chair near the fireplace) you take a break from our conversations and contemplate what we have just discussed. Take two hours or two days or a week to consider the work of the Holy Spirit in your life, how He interacts with you and how you will respond to His work in you. Confess to God your acceptance of Jesus as Lord and Savior and accept His gift of the Holy Spirit into your life.

He can work through *us— or* around *us. But His work is of no benefit to us until we choose to allow Him to work in us.*

This is not about whether you are in a saving relationship with God. God has already provided salvation for the entire world (1 John 2:2) and made it available to each of us when we accept it (John 3:3, 5). This is about our cooperating with the work of the Holy Spirit to be made alive. He can work *through* us—or *around* us (think Pharaoh of Egypt or King Saul)—to accomplish His purpose. But His work is of no benefit *to* us until we choose to allow Him to work *in* us (see Ezekiel 37:14).

I realize that it's risky to tell you to take a break, but I will. Let's break off our conversation for now. Put down the book, go off by yourself, pray and meditate. For me *and* for you, this is important enough to risk losing your attention for just a bit. When you are ready, come back. I'll be waiting.

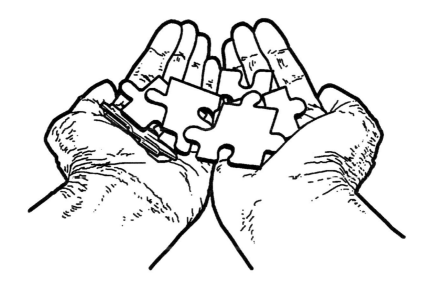

Chapter 7

Do You Know You Are to Keep the Commandments?

"Here is the perseverance of the saints who keep the commandments of God and their faith in Jesus." Revelation 14:12

Hello, again. I did not expect to see you so soon. However, I'm glad you came when you did. I've been thinking about, actually studying in my Bible about, something that I want to share with you in just the way it was shared with me. And this is a good time to do it. Oh, and one more thing. Keep your Bible handy. As you can tell, I've stopped warning you whenever I've added extra Bible texts in parentheses. If they are familiar, move on. If they are not, look them up.

As I've been discussing with you the Covenant Grace-Faith Relationship, I realize that I've been emphasizing the Faith part, mostly because I think many people don't know how that "actually works." But here's the rub. I suspect that people don't know how "keeping the commandments of God" actually works, either. I've been looking at the multiple times that Revelation mentions the two phrases: "keeping the commandments of God" and "the faith of Jesus" (the last phrase being expressed differently in various places, such as, Revelation 1:2, 1:9, 12:17, 14:12). These two phrases represent the Covenant Grace-Faith Relationship from two different viewpoints: thoughts versus actions, internal changes versus external results. The fact is, what we've been talking about—the *choice* on our part to "surrender" and to "present ourselves" and to "abide"—happens internally. But it must eventually result in useful actions externally. The "faith of Jesus" *must* result in "keeping the commandments." Otherwise we're just playing church, just going through the motions, just pretending to be Christ-followers.

I think it's time that you and I discuss this topic. If we don't, you'll hear it discussed at the potluck after next Sabbath's sermon or at the next prayer meeting you attend. Someone will lament or complain (it can take either form) that they can't keep the commandment that says _____ (fill in the blank as you choose) because _____. Here they recount their unsolvable dilemma between two equally unpalatable choices. Or, you will hear it discussed at the next church board meeting or elder's meeting when someone addresses the obvious difficulty that someone else ("who will remain nameless") is having in "keeping" the commandment that says _____ (again, fill in the blank with your favorite sin that you like to catch other people doing).

As Seventh-day Adventists, we are very concerned about "keeping the commandments of God." It's important. It's integral to who we are. We become exercised if we think we or someone we know is not "keeping" the commandments. We understand that the People of God at the Time of the End will be "keeping the commandments of God," and we don't want any of our friends to be missing in heaven because we didn't stridently remind them to "keep the commandments."

"Keeping" is one of those metaphorical phrases like the ones I mentioned in our last conversation. I don't think we Seventh-day Adventists understand what that word means, even though we use it constantly to describe ourselves in our favorite Revelation passages.

"Keeping" the commandments. Actually *doing* what God wants us to do. Do we know what we're talking about?

Do you know who you are?

My wife has a small china hutch that is full of teacups. The cups belonged to her Aunt

> *The "faith of Jesus" must result in "keeping the commandments." Otherwise we're just playing church, just going through the motions, just pretending.*

Hennie. (Her name was Helen, but I never heard anyone call her anything but Hennie or Hennie Pen.) When we moved to Florida, we kept those cups in a box for six years, never opening the box, never taking them out. Only since we have moved to a larger house in North Carolina have the cups come out of the box and are now in the china hutch. Although not a hoarder by nature, my wife never talked of getting rid of the teacups. She "kept" them.

My wife also "kept" her cookbooks on her special bookshelf near her kitchen workspace. She probably had twenty or thirty of them all lined up on two shelves, covering every conceivable culinary possibility in the vegetarian line—from tofu to quinoa, from soups to ethnic foods. My son Christopher (who as a student of her culinary skills also cooks well) suggested that she didn't need all of these cookbooks. All of the recipes were online, to be downloaded whenever needed.

My wife answered him in this way: "When I open one of these cookbooks, my mother or Aunt Hennie is standing here beside me. As I read these cookbooks, see the stains on their pages, and cook from them, I am again in the presence of my mother or Aunt Hennie or Aunt Libbus. My cookbooks and my cooking are an extension of my relationship with these people that I love. That's why I 'keep' them."

Do you know about this kind of "keeping," this kind of "treasuring" of a memory, of a favorite vacation photo, of a family heirloom? I know that I have special treasures that belonged to my family. They include my father's pocket watch that he won for achieving first place in his eighth grade class exams and my uncle's violin that he passed on to me when I learned to play "Ragtime Annie." I'm sure you have these kinds of treasures as well. We call these treasures "keepsakes." We *keep* them for the *sake* of remembering a special time, place, or person that we loved.

Now let me ask you, do you know the fourth commandment? Yes, the Sabbath commandment. Can you say it from memory? Do you know how it begins?

Of course, you remember it. "Remember the Sabbath day to keep it holy" is how it begins (Exodus 20:8). Did you hear those two words: "remember" and "keep"? Now let me ask you the next obvious question: Why do *you* "remember" to "keep" the Sabbath day holy?

Do you know who you are?

Why *do* we "keep" the commandments? What's so great about the Ten Commandments, anyway?

Most Christians think of the Ten Commandments as a list of ten rules that God says you have to obey—or else God will frown on you, maybe even strike you down. They live in fear of breaking one of these rules. Have you known someone like this? Or is this how *you* view the Ten Commandments? After our previous conversations, I am hoping it is not, but it's because of this possibility that we're having this conversation. Some people are fearful of getting on the wrong side of God, either by accident (fearing that they might not know when they have broken one of the rules) or on purpose (wanting and insisting on doing their own thing, then living in fear that they

might have permanently excluded themselves from God's grace.)

Consider a different description of the Ten Commandments. Consider them to be a description of the character of God.

For a moment, consider a different description of the Ten Commandments. Consider them to be a description of the character of God, a description of who God is. So that you can follow my thoughts, I will describe the Ten Commandments in the order of their classic presentation in Exodus 20, but I will describe them in their positive sense as a description of who God is. Understand that these ten—and many other commandments—are presented both in the Old Testament as well as in the New Testament, all of them being a reflection and a description of the character of God. As added illustrations, I'm going to suggest other Scriptures as well for you to look up now or later, if you choose, in the Bible that you always have with you when we're having a conversation.

- **Commandment 1:** As the Savior of mankind, God is unique and stands alone, stronger and more reliable than other supposed gods (Exodus 20:2, 3; cf. Isaiah 43:10–13, 44:6–8; 1 John 4:9–19).

- **Commandment 2:** God is more immense, more complex, more knowledgeable, more powerful than all of creation collectively; therefore, any created symbol, icon, entity, or being is too restricted, too limited, too small to adequately and appropriately represent Him (Exodus 20:4–6; cf. Isaiah 45:18–46:5; Romans 1:20–23)

- **Commandment 3:** God's name "I AM WHO I AM" (Exodus 3:14) symbolizes the breadth, depth, and height of His character. In attaching His name to worlds, to things, and to peoples, He declares and establishes a relationship with that entity in which and through which His character is reflected. Further, He allows that world, thing, or people to use His name to signify that they are in relationship with Him (Exodus 20:7; cf. 1 Kings 11:36; Psalm 91:14; Revelation 3:12).

- **Commandment 4:** In His creativity, even of Time itself, God establishes a moment of time that He sanctifies, specifically sets aside, as representing the completed sufficiency of His work in providing for His created beings. In this specific time period, they can "rest"—relax, contemplate, recognize, and celebrate—in their relationship with Him in His complete provision for them (Exodus 20:8–11; cf. Ezekiel 20:12; Isaiah 66:22, 23; Hebrews 4:1–11).

- **Commandment 5:** God establishes the concept of "family," for which He has appointed responsible mentor/teachers, in which His created beings can safely experience leadership and security, love and fellowship, accep-

tance and growth (Exodus 20:12; cf. Malachi 4:5, 6; Matthew 15:3–6; Ephesians 4:11–16).

- **Commandment 6:** As the giver of life, God holds this Gift of Life in the highest regard and does not withdraw this gift, except by the demanding choice of any created being who insists on withdrawing from fellowship with God (Exodus 20:13; cf. Ezekiel 18:31. 32; John 10:10).

- **Commandment 7**: God is forever faithful to His relationships: steadfast, unmovable, unchangeable in His grace, His hope, and His peace (Exodus 20:14; cf. Jeremiah 31:3; Hosea 2; Malachi 3:6).

- **Commandment 8:** God respects the individuality and the choice of each created being. He accepts in worship from these created beings only that which is freely offered (Exodus 20:15; cf. Joshua 24:15; 2 Corinthians 9:7; Romans 6:17).

- **Commandment 9:** God is truthful to Himself and to every created being—about Himself and about His created being (Exodus 20:16; cf. Exodus 34:6, 7; John 5:32).

- **Commandment 10:** God rejoices over the position, power, or prestige that other beings have achieved (Exodus 20:17; cf. Isaiah 62:1–5; Psalm 35:27; Zephaniah 3:17; Song of Solomon 2:4).

My first discovery from my Bible study was this: The Ten Commandments and all other commandments are a description of who God is, the God who wants to be in a Covenant Grace-Faith Relationship with us.

Likewise, I discovered that the Ten Commandments are a description of what God desires our response to be to Him—and to His other creatures. As I have said before, God desires that we be "partakers of the divine nature" (2 Peter 1:4). Therefore, as an extension of His relationship with us, He wants the Ten Commandments to be a description of *who we are* as we reflect His character to the world.

> *As an extension of His relationship with us, He wants the Ten Commandments to be a description of* who we are *as we reflect His character to the world.*

My second discovery came to me while I was praying for my granddaughter Amber, a freshman (as I write this) studying in the university. I had been praying for her as she faced a multitude of adult decisions, some for the first time, as she struggled to establish herself as an independently functioning adult. I desperately desired (it was *my* will) that she avoid many of the distractions, temptations, and difficulties that I—and so many others before me—had fallen into. I had been praying earnestly to the Lord that He would protect and keep her from …

And then it occurred to me: The Lord has His own will concerning Amber. The Lord knows how best to lead Amber, what temptations or difficulties she will learn best to avoid by hearing about

them from me or by learning about them on her own. The Lord knows best what she is ready for and what may not be as important to her growth and happiness right now, as it was to mine. I was not praying in the Lord's will, but in my own will, what I thought was best for Amber.

So, what's the Lord's will for you and me? What does the Lord passionately, lovingly, thoughtfully, hopefully desire for us? We have spent the last several conversations exploring the will of God for us; that is, through a discussion of the three Gifts (Chapter 4), by outlining the impact of living in the Gospel of R-G-B (Chapter 5), by discovering what it means to walk with God (Chapter 6).

However, in the context of *this* conversation, Jesus expressed the will of God when He said: "Abide in Me, and I in you. As the branch cannot bear fruit of itself unless it abides in the vine, so neither can you unless you abide in Me. I am the vine, you are the branches; he who abides in Me and I in him, he bears much fruit, for apart from Me you can do nothing. If anyone does not abide in Me, he is thrown away as a branch and dries up; and they gather them, and cast them into the fire and they are burned.

"If you abide in Me, and My words abide in you, ask whatever you wish, and it will be done for you. My Father is glorified by this, that you bear much fruit, and so prove to be My disciples" (John 15:4–8).

Jesus has summarized nicely our last three conversations: By receiving the Gifts and abiding in Him, we are empowered to function like Him, to reflect His character to the world, letting our "light so shine before men that … they glorify [our] Father which is in heaven" (Matthew 5:16).

To make this interaction with God—and the transaction with the observing world—function consistently, you and I need a driver, a motivator, a force so powerful that it can work successfully "against the rulers, against the powers, against the world forces of this darkness, against the spiritual forces of wickedness in the heavenly places" (Ephesians 6:12). Where do you think we can find such a powerful, consistent motivator?

After our previous conversations, I'm sure you know the answer to this question. But let me say it again: When Jesus was asked, "What is the greatest commandment," He answered, "'You shall love the Lord your God with all your heart, and with all your soul, and with all your mind.' This is the great and foremost commandment. The second is like it, 'You shall love your neighbor as yourself'" (Matthew 22:37–39). In giving His answer, Jesus essentially described the Ten Commandments in this way: Draw a circle around the first four commandments and label the circle "Love God." Draw a circle around the second six commandments and label the circle "Love your neighbor." Jesus was saying, in essence, that the basis for the Ten Commandments is love—to God and to your neighbor.

Therefore, in my roundabout way, I made the following connections:

1. The Ten Commandments describe the character of God in the Covenant Grace-Faith Relationship.

2. The will of God is that we reflect His character and join Him in this relationship.

3. This Covenant Grace-Faith Relationship is based on love.

However, two issues still trouble me. First, I want to make doubly sure of something. What do *you* think? Does God actually love *you*? I know, I've asked this question before (in our very first long conversation in Chapter 2), but it's at the

core of who you are, so it's doubly important that you know the answer for yourself. Does God love you?

Jesus says He does: "… for the Father Himself loves you …" (John 16:27). God says He does: "For God so loved the world that He gave His only begotten Son …" (John 3:16). I think God is trying to tell you (and me) something: "I have loved you with an everlasting love; Therefore I have drawn you with lovingkindness" (Jeremiah 31:3).

So, do we have that settled? Do you know that God loves *you*? Good. I hope you will always cherish that line from the old praise song written about John 3:16—"God so loved the world … that whosoever believeth …" The line from the song says: "'Whosoever' surely meaneth me." It's one of the first of several answers to my original question—do you know who you are?

And the second issue is this: Jesus suggests that the appropriate response to such a love (see Ephesians 2:4; 3:19) is the instruction that Moses gave the children of Israel several millennia ago in Deuteronomy 6:5: "And you shall love the Lord your God with all your heart and with all your soul and with all you might." The Ten Commandments describe love—God's love for us and our love for Him and for others. But why love? Why not physical strength, why not moral fortitude, or cultural correctness, or intellectual assent and agreement? Why does God insist, "Not by might, nor by power, but by My Spirit …" (Zechariah 4:6) that it has to be done this way?

To answer this question I'd like to discuss three stories from the Bible. The first is one of the few stories that appears in all four of the Gospels. It's the story of the woman who anointed Jesus prior to His crucifixion at the feast of Simon the Pharisee. Luke 7:37 tells us that the woman was a sinner. Matthew 26:6 tells us that it happened at the house of Simon the leper. (One of the ten lepers healed by Jesus in Luke 17:11–19? Perhaps he was.) Mark 14:3 tells us that the woman brought an alabaster vial of very expensive perfume, pure nard.

And in John 12 we discover the most revealing information. Verse 1 tells us that this scene takes place where Lazarus lives, in Bethany. Verse 2 says that Lazarus and Martha are both there. And in verse 3 we learn that the woman is Mary. Putting all of this information with Luke 11:1, we understand that the woman is Mary, and she is the sister of Martha and Lazarus.

When Simon the Pharisee (previously a leper?) observed that Jesus made no protest over Mary's ministrations to Him, Simon concluded that Jesus could not be a prophet. Otherwise, he thought, Jesus would have known the kind of woman she was and would not have allowed her to touch Him and defile Him. In response, reading Simon's mind, Jesus told the story of two debtors who were forgiven debts by a moneylender. One owed a large sum; the other owed a small sum. Jesus asked Simon: "'Which of them therefore will love him more?' Simon answered and said, 'I suppose the one whom he forgave more.'"

I propose to you that love is the strongest motivator to establish and maintain a relationship *because* God has chosen to pay for us the sacrificial price that was impossible for us to pay ourselves for our Salvation (John 3:16). As we recognize this incredible act of God on our behalf, we choose to respond with our own sacrificial offering: "to present your bodies a living and holy sacrifice, acceptable to God, which is you spiritual service of worship" (Romans 12:1). "We love, because He first loved us" (1 John 4:19). We love because we are forgiven much. (And you have to know who you are in order for you to know how much you are forgiven. Yes?)

The second story is told in Luke 15:11–32, the story of the prodigal son which we have studied previously. However, the part I want to emphasize

is the attitude of the older brother who did not want to rejoice at the return of his younger sibling. Notice what the father says to him: "But we had to be merry and rejoice, for *this brother of yours* was dead and has begun to live, and was lost and has been found" (italics supplied).

The reason for rejoicing, the reason for loving his brother was because he is "this brother of yours." He is family. Our family, of course, is the body of Christ described by Paul in Ephesians 4:12–16 and Colossians 3:11–17. (I'll let you study these for yourself on your own time.) Jesus helps us to recognize how important it is for the world to see us while we are loving our family when He says, "By this will all men know that you are my disciples, if you have love for one another" (John 13:35).

Again, love is the strongest motivator to establish and maintain a relationship because we are family and you are my brother or my sister. God is our father. (A fact, which is first hinted at in Deuteronomy 1:31 and 32:6, then stated explicitly in Psalm 68:5 and 89:26, and further revealed in Isaiah 9:6 and Malachi 2:10.) And we are all members of "God's household" (Ephesians 2:19; cf. Galatians 3:26, 29). We love each other because we are brothers/sisters.

Do you see yourself as part of the family of God? Is that who you are?

The third story is from Luke 10:30–37, the story of the Good Samaritan. However, this story exhibits no connection between the Samaritan and the man he finds stranded and left to die on the road to Jericho. The only reason the Samaritan helps the wounded man is because the man is in need and the Samaritan has compassion on him. The Samaritan ignores all traditional, cultural rules and taboos and responds because the wounded man is a fellow human being.

In a later conversation I will explore with you this kind of compassionate effort for our fellow man and how it contributes to another answer to my continuous, curious, (dare I say, irritating) question: Do you know who you are? But for now, understand that love is the strongest motivator to establish and maintain a relationship because we share the designation of *human being* with our fellow man. We recognize the value of a human being in the sight of God and act as if we think and feel the same way that He does. We love.

The ability to love as God loves—intensely, unreservedly, sacrificially, eternally (from our conversation in Chapter 2)—is one indication that we have "become partakers of the divine nature," which is described elsewhere as the first of those character traits known as the Fruit of the Spirit—"*love*, joy, peace, longsuffering, kindness, goodness, faithfulness, gentleness, self-control" (Galatians 5:22, 23).

One of my favorite things—besides raindrops on roses and whiskers on kittens (thank you, *Sound of Music*)—is to find Bible passages that so beautifully express a concept that I've been studying to understand. John 15:9–11 is just such a passage. "Just as the Father has loved Me, I have also loved you; abide in My love. If you keep My commandments, you will abide in My love; just as I have kept My Father's commandments and abide in His love. These things I have spoken to you so that My joy may be in you, and that your joy may be made full."

To summarize, I understand Jesus to be saying that our ability to reflect the character of God— to "bear much fruit [of the Spirit]"—is directly related to our relationship with Him, expressed as "abide in Me, and I in you." And our relationship with Him and with the Father—our "abiding"—is motivated by and is expressed as *love*. Our abiding in His love is most clearly expressed as "keep my commandments."

We spent a great deal of time in Chapters 4, 5, and 6 discussing how utterly impossible it is to "obey" on our own—by trying hard. We explored and explained the concept that as we choose to allow the Holy Spirit to work in us (see Ezekiel 36:26, 27), He changes our heart so that obedience—which was impossible before—is now possible.

Therefore, "keeping" the commandments becomes possible, *not* because we try hard, but because we love hard. Jesus expressed it: "If you love me, you will keep my commandments" (John 14:15). Paul expressed it in one of those beautiful summary scriptures this way: "For in Christ Jesus neither circumcision nor uncircumcision [nor any other "trying hard" effort of man (Ephesians 2:9)] means anything, but Faith Working by Love" (Galatians 5:6). My use of caps was intentional to emphasize R-G-B. Did you see it?

"Keeping" the commandments becomes possible, not *because we try hard, but because we love hard.*

More than this, "keeping" the commandments now becomes a way of life. Like my wife's treasuring her aunt's teacups or her mother's cookbooks, we daily learn to "treasure," we learn to "keep" the love relationship we share with God. In concert with the will of God, reflecting to the world by the power of His love the character of God expressed in the commandments, we "no longer … live, but Christ lives in [us]; and the life which [we] now live in the flesh [we] live by faith in the Son of God, who loved [us], and delivered Himself up for [us] (Galatians 2:20).

Even more than this, "keeping" the commandments is daily, hourly, minute-by-minute *worship* as Paul expressed in Romans 12:1, writing, "… daily [we] present [our] bodies a living and holy sacrifice, acceptable to God, which is [our] spiritual service of worship."

So this is the result of my Bible study that I wanted to share with you. This is my witness. I *keep* the commandments because I want to Receive From, Grow In, and Become Like God. I keep the commandments because they are "my precious keepsake," my "memorial reminder" of my relationship with God. I *keep* the commandments because I love Him and worship Him. I *keep* the commandments because they symbolize who I am. I invite you to do the same.

All that we have been discussing for the last six chapters is absolutely critical to understand before we can move deeper into the rest of our conversations. As I said to you at the beginning of our last conversation, we've turned the corner and are headed into a deeper, more intense discussion of our Covenant Grace-Faith Relationship with God. Unless we grasp these concepts, studying further into the role of the Seventh-day Adventist Church in the Time of the End would be a waste of time. These basic Christian activities—believing, abiding, and loving—must be expressed and activated in the life of the Seventh-day Adventist Christian before we are able to have a witness before the world. But I am getting ahead of myself (as usual). So I will pause for a moment and take a deep breath—before I move on to our next conversation. Please join me, if you are ready.

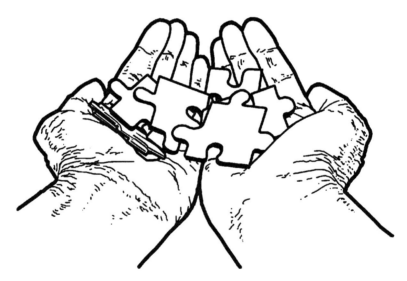

Chapter 8

Do You Know You Are a Ministering Priest?

"But you are a chosen people, a royal priesthood, a holy nation, a people of God's own possession, that you may proclaim the excellencies of Him who has called you out of darkness into His marvelous light." 1 Peter 2:9

Good morning, tour guests, and welcome to our special tour for the morning. I trust you slept well last night and are ready for the activities of the day.

(*Shh*. Come over here and join me. For something a little different—a bit of relaxation after our last conversation—I've arranged for a special tour. Put on your walking shoes, engage your imagination, and embark with me on an adventure as we begin our conversation for today. Come on, get out of your chair. Try it, you'll like it.)

Today we are visiting a replica of the Old Testament Sanctuary, or as some call it, the wilderness Tabernacle. I can assure you that no expense was spared to enable you to once again view the Sanctuary—and at no extra cost to you. The cost of this morning's tour is part of the package that

you purchased when you first signed up for our tour group. (Yeah, I got our tickets at a special price, too.) So you can take your hands off your wallets and relax while we walk through the Old Testament Sanctuary and examine the items of furniture that we find here. If you want to follow along, this part of our tour is described in your guidebook: Exodus 25–27.

Currently we are standing inside the courtyard of the Old Testament Sanctuary. Around us are the walls of the courtyard grounds surrounded by 7½-foot high white linen curtains mounted on posts with bronze bases and silver tops. This courtyard is 150 feet long and 75 feet wide. The curtains just behind us that serve as the gates to the courtyard are 35 feet wide, and—as you can see—are blue and purple and scarlet.

Here at this end of the courtyard is a large box that looks like it's made of bronze and smells like there's been a fire burning here. Does anyone know its name? Yes. Very good. It's the altar of burnt offering. Twice daily a lamb was offered on this altar and the fire burned continually. In fact, all sacrificial offerings—whether for the whole nation of Israel or for individuals—were offered here. It's stunningly large in its original form—7½ feet square and 4½ feet tall. Quite an imposing sight when one first enters the sanctuary grounds, wouldn't you say?

Okay, let's move forward to that basin sitting just ahead and to our left. Does anyone know what this is? Very good. It is called the laver. Like the altar, it is also made of bronze. Although its original size is not certain, its purpose is well known. It held water so that the priests could wash before they entered into the Tent of Meeting itself.

And now we come to the tabernacle proper, a large building, a tent actually, but with wooden walls, which are 15 feet high, 45 feet long and 18 feet wide with a special screen of curtains—sometimes called a veil or a gate—of scarlet and purple and blue here in the front.

Let's go in and see what's in the first section or first apartment of this Tent of Meeting. The walls of this apartment are made of wood overlaid with gold. The whole building is covered with four layers of curtains so that the inside would be totally dark were it not for the light from the lamp stand, which reflects off the golden walls and bathes the entire inside in a golden flickering light—like fire.

Here on our left is the golden lamp stand, which uses special olive oil and is kept burning twenty-four hours a day. To our right is the low table—covered with gold—with the showbread and the jars for the wine. And straight ahead of us, in the back of this first apartment, is the altar of incense—again overlaid with gold—where special incense is burned. You will notice that this altar is positioned directly against a dividing curtain.

While the other curtains in the Tent of Meeting are sometimes called veils, this particular curtain is always called "the Veil," because it divides the tabernacle proper or Tent of Meeting into two equal parts.

Who knows what is just behind this dividing veil?

Very good. It is the sacred ark of the covenant. We are not going to show the ark today for two reasons. The first reason is that we ordinary people are forbidden to go into that second apartment. And two, even with the description given in Exodus 25, we aren't certain what the ark looked like because so few people ever actually saw the original.

(I'm pretty sure that you know your way around the wilderness Sanctuary, so let's leave the tour and go somewhere where we can talk—above a whisper—about what we just saw.)

There—that's better. Well, that was interesting, wasn't it, to see the sanctuary and all its furniture up close—just as if we were priests going about our daily duties? I'm curious, what were your thoughts? Did you wonder why I brought you on this tour? Did it occur to you to think about the question I've been asking you, Do you know who you are?

Open your Bible and turn to Leviticus 1:2. (I know you're keeping your Bible right beside you, aren't you?) "Speak to the sons of Israel and say to them, 'when any man of you brings an offering to the Lord, you shall bring of animals from the herd or the flock.'"

Who came to this altar of burnt offering? Who brought those sacrifices for a sin offering and a burnt offering and a peace offering—for offerings of various kinds? Yes, the pious and the penitent. Those who were following the Lord's will and those who were struggling to do so. These were ordinary people like you and me. They were sinners.

(Just a quick aside: this world has two kinds of people: sinners and sinners who have been forgiven. All of us are in one category or the other. Just so you don't forget our second conversation—back in Chapter 2—and just so you don't forget who you are.)

And when they came to this altar of burnt offering and made their sacrifice, when they said their penitential prayers while pressing their hand upon the animal's head and cut the throat of the animal with their own hand and watched the blood run out until the animal died—in their place—for their sin, they left forgiven. They went back out through those curtained gates at the entrance to the courtyard as a sinner who was forgiven, *in other words* (the Greek word *kai*—did you remember?), a saint. And greatly beloved of God.

This is where most people today who profess to be Christians stop. This is where the people of Romans 3:19–26 stop—where God displays publicly the redemption that is in Jesus Christ, that He might be just and, at the same time, be the justifier of those who have faith in Jesus. This is where the people of 2 Corinthians 5:21 stop—where Jesus was made to be sin for us that we might become the righteousness of God in Him. This is where the story of the Philippian jailer stopped. Look at Acts 16:30, 31: "And after he brought them out, he said, 'Sirs, what must I do to be saved?' And they said, 'Believe in the Lord Jesus, and you shall be saved, you and your household.'" So many people today want to stop here at the altar of burnt offering.

To be sure—just as we discussed in our last conversation—the precious, beloved Christian comes here to the altar of burnt offering, but the Christian doesn't stop here. Let's see what Peter says in Acts 2:38. "And Peter said to them, 'Repent, and let each of you be baptized in the name of Jesus Christ for the forgiveness of your sins; and you shall receive the gift of the Holy Spirit.'"

Did you notice what else was mentioned that was not in the story of the Philippian jailer? Correct. You will receive the gift of the Holy Spirit. In John 3:5 Jesus said, "Unless one is born of the water *and the Spirit*, he cannot enter into the kingdom of God" (italics supplied). There is something more to the Christian life than just the altar of burnt offering. Yes, I'm picking up where we left off in our last conversation. I'm ready to talk with you about one of those metaphors for God's People. But the basic question remains the same.

Do you know who you are?

When God was establishing His people under the leadership of Moses, He said, "You yourselves have seen what I did to the Egyptians and how I bore you on eagles' wings, and brought you to Myself. Now then, if you will indeed obey My voice and keep My covenant, then you shall be My own possession among all the peoples for all the earth is Mine; and you shall be to Me a kingdom of priests and a holy nation" (Exodus 19:4–6).

Because of His salvation, which *He had done* for them—precisely what the altar of burnt offering represented for them—He now claimed them as His own. He set them apart as a kingdom of priests and a holy nation.

In exactly the same way, when God was establishing His people after the life, death, and resurrection of Jesus Christ, He said, "But you are a chosen race, a royal priesthood, a holy nation, a people for God's own possession, that you may proclaim the excellencies of Him who has called you out of darkness into His marvelous light" (1 Peter 2:9).

If you have made the choice to be a Christian, you do not stop at the altar of burnt offering. Instead, continuing in the Covenant Grace-Faith Relationship, when you make the second choice to receive God's second Gift of the Holy Spirit, you are now set apart for service to God. You are a Priest in the house of God.

Does this shock you?

Do you know who you are?

No? Then let me show you.

Do you remember the laver that we saw on our tour of the wilderness Sanctuary? What happens at the laver? Read it for yourself in Exodus 30:18, 19. (I'll wait while you look it up again.) What happens at the laver? Yes, the priests were to wash there—their hands and their feet.

Why?

What does it say in Exodus 30:20? "… that they may not die."

Why would they die? Because they are about to enter into a sacred and holy place to minister. They are coming into the presence of God who is "… the fury of a fire which will consume the adversaries" (Hebrews 10:27). As His "set apart" people, as His priests, they are going to minister in the presence of a holy God and yet be preserved. They must be protected "that the glory of the Lord may appear unto you" (Leviticus 9:6) and not be consumed by that glory.

(For the sake of time and space, I must move on. I leave you to a more in-depth study of the specialness of priests in Leviticus 8–10, 21 and Numbers 18. For a more in-depth study of not being consumed by the presence of God, study Psalm 15:1–5 and Isaiah 33:14–16 in conjunction with Isaiah 6:5–7 and Deuteronomy 30:6—in light of our conversation in Chapter 6. It's a big assignment, I know. But I think you can handle it.)

Okay, back to our discussion of the laver. What was Jesus doing when He washed the disciples' feet in the Upper Room? Was this just a ceremony that showed how humble Jesus was and how humble the disciples should be in serving one another?

No. Jesus was preparing the disciples to be priests and to serve in His temple where He would be the High Priest.

As Jesus told Peter, the foot washing ceremony is symbolic of the cleansing of the heart, the cleansing on the inside (compare John 13:10 with Matthew 15:17–20). This cleansing of the feet (the heart) should take place before participating in Communion—just as the priests washed their hands and feet before going into the first apartment of the wilderness Sanctuary.

As you can see, this business of being a Christian, of entering into the service of the Lord is serious business. Our hearts need to be properly cleansed—because we have been set apart to serve. That is why I insisted on the importance of having our last two conversations before we have these next several conversations about the metaphorical word symbols.

Now, please, this is not about following rules. This is not about cleaning yourself up before you can enter God's service. This is about surrendering the heart to the Lordship of Jesus Christ. This is not about being perfect. This is about letting Jesus Christ make you perfect.

Remember, in the service of humility, you don't wash your own feet—just like you can't cleanse your own heart. You may review this concept in Romans 12:2, from our last conversation,

> *In the service of humility, you don't wash your own feet— just like you can't cleanse your own heart.*

if you like. The disciples' feet were washed by Jesus. His Lordship, His righteousness is what makes you and me clean for service (Jeremiah

23:6). Therefore, in the Ordinance of Humility you don't wash your own feet.

So, now that we have properly prepared our feet—and our hearts—as priests, let's move into the first apartment of the Sanctuary.

What did we find here during our tour? That first article of furniture just to the left, what was it? Yes, the golden lampstand, which is symbolic of … ? What does it say in Psalm 119:105? The light of God's word. The Scriptures. Do you remember it best as a scripture song? Go ahead, sing it aloud with me now. "Thy word is a lamp unto my feet, and a light unto my path. Thy word is a lamp unto my feet, and a light unto my path."

John 8:12 records that when Jesus attended the Festival of Lights in Jerusalem, He said, "I am the light of the world." And in so many ways Jesus is the Word and the Light. At this point I could take you through multiple scriptures that describe what Jesus taught His disciples—and us—showing us the way, describing the character of God, teaching the principles of discipleship, demonstrating agape love in action and, most importantly of all, helping us to know the Father.

Second Timothy 3:16, 17 describes what the Scriptures and Jesus' life were designed to do. "All scripture is inspired by God and profitable for teaching, for reproof, for correction, for training in righteousness; so that the man of God may be adequate, equipped for every good work."

Jesus is the Light of the world. Jesus is the Word, giving His Priests knowledge and understanding, equipping them for their work.

Is it coming to you? Do you know who you are?

In 1995 I hiked a portion of the Appalachian Trail with my sons, John and Christopher. I wanted to be equipped. I wanted to be ready for any eventuality. So in addition to my backpack with cooking utensils, stove, food, clothes, extra shoes, medicines, plus maps and guide books, I was carrying rain gear that covered the entire backpack and me, drinking flask, flashlight—and the eleventh essential, toilet paper. Oh, yes, I was also carrying a tent complete with metal poles. I was equipped; I was ready.

After a hearty breakfast we began our ascent up the first part of the trail. About two miles out, I began to feel faint. My pulse was racing; my head was light. And I had to lie down in the middle of the trail. The boys were worried that they'd have to go get help and end the three-day hike before it had even begun.

Fortunately, I recovered quickly. The boys split up some of the "extra" gear I was carrying. We continued on the hike and did well for the next three days.

My point is this: It is one thing to be well-equipped. It is quite another thing to have to actually go on the hike. It is one thing to be well-educated, well-versed in the Word. It is quite another to actually have to use this information to minister. And that takes us to our next piece of furniture in the first apartment of the Sanctuary.

On our tour in the first apartment, what did you see to the right? There was a table and unleavened bread. There were pitchers and bowls and serving trays. Bread and wine. Sound familiar?

Let's look at Exodus 25:30. What was this table and this bread called? It was called the Bread of the Presence—actually the Hebrews words read "the Bread of the Face." We are talking about an up front and close encounter here. We are talking about an "in-your-face" experience.

Turn in your Bible to John 6:48. Do you remember this controversial sermon? Jesus said, "I am the bread of life." Now notice verse 53 where He said, "Unless you eat the flesh of the Son of man and drink His blood, you have no life in yourselves."

Jesus' disciples found this to be a hard saying. So let's help them out by connecting this scripture with what Jesus said in John 4:34. "My food is to do the will of Him who sent Me and to accomplish His work." And our food is to be the same as Jesus' food.

Do the words in John 6:53 make sense to you now? No? Okay, let me explain further.

The Table and the Bread of the Presence represents the active ministry you will experience as a Priest of God. The experience of Christ (you now have to *face* it and begin to *experience* it for yourself)—what Jesus said, what He did; how He felt, what He thought; His loyalty to the Father; His faithfulness in the face of persecution; His forthrightness to His enemies; His compassion for the multitudes; His focus on the path marked out for Him by the Father—is to be yours.

Just as He told James and John, Peter and Andrew, and Matthew, He now tells you and me. "Follow Me."

When you pick up the bread and when you drink the wine, this is what you are promising to do. Have you done that? Picked up the bread and drunk the wine? Of course you have. We call it Communion.

I think it is becoming clearer to you, yes?

Do you know who you are?

You are not here to stare at the pretty lights. You are here to learn all you can at the lampstand over there to your left. Having been filled with knowledge and understanding, you are about to go on a journey with Jesus—at the table of showbread, the table of the Presence. As you pick up the bread and the wine, you are promising to join Jesus in His ministry. Don't do it unless you mean it. When you participate in your next Communion service, consider that you are preparing to enter into sacred service for Jesus. Just like the priests of the wilderness Sanctuary, to enter "unworthily" puts you in grave danger of dying.

In 1 Corinthians 11:18–22, Paul addresses a problem among the Corinthians and tells them that they are factious, greedy, gluttonous, and drunk. Then they come to Communion. As a result, Paul says, in verse 30, that many of the saints at Corinth were sick and weak and dying. (Sort of reminds me of Leviticus 10:1–11, what do you think? I purposefully didn't tell you what these verses say in hopes you would look them up. Did you?)

Now again, please—let's not have any human traditional interpretations here about eating unworthily—such as sharing Communion with your children in a training situation—when the interpretation is already given to us. This is serious business. This is about people who are coming to Communion with no love in their hearts for one another, with no intention of entering into the compassionate ministry of Christ.

This smacks of the same problem as "taking the Lord's name in vain"; that is, accepting the family name of God at your baptism/adoption, but living as if you didn't belong to the family at all. This is behaving as if you didn't care that the family name is being dragged in the dirt, that God's reputation is being tarnished, that His Name is being treated as a "vain" (empty) thing, that your promise to live as His child is a "vain" (empty) promise. This is not "keeping" (treasuring, cherishing) the Commandments and the Covenant Grace-Faith Relationship, and it grieves the heart of God when we do it.

Do you know who you are?

If you have entered the curtained gate into the courtyard and accepted the sacrifice given for you,

---

As you pick up the bread and the wine, you are promising to join Jesus in His ministry. Don't do it unless you mean it.

then as Paul says, "You are bought with a price." You belong to God and are set apart by God. You are a ministering Priest.

Look at Leviticus 7:6, 7 with me for a moment. The early part of this chapter is about the guilt offering; that is, a sin done thoughtlessly—as described in Leviticus 5:4. But Leviticus 7 addresses the priest's role in the guilt offering. Notice verses 6 and 7. Do you see who eats the guilt offering? The priest eats it and bears in his own body the sin and guilt of the sinner—just like Jesus. (For a check on this concept, compare with Numbers 18:1.)

In Galatians 6:2 when Paul says to bear one another's burdens and so fulfill the law of Christ, he's as serious as a heart attack. Bearing one another's burdens and ministering to one another is the training we need for learning to minister to others. When strangers come through the door of the church needing ministry, the Lord doesn't want them to find a bunch of amateurs. We practice on each other until we get good at it. We practice our loyalty and faithfulness and forthrightness and compassion and focus in love—on each other.

In medical school we learned that the practice of medicine required "practice." So we practiced on each other. We learned to draw blood by drawing from each other. I have huge veins in my forearms—exceptionally huge veins. My friend in medical school, Ken, pushed his needle right through my vein and into my elbow joint. I fainted (again). He obviously needed more practice.

Every time you take the bread and wine at Communion you are committing yourself to this ministry of Jesus Christ—with whatever gifts the Holy Spirit has gifted you with in whatever place where He has assigned you. You are a ministering Priest—to each other and to others who come your way.

Do you know who you are?

You are a ministering Priest.

Let me add a quick word. In fact, let me add the words of Deuteronomy 6:6, 7: "And these words which I am commanding you today, shall be on your heart; and you shall teach them diligently to your sons and shall talk of them when you sit in your house and when you walk by the way and when you lie down and when you rise up."

At every opportunity you should be teaching these things to your children. Every child should be trained from the time they are old enough to sit with you in church. From three years old and up they need to know about the laver. They should be watching, and they should be participating as learners. That's why we have family rooms for foot washing. When you are holding the bread and the wine at Communion, they should be sitting with you, and they should be sharing with you. Let them participate. No, they don't have their own bread and wine. They participate *with you.*

When strangers come through the door of the church needing ministry, the Lord doesn't want them to find a bunch of amateurs.

You must teach. You must share. Give them a small piece of your bread, a small sip of your cup. Let them know that when they have made the same commitment that you have made, they will receive their own Communion bread and wine—and their own ministry.

That, of course, assumes that you have made your own commitment. Have you?

Do you know who you are?
A ministering Priest.

And now we come to the third piece of furniture. Do you remember it from our tour? Very good. It's the altar of incense that's described in Exodus 30.

Do you know what happens here? Yes, prayers. Revelation 8:3, 4 describes what takes place at this altar: "… and much incense was given him that he might add it to the prayers of all the saints upon the golden altar that was before the throne" (verse 3).

This altar symbolizes the prayers of the Priest. That's you. This altar is for intercession.

Let's look in Exodus 30:6 again. Please notice how carefully the Lord describes the placement of this altar. It's in front of the Veil (the third veil, the one that's always called "the Veil") which is just in front of the ark of the covenant—just in front of the mercy seat which sits over the ark that contains the Ten Commandments written on stone and the manna and Aaron's rod that budded—"where I will meet with you." Did you see those words in Exodus 30:6?

This is the closest you will ever be to God—when you are interceding for someone else.

Do you write in your Bible? Take notes in your Bible? If you do, take out your pen and underline those words: "… where I will meet with you." This is the closest you will ever be to God—when you are interceding for someone else. "Where I will meet with you."

God is in the salvation business and nothing supersedes that mission—not the keeping of the stars in their places, not the rise and fall of nations, not even the life of Jesus Christ Himself. And when you are interceding for someone, God is there.

Do you know who you are? A ministering Priest.

Are you overwhelmed yet? I am.

There are six people on a volleyball team. Do you play volleyball? If you do, then you know the game and you know the purpose of each person and the position they play. And you should be able to answer this simple question. Who's the most important person on the team? Depends on where the ball is, doesn't it? When the ball is in your part of the court, you are the most important person on the team.

So let's go back to the courtyard of the Sanctuary at the altar of burnt offering. Which member of the Godhead is most important here? Yes, I know that all of the Godhead is involved throughout the Sanctuary. But which One is represented here? Which One's responsibility is most obvious? This is the place of sacrifice. This is the place of the Lamb of God, Jesus the Christ.

As we move forward to the first apartment, Whose path are we following? Yes, Jesus' path (see John 14:12). And as we enter the first apartment—as we contemplate our need to understand the Word, our need to engage in ministry, our need to intercede for others—as we contemplate the awesomeness of what we are expected to do as ministering priests, we know that we need a helper. Who is going to help us?

Turn to John 16:13. Who is going to see to it that we understand what we need to understand? Turn to 1 Corinthians 12:7–11. Who is going to see to it that we have the gifts we need to do our ministry? Turn to Ephesians 4:12, 13. Who is going to see to it that we minister together, each one contributing to the body of Christ, and that we are drawn closer to each other? Turn to

Romans 8:26, 27. Who is going to see to it that we know how to pray and for whom to pray? And when we are overwhelmed, who will pray for us?

This area here, this first apartment is the special responsibility of the Holy Spirit. Yes, the furniture and symbols are about Jesus, but without His second Gift of the Holy Spirit:

We would be like children—unprepared to minister

Afraid to touch them—paralyzed by fear

Wanting to play with them—playing church

Thinking we know how to use them on our own—spiritual pride.

Do you know who you are?

You and I—we are ministering Priests for Christ, ministering Priests who are empowered by the Spirit.

As we enter into our ministry:

1.   We need the deep sense of awe that comes from knowing why our feet are washed and by Whom they are washed—at the laver.

2.   We need the deep sense of wonder at all that Jesus has for us to learn as He is equipping us for service—at the lampstand.

3.   We need the deep sense of empowering as we realize the truth of Ephesians 2:10—"For we are His workmanship, created in Christ Jesus for good works, which God prepared beforehand that we should walk in them"—at the table of the Presence. Did you notice Who has prepared our ministry, the good works beforehand?

     – opening a door

     – offering a glass of water

     – sharing the fellowship of a meal

     – teaching a memory verse to a child

     – listening to a sick person tell about their sadness at being ill.

These opportunities are all prepared beforehand by God that we should walk in them.

That's our part—the "walking" part. Look at Romans 6:17 with me. "But thanks be to God that though you were slaves of sin, you became obedient from the heart…"

We are here as ministering priests to be "obedient from the heart," to eat the bread and drink the wine of ministry.

4.   We need the deep sense of the burden of interceding for others—at the altar of incense.

We are ministering Priests.

(Bible Study Alert: Hebrews 9:1–6 describes the work of the priests in the earthly sanctuary and concludes with these words: "the priests are continually entering the outer tabernacle, performing the divine *worship*" (italics supplied). This is the third time we have discovered the word "worship" in our discussions, in the culmination of the Covenant Grace-Faith Relationship (Psalm 95:6, 7), in the "presenting yourselves" description of "obedience from the heart" (Romans 12:1), and now here in the Sanctuary where we function as priests. Watch for this word "worship," which will appear again in the Time of the End scenarios (Revelation 14:6, 7). Study these Scriptures together and see what they can tell you about what "worship" is, another misunderstood word in the Seventh-day Adventist lexicon.)

Do you remember the Chicago Bulls in their 1996–1998 seasons? Do you remember Michael Jordan—fantastic playmaker and shooter from anywhere *but* not an especially good rebounder, especially under the basket? Do you remember Scotty Pippen—the field marshal who called the plays, a good shooter from the top of the circle *but* not the corners, and *not* a great outside shooter from beyond the three-point line? Do you remember Dennis Rodman—the wild, tattooed man, the lone wolf who was a terrible shooter *but* was a fantastic rebounder under the basket or at mid-court and a great feeder to other players?

Who was the most important player for the Chicago Bulls? Michael, Scotty, Dennis? Let me suggest that it was—none of these.

The most important person was Phil Jackson, the coach. He knew how to get the lone wolf Rodman to play team ball; he knew how to communicate to Pippen what plays to call; he knew how to set up for Jordan's great shooting strength. Phil Jackson knew how to coach toward the team's strength and away from their weaknesses.

The coach is the most important team member. Our coach is the Holy Spirit.

Remember what we read in John 3:5. Jesus said, "Unless you are born of the water and the Spirit, you cannot enter the kingdom of God." You cannot be a live, functioning Christian (don't forget Ezekiel 37:14) until you step past the altar of burnt offering, until you accept the second Gift of the Holy Spirit who gives you your new heart and breathes life into you, until you step into the role of a functioning priest.

Do you know who you are?

First of all, you are a forgiven, beloved saint. (Level 1)

Secondly, you are washed, you are gifted, you are coached, you are drawn to God and to each other into a cooperating team, a functioning body, a ministering church. (Level 2)

If you are willing to make Jesus Christ the Lord of your life, and if you are willing to be obedient from the heart to the leading of the Holy Spirit, then you *are* one of the ministering Priests among the People of God.

(Just like R-G-B, there is a *thirdly*, but we will discuss that in a later conversation. Stay tuned.)

This was our second conversation about the metaphorical words and concepts that I wanted to discuss with you in the "middle section" in preparation for discussing the unique role of the Seventh-day Adventist Church in the Time of the End—which will help us answer the question, "Do you know who you are?" I am watching your face as your mind frames the question, "Yes, so how does this fit in?"

Imagine the end time world where all the clear-thinking, godly pastors—both Seventh-day Adventist and non-Seventh-day Adventist—are either dead or in jail. (They are the obvious first targets—always have been—in a world of persecution.) Imagine a world where all normal relationships are being pulled asunder, where all human compassion has been obliterated, where "… every intent of the thoughts of [their] heart[s] was only evil continually" (Genesis 6:5). Imagine a world where all thoughtful considerations of God have been hijacked, where all religious allegiance is being commanded by and focused on an earthly power.

Imagine the people of this world floundering about, wondering, "What's going on?" They are looking for someone who *knows* what's happening and is willing to *teach* them, who has compassion for them and is willing to *minister* to their needs, who is willing to bear their burdens and to *intercede* for them.

God is preparing His people to be Priests to a world in chaos. God's preparation for His people to function as Priests in the "chaotic" world is to empower them (comfort them, teach them, remind them, focus them, convict them, gift them, John 14–16) to function as Priests in the comparatively "normal" world. When we say that God's people are to be Priests, that word "Priest" is a job description which is loaded with meaning, loaded with activity—exceedingly, overwhelmingly more than we normally associate with being a church member. Is it any wonder that the heart needs to be transformed (Romans 12:2) before the job can be undertaken?

Now that we have discussed the job description, we need to discuss the attitude of those who are functioning in the power of the Holy Spirit. But that's for our next conversation. If you like, we can move right into it—or we can take a break. Either way, I'll be waiting for you (on the next page).

God is preparing His people to be Priests to a world in chaos.

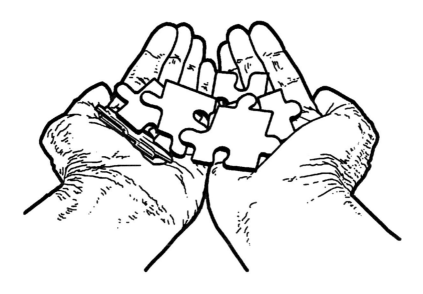

Chapter 9

Do You Know You Are Called to be a Faithful Steward?

"Do nothing from selfishness or empty conceit, but with humility of mind regard one another as more important than yourselves; do not merely look out for your own personal interests, but also for the interests of others." Philippians 2:3, 4

Welcome back. If you're ready, it's time to take on another of the metaphorical phrases that Seventh-day Adventists are so fond of—Steward. In our last conversation (our last chapter), we discussed the job description of God's People. Now I want to discuss with you the attitude of God's People as they undertake their assignment, the attitude of a Steward.

By way of reminder, I am still in the "middle section," that series of conversations where we talk about the deeper, more intense Covenant Grace-Faith Relationship, that part that is not the exclusive purview of Seventh-day Adventists. We'll get to that exclusive part soon enough. But for now,

just consider yourself one of millions of Christians who have been called by God to a clearer understanding of who He is and—who you are.

Eliezer stands by the city well in the town of Nahor. His camels are all kneeling. Those who have accompanied him in the large caravan are milling about beside their animals, not straying too far in this foreign market place, uncertain as to whether they are to unload or to prepare to move on. It is the time of evening when the women of the city come to draw water. But now there is no water, at least not above ground.

In that part of the world, water is like gold. You don't just help yourself to someone else's gold. So they're all waiting—while Eliezer prays. Eliezer, the servant, the oldest member of the household of Abraham. Eliezer, the steward.

Why is he called a "steward"? Because he has charge of all that Abraham owns. Everything. It does not belong to Eliezer—none of it. But he has charge of all of it.

Eliezer has been given an assignment by his master Abraham. Even now he can hear his master's voice. "Do not take a wife for my son, Isaac, from among the Canaanites. Go to my country and my relatives. Find a wife for Isaac there." (The story is in Genesis 24 if you want to follow along.)

Abraham had received the promise from the Lord. Through Isaac would be the lineage from which would come the Savior of the world—Messiah, the Promised One (see Genesis 12:3). Abraham has entrusted one aspect of the fulfilling of this promise to the man who has proved himself to be a trusted servant, the steward of all his possessions, Eliezer.

On arriving at the city gate of the city of Nahor, Eliezer *prays.*

His notion of success is simple: to seek the will of God, that it will be a kindness to his master. His journey is not an ego trip; he is about his master's business. His prayer is not an empty ritual; he prays from his heart. Eliezer believes in a God who answers prayer. (My focus is Eliezer and not his prayer, but the actual prayer, which is beautifully practical, is in Genesis 24:12–14).

When God answers his prayer by sending Rebecca to water the camels, almost before he is finished praying, Eliezer is *persistent.*

On arriving at the house of Bethuel—who is the son of Abraham's brother Nahor, Eliezer refuses to eat until he has concluded his business for his master (see Genesis 24:33). He is not sidetracked from his priorities. His only concern is for the success of his mission. He is offered a lengthy stay, wonderful food, and pleasures. But Eliezer is a man of one focus: his mission for his master. He is *persistent.*

Eliezer had asked God for a sign, that the young woman who would come and offer to water the camels would be the woman he sought for Isaac. When this young woman turned out to belong to Abraham's family, Eliezer knew that God had sent her to him. But now he needs to know if her family also understands this. Eliezer becomes *persuasive.*

Eliezer gives his witness, telling the story of his assignment, his prayer, and the answer to his prayer (Genesis 34:34–47). Then he adds, "I bowed low and worshiped the Lord, the God of my master Abraham, who has guided me in the right way to take the daughter of my master's kinsman for his son." Eliezer is building his case. He lets that last message sink in.

Then he says, "If you are going to deal kindly and truly with my master, tell me. If not, tell me know, that [I will know what I should do]" (verse 49).

Now he waits to see what this family will answer.

Bethuel and Laban quickly agree to Eliezer's persuasive argument, realizing that God is with this faithful steward. But only when they concede, "This is from the Lord," does Eliezer present them with costly gifts from Abraham. Eliezer is not going to waste his master's precious gifts. He is not the owner. He is the steward.

Eliezer is one of the Bible's best examples of a steward—in handling all that Abraham possesses—including the promise God has given to Abraham. By praying, being persistent, and arguing persuasively, Eliezer is a faithful steward.

But what, exactly, is a steward?

If you had asked that question of your grandfather, he would have said that it was the man who made up your bed in the Pullman cars on a train. Today we would say that a steward is a male flight attendant on an airplane. But the biblical description of a steward is far different.

Notice what Eliezer is called. Look at Genesis 24:2: "And Abraham said to his oldest servant …" Eliezer is called a servant.

Now turn in your Bible to a description that Jesus gives in Matthew 24:45. "Who then is the faithful and sensible slave whom his master put in charge of his household …" This person is called a slave.

In both instances the person being described —the servant or slave—has a function to fulfill, the function of a steward. In both instances the person is an underling who has been elevated to a position of high responsibility. This person is being put in charge of something that does not belong to him. This person is asked to solely manage something that is not his. Conclusion: This person is acting as a steward. In fact, in today's language, a steward is a manager.

The Bible is full of stories about stewards: Moses, Joseph, Abraham, Paul. They are all Stewards. Question: As stewards, what was it they were asked to manage that didn't belong to them?

Moses was to manage the care and keeping of people, specifically, the children of Israel, through whom was the lineage to the Messiah (Exodus 33:12–17). Moses was to explain to them the character of God—through the Ten Commandments (Exodus 19:3–9). Moses was to instruct them in the symbolism of God's ministry, which was to be their ministry—the wilderness Sanctuary (Exodus 25:8, 34:6–9; Leviticus 19:2). However, this revelation of God's ministry would be explained more clearly in the life, death, resurrection, and heavenly Sanctuary ministry of Jesus (Hebrews 8–10).

The children of Israel did not belong to Moses. They belonged to God. However, God placed the management of them in the hands of Moses. Moses was a Steward.

Joseph was to manage power, the power of Egypt. Joseph was made steward of Pharaoh, the most powerful ruler on earth at the time. But this was only a training ground for the management of the power to preserve God's people—his own brothers who had sold him into bondage. Joseph had the power of vengeance, but these brothers did not belong to him. Vengeance did not belong

---

In today's language, a steward is a manager.

---

to him (Genesis 45:5–8; 50:19). These things belonged to God. Joseph was asked to manage them, though he did not own them. Joseph was a Steward of God as well as a steward of the Pharaoh.

Abraham was to manage the Promise, specifically God's promise to send the Messiah through a miracle baby—Isaac. Abraham was to manage faith in God by trusting that God could resurrect this miracle baby, Isaac, if need be, to carry out His promise (Hebrews 11:18, 19). Abraham was a Steward of the most precious thing God owns and has to offer—life.

Paul was to manage the Gospel—the mysterious theological explanation of the Messiah. He was to teach it to new Gentile Christians, a few of whom had a meager synagogue school understanding of the Scriptures, most of whom had only a Gentile, superstitious understanding of spirituality.

Here, let's let Paul tell you himself in what way he is a steward.

"Of this church I was made a minister according to the *stewardship* from God bestowed on me for your benefit, so that I might fully carry out the preaching of the word of God; that is, the *mystery* which has been hidden from the past ages and generations; but has now been manifested to His saints, to whom God willed to make known what is the riches of the glory of this *mystery* among the Gentiles, which is: Christ in you, the hope of glory" (Colossians 1:25–27, italics supplied).

Without Paul's stewardship of the gospel, we wouldn't know this, wouldn't have this explanation, this justification for our hope. By Paul's own description in various letters, he sees himself as a slave, a servant, a Steward for God.

Are you getting a picture of the attitude required to be a steward? Yes, I can see that you understand. But do you know where I'm going with this? Let me press the issue even further, and keep my curiously hard question before you.

Do you know who *you* are?

What is the most important characteristic of a steward? Let's look at Matthew 25:21, "Well done, good and *faithful* slave " (italics supplied). The most important characteristic of a steward is faithfulness.

And what is faithfulness?

Let's go to the faithfulness chapter—Hebrews 11. Specifically read Hebrews 11:5: "By faith Enoch was taken up." (Familiar, isn't it?) From our previous conversation we know that Enoch was taken up—but why? And what did his faith have to do with it? (This should be looking very familiar to you!) Look at the last part of the verse. "… before his being taken up he was pleasing to God." Now *very* quickly turn to Genesis 5:24. "Enoch walked with God; and he was not, for God took him."

Compare those two scriptures. "… he was pleasing to God." "Enoch walked with God." Do you see it? They mean the same thing.

"Pleasing" does not mean bowing and scraping. It doesn't mean struggling to be good. "Pleasing" means "walking with God." The word in Hebrew means being in intimate friendship with,

trusting in, wanting to be like. (Review the connection of "pleasing to" and "walking" in 1 Thessalonians 4:1 and Colossians 1:10; scriptures you looked up for me two conversations ago. That was in Chapter 6, for those who are on that mountain hike.)

In what does Enoch trust? What does it say in Hebrews 11:6? (A verse that we've always found to be a bit of a mystery, but one which I hope you now have a better understanding of.) "Without faith it is impossible to please Him." That is, without faith it is impossible to want to be in intimate relationship with—to trust in—to want to be like God. Without faith it is impossible to walk with Him. It's always about relationship.

And what is our faith in? Continue in Hebrews 11:6. Our faith is in the fact "that He is and that He is a rewarder of those who seek Him." Our faith is in the fact that God is who He says He is, and that He can do what He says He can do. I want to be close to Someone like that. I can trust Someone like that. I want to walk with Someone like that. Don't you?

"Well done, good and *faithful* [steward]." Faithfulness is not about our doing the right thing. Faithfulness is trusting that God is God and that He can do the right thing.

What makes Eliezer such a good steward? Whom does Eliezer trust? He trusts the promise of God that his master Abraham has told him about. And ultimately He trusts God. "And I bowed low and worshiped the Lord … the God of my master

---

"Pleasing" does not mean bowing and scraping. It doesn't mean struggling to be good. "Pleasing" means "walking with God."

Abraham, who had guided me in the right way to take the daughter of my master's kinsman for his son" (Genesis 24:48).

Whom did Moses trust? Whom did Joseph trust? Whom did Abraham trust? Whom did Paul trust? Certainly not themselves. They were stewards. They trusted their master. When He said it, they believed it and they acted on that trust.

It is called faithfulness. Faithfulness is acting like you really believe God is God and that He can be trusted to do what He says He will do. This is what makes a steward *faithful*: he trusts in his master. It's not about *doing* the right thing; it's about a relationship of trust. When the *trusting* comes first, then the *doing* comes as a natural consequence. The secret of the Christian life is relationship.

During His conversation with His disciples at the Last Supper, Jesus assured them, "I will come again" (John 14:3). Just a short time later under the light of the full moon shining on the Mount of Olives, Jesus told this parable in the context of Time of the End events. "Who then is the faithful and sensible [steward] whom his master put in charge of his household to give them their food at the proper time?" (Matthew 24:45). Then Jesus compared this faithful steward with the evil steward described in verse 48. "But if that evil [steward] says in his heart, 'My master is not coming for a long time.'" (If your translation says "slave" or "servant," cross-check the story with Luke 12:42 which uses the word "steward" in the very same story.)

What is the difference between the faithful steward and the evil steward?

The faithful steward believes (in his heart) in what his master has said—that he will return. Therefore, the faithful steward is faithful. The evil steward does not believe (in his heart) in his master. He thinks he will be waiting for his master "for

a long time." And therefore, the evil steward is not faithful. This is what makes a steward faithful. He trusts in his master.

Now consider prayerfully as I put these questions to you. What have you been given to manage that is not yours? What task or truth, what person or project, what assignment has He gifted you for

---

This is what makes a steward faithful: he trusts in his master.

---

and given to you? What has God entrusted to your care, asking you to be a steward of this thing that doesn't belong to you but has been placed under your management—your stewardship?

Most importantly, is your job description of being a Priest and your attitude toward that assignment becoming clearer to you? Do you believe in your heart in your Master? Are you part of the deeper, more intimate Grace-Faith Relationship with God?

Do you know who you are?

To bring it home, look at these biblical facts with me:

1. "For we are His workmanship, created in Christ Jesus for good works, which God prepared beforehand, that we should walk in them" (Ephesians 2:10). You were created to do a good work that God has designed specifically for you.

2. "But to each one is given the manifestation of the Spirit for the common good… one and the same Spirit works all these things , distributing to each one individually

just as He wills" (1 Corinthians 12:7, 11). You are gifted and you are empowered to carry out this good work of stewardship.

3. "He hath shewd thee, O man, what is good; and what doth the LORD require of thee, but to do justly, and to love mercy, and to walk humbly with thy God" (Micah 6:8, KJV). A steward chooses to walk humbly with God. That is, a steward humbly remembers that God is God and He is the owner. The steward is not the owner of anything, God is.

By walking with God, a steward wants to be "pleasing to God"; that is, to be close to God and to trust God that He can assign him a task, gift him for the task, and enable him to carry out that task. A steward is given what does not belong to him and manages it for God. A steward is pleasing to God. A steward is faithful.

Remember Eliezer as he prays and persists and is persuasive. How does he do this? He doesn't do this on his own. He is able to be a good steward because he trusts his master. He trusts the God of his master. Therefore, he is faithful.

Do you trust God?

Steward, look around you. Look at who is nearest and dearest to you—your blood family and your church family. Look at where you live, what you have in your house, what you drive, what you earn. Look at the people in your neighborhood and where you work. Look at your recreational toys and your hobbies. Look at all your time, all your talents, all your finances, all your "stuff."

You don't own any of these things. You are a Steward for God.

What has God given you to manage for Him?

Do you trust God?

Do you know who you are?

This particular topic always stops me in my tracks. More than any other, this metaphorical concept of being a steward makes me discover just how worldly is my mindset. I say "discover" because although I know intellectually that I am a steward, a manager for God, not an owner of anything, my human mindset thinks and the world around me reinforces otherwise. I have to "discover" this concept again and again, not on my own, but with the prompting of, and under the conviction of the Holy Spirit.

Sanctification is the Holy Spirit's work of retraining the human heart to choose a different set of values, to function from a different mindset.

Level 2, the second part, sanctification is the work of a lifetime. Sanctification is the Holy Spirit's work of retraining the human heart to choose a different set of values, to function from a different mindset. Read Romans 8:5–11 again for yourself and let this concept sink deep into the very core of your being. Let it sink into your heart.

I'm sorry if I seem to be hammering on this one topic. But it is the one topic that we as Seventh-day Adventist Christians understand the least and the one topic that we resist the most—"to be transformed by the renewing of your mind, that you may prove what the will of God is, that which is good and acceptable and perfect" (Romans 12:2).

If you'll excuse me, I need to go pray by myself for a little while. When I return, I'm ready to turn a significant corner with you. We'll get into the specifics of being a Seventh-day Adventist Christian and how we gain a deeper, more intimate Covenant Grace-Faith Relationship with God.

I'll be back with you in just a bit.

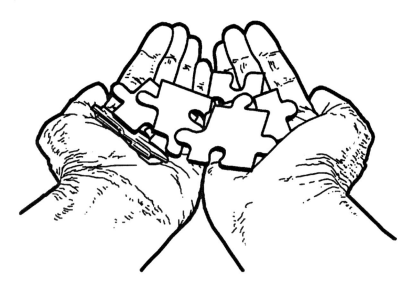

Chapter 10

Do You Know You Are a Seventh-day Adventist Christian?

"Then the voice which I heard from heaven, I heard again speaking with me, and saying,
'Go, take the book which is open in the hand of the angel who stands on the sea and on the land.'
So I went to the angel, telling him to give me the little book.
And he said to me, 'Take it and eat it; it will make your stomach bitter,
but in your mouth it will be sweet as honey.'
I took the little book out of the angel's hand and ate it, and in my mouth it was sweet as honey
and when I had eaten it, my stomach was made bitter." Revelation 10:8–10

Hello, again. Now that you've returned, I'm ready, even anxious, to turn that corner that I talked about. I'm ready to concentrate on the unique spiritual and historical description of the Seventh-day Adventist Church—and you as a Seventh-day Adventist Christian. Remember, I ask my curiously hard question, not only of the church body, but of you.

Do you know who you are?

Now for that corner we'll turn. I'm going to take all that we have studied thus far, all that the Bible says pertaining to all seriously seeking Christians, and apply it specifically to Seventh-day Adventist Christians.

Fair enough, you say.

But now—add to it all that the Bible says pertaining to us as Seventh-day Adventists.

And immediately, I hear you ask: Really? What makes us think that we're so special? Aren't we being a little arrogant?

What makes us think that we're so special? Aren't we being a little arrogant?

Believe me, it's not about arrogance—as the surprise or shock (depends on how you look at it) will reveal at the end of our conversation. It's about God's agenda and the way He makes known His agenda to His world. He has always had a special group with whom He has developed a Covenant Grace-Faith Relationship, through whom He transmits His character and His messages to the world. We even have a special name for this group. They are called the Remnant—another of those metaphorical words we want to explore. But before we discuss Seventh-day Adventists as the Remnant, let me explore with you whether we should even be considered as part of that special group that God has always had in every age, especially in every age of crisis.

Let me say right here that this exploration requires something that many people find difficult to do. Some don't have the patience for it. Some don't think it's worth the effort. Many don't think that God or His Word has anything to say worth exploring.

I am proposing that you and I do something that many find inconvenient. I want to do a Bible study with you. Unlike the Bible studies we had in our previous conversations, this one won't be easy. This will be an extended Bible study that requires some flipping through the pages and some thoughtful contemplation on your part.

I will not apologize for studying the Word of God, because in it we find the self-revelation of God, the plan of Salvation, and the hope that we as humans need to enable us to be rescued from the dilemma of Sin. Secondly, studying the Word of God is absolutely essential to enable us to be in a Covenant Grace-Faith Relationship with God. We have to talk with Him and, especially—the part we frequently leave out—He has to talk with us. No communication; no relationship.

So, if you are up for this, I promise to go slowly and allow time for you to think about each step. Patiently follow in your Bible that you always bring to our conversations. I think you will agree that the final product at the end of our study will be worth the effort.

To begin this exploration, let's attempt to understand one of those Bible teasers that God is famous for, like a Sudoku grid with only half the parts supplied, a "mystery" which God sets before us and says, "Consider the evidence. See if you can piece this one together." And I will begin, as usual, with a story.

It was one of those hot days when there were no clouds in the sky and the sun beat down unmercifully. Actually it had been hot and dry every day for the last three and a half years. There had been no rain. No early rain, no latter rain. No rain at all.

Elijah, the "hairy" prophet (according to 2 Kings 1:8), had called a meeting of all Israel, including King Ahab and his band of 450 prophets of Baal. Amazingly they all came. Imagine it, if you can. The entire mountainside was covered with people, people curious to see what would happen.

"Have you heard?"

"Do you know what's going to happen?"

"I heard Elijah threatened the king."

"I heard there's going to be a fight."

"Do you think the king will kill Elijah?"

"Isn't Elijah a prophet of God? You can't kill God's prophets, can you?"

Everyone had an opinion. Everyone had something to say. No one was certain but everyone wanted to know. It looked like a showdown, and everyone wanted to watch. They weren't about to get involved, of course. It was way too dangerous. They weren't committed one way or the other: neither cold nor hot, only lukewarm. They were onlookers only. They stayed close enough to see but far enough away not to get involved.

Then Elijah appeared over the crown of the mountain. As he came down the mountain, he did not approach the king or his prophets. In fact, he ignored the king altogether.

Instead he came near to the people. His eyes were like burning coals and his face was set like that of a stern schoolmaster. The spectators began to back away from him, but there were so many that it was difficult for the front rows to back up at all.

Elijah strode to within a few feet of the crowd and then demanded, "How long will you hesitate between two opinions? If the Lord is God, follow Him. If Baal [is god], follow him" (1 Kings 18:21).

These people were to make known the Creator God of Heaven to the world. These people had been given a job to do, but they weren't doing it.

Elijah scanned the crowd. These were the people of the Lord Most High. At least, these were the descendants of the people whom the Lord had placed at the crossroads of civilization: between Egypt and Assyria, between the north and the south, in the land through which everyone had to travel to go from one part of the known world to another. Here in this place these people were to make known the Creator God of Heaven to the world. These people had been given a job to do, but they weren't doing it and hadn't been doing it for some time.

"How long will you hesitate between two opinions?" he cried out again. But no one said a word.

Then Elijah realized that these people had forgotten. These people didn't know what they were supposed to do. They didn't know who they were.

(Bible Study Alert: For a study on your own, start with the sentiments expressed in Isaiah 1:3; Jeremiah 4:22; Hosea 5:4 and follow this with a word search of "do not [or] did not know" in a Bible program looking for similar ideas. Note the differences and similarities between those who are ignorant and those who are evil. It is chilling to discover the eventual outcome for people who "do not know" who they are.)

Do you like to do puzzles—jigsaw puzzles? For the sake of my discussion, I'm going to assume that you do, so I will ask: Where do you start on a jigsaw puzzle? Do you start with the corner pieces? Do you start on the edge pieces? Do you start gathering all the pieces of a particular color?

What's the biggest help you can have when doing a 1,000-piece jigsaw puzzle? Exactly! The picture on the box. I want to take you to one of the biggest puzzles in the Bible—the book of Revelation—where we will look at the "picture on the box." The book of Revelation has lots of puzzles contained in one big puzzle. I don't intend for us to attempt to resolve all the puzzles in the book of Revelation, but I do want us to tackle one of them.

But first, before taking on the smaller puzzle, let me give you the biggest clue, the equivalent of the "picture on the box" for the book of Revelation. This is a simplified, overall outline of the book of Revelation. You can open your Bible and flip through the various chapters as I proceed or you can just cruise through this short section. Your choice.

Chapter 1

Introduction and purpose of the book

Chapters 2–11

The series of the Sevens:

- Seven Churches (God's knowledge, wisdom, counsel, and advice to His People)

- Seven Seals (the People of God's experiential ministry and their interaction with the forces and minions of the enemy)

- Seven Trumpets (the historical outworking of the People of God in intercession and of the enemies of God's people in judgment).

Each of the Sevens describes the experience and progress of the People of God from the time of John to the Second Coming of Jesus

Chapter 12

The beginning of a complete, historical three-chapter review of the good versus evil conflict in the history of the People of God (aka The Great Controversy)—in three parts:

1. The conflict of the Dragon with the Jewish People of God

2. The conflict of the Dragon with the People of God in the Christian church, including the 1260 prophetic days-years (first described in the book of Daniel), and concluding with

3. The conflict of the Dragon with the People of God at the Time of the End.

Chapter 13

A review of the activities of the agents of darkness against the People of God, again in three parts:

1. The Dragon's call for, and the activities of, the dreadful and terrifying seven-headed beast (with characteristics from all the beasts of Daniel 7); that is, the Sea Beast of Revelation 13,

2. The Land Beast, and

3. The final activities of the Image to the Beast.

Chapter 14

The conclusion of the three-chapter historical review highlighting the response of the People of God to the activities of God (Chapters 7 and 10) and to the activities of the enemy (Chapters 11, 12, and 13), concluding with the Second Coming of Jesus.

Chapter 15 and 16

These give an expanded description of the results of the Close of Probation, closing the activities of all of the seventh and final phases of the Seven Churches, Seven Seals, and Seven Trumpets:

1. The consequences incurred by the People of God and their reactions, and

2. The consequences incurred by the enemies of God's people (the Seven Last Plagues), especially emphasizing the Sixth Plague (the demonic

delusion leading up to the final battle, Revelation 16:13, 14) and the Seventh Plague (the events just before and surrounding the actual Battle of Har-Megadon (Armageddon)) from the viewpoint of the enemy forces and their reactions (Revelation 16:17–21).

Chapter 17–19

An expansion of the events of the Seventh Trumpet, including:

- Chapter 17 reveals the connection between and the joint activities of the Scarlet Woman from the Wilderness (compare Revelation 12:6 with Revelation 17:3) and the Sea Beast from chapter 13, including an introduction to the Battle of Har-Megadon from the viewpoint of the conquering Christ and His allies, the People of God (verse 14), ending with the destruction of the Scarlet Woman (Babylon) by her own supporters.

- Chapter 18 is an expansion and explanation of God's intervention for His people in carrying out the events of chapter 14 and a review of the shocked reaction of the enemy to their own destruction of the Scarlet Woman (Babylon).

- Chapter 19 is a detailed review of the reaction of the People of God using two metaphors, Bride and Wedding Guests, to the results of Christ's return. The chapter concludes with a description of the actual Battle of Har-Magedon, told as a repeat description of the Second Coming of Jesus and the destruction of the Beast and False Prophet.

Chapter 20

A review of the events immediately following the Second Coming of Jesus, the events of the Millennium, and the events of the Great White Throne Judgment.

Chapter 21 and 22

A description of the New Heavens and the New Earth.

That's the picture on the box of the book of Revelation. We see a lot of activities and a lot of puzzles.

We will not attempt to solve all the puzzles in Revelation. Instead, I want to concentrate on only one small part of that "picture on the box," as my grandson Braeden does when he works on one of his favorite puzzles. His puzzle is a picture of Thomas the Tank Engine (who is blue) with his friend Percy (another tank engine, this one green) in their round house at night in the shadows under a nightlight. Braeden usually begins by working on just one part of the puzzle. He picks out all the pieces that display a blue engine, concentrating on just the parts that are obviously Thomas.

In the same way, let's go back and look at just one part of the puzzle in the book of Revelation. This time we will use another of Braeden's toys, a Slinky.

To refresh your memory, a Slinky is a tightly coiled, flat wire that when set on the first step of a stairway and pushed forward, will uncoil onto the next lower step, then fall forward and coil again on the next lower step, repeating this process on each succeeding lower step, "walking" down the stairway. You also know that the Slinky can be stretched out by grasping it on each end and pulling, stretching it out and revealing gaps between the wire coils.

That's what happens in the book of Revelation. Throughout the book there are "interludes" where John pauses, stretches out a section of the book, and inserts some extra descriptive material. We will investigate these interludes together, asking the purpose of these interludes. Who or what does John describe in these interludes? And why are these interludes placed in the narrative at these particular places? This is the smaller part of the larger puzzle I want to try to put together with you and, in the process, relate all of this to my opening story about Elijah.

Remember, this is going to take some careful Bible study. I will suggest Scripture references along the way (in parentheses, as a visual aid). If you are familiar with the ideas in these scriptures, feel free to *not* stop and look them up. Just be sure that you understand the ideas conveyed by these scriptures before going on. If you need to look up a scripture or you need to pause and reflect on a concept, please do so. I'll wait for you. If you need to write down some notes or make an outline (see the outline provided in the Discussion Questions for Chapter 10 in the Appendix) to keep track of the concepts as they are introduced, do that. I want you to understand each step along the way so that you can appreciate the conclusion at the end of our puzzle solution. Okay, are you up for this? Good.

Here's the first puzzle piece. Open your Bible to Revelation 6:12–17. Yes, like physically pulling out the Slinky, you really need to open your Bible to see these interludes as they occur. Okay, here is Revelation 6:12: "And I looked when He broke the sixth seal …" From here to the end of the chapter is a description of the activities in the

Sixth Seal. I'm sure you recognize the earthquake, the dark day, and the falling of the stars—all standard Adventist fare. This passage continues the narrative right up to the activities of verses 15–17 that anticipate and spill over into the Seventh Seal. But before the Seventh Seal is described, there is a pause in the action. The First Interlude is inserted here at the end of the Sixth Seal. Revelation 7 is the First Interlude.

In Revelation 7 we find described the 144,000 and the large group of victors who will be present in the throne room in heaven after the judgment. In whatever way you understand the 144,000, notice that they and then the large group—all these people—are introduced and described in this First Interlude immediately after the earthquake, the dark day, and the falling of the stars and right before the Seventh Seal discussed in Revelation 8:1. Pause a moment and think about where in historical time these events occurred— and where this First Interlude occurs. Remember the historical dates of the earthquake (1755), the dark day (1780), and the falling of the stars (1833). Store this general time period in your mind as your first clue to the puzzle.

Now look at the next puzzle piece, a description of the Second Interlude. Look at Revelation 9:13, 14 and onward. "And the sixth angel sounded, and I heard a voice from the horns of the golden altar which is before God, one saying to the sixth angel who had the trumpet …"

Under the activities of the Sixth Trumpet we find the release of the four angels at the River Euphrates and the consequential judgments that are about to fall on the people of the earth. While not attempting an interpretation of these activities (another part of the Revelation puzzle entirely), notice that before the Seventh Trumpet can be sounded, the Slinky is pulled out again and an interlude is inserted. The Second Interlude is Chapters 10 and 11.

Chapter 10 describes a strong angel—whom I'm sure you've heard called the Angel of the Loud Cry (see verse 3 for the reason why it's called "the loud cry")—who announces that "there will be time no longer"; that is, the end of prophetic time. If you're not sure that this "time" is a prophetic time, compare Acts 1:7 and 2:17 with Daniel 8:14, 17, and 19. Now note that we are talking about the Sixth Phases of the Seals and Trumpets (so far), right near the end of time. I don't want to go too fast here. Take your time; look this up. I'll wait.

Okay, now that you understand prophetic time, which prophetic time would that be? What is the longest prophetic time period of the Bible and the last one to be fulfilled? Yes, good for you. It is the 2300 day-year prophecy of Daniel 8. This strong angel of Revelation 10 says that prophetic time has now ended according to this Second Interlude. Then this angel displays a little book and the text takes some pains to make sure the reader knows that the book is now opened. Obviously the book was originally shut but has now been opened.

Do you know which book of the Bible was written, and then the writer was told, "… but as for you, Daniel, conceal these words and seal up the book *until the time of the end* … [my italics]"? Correct. I'm sure you recognized Daniel 12:4. Please note my emphasis here on *the time of the end*. Noting the italicized words, the end of prophetic time, that is, the end of the 2300 day-year prophecy (which marks the beginning of the Time of the End—Daniel 8:17, 19) has arrived and now the book of Daniel is to be opened and understood. "The mystery of God is finished."

Are you following this? Do you know what the mystery of God is? (If you are not sure, check Ephesians 3:9–12 and Colossians 1:26, 27. Compare these with Titus 2:13, 14.)

Apparently the information in the book of Daniel, especially that information which pertains to the Time of the End, is about the complete unfolding and final outworking of this mystery of God. This mystery is the complete revelation of the salvation of the People of God in the life, death, resurrection, ministry, and final rescue mission of Jesus Christ.

Revelation 10:8, 9 goes on to say that John is to take "the book which is open" and eat it. Eating is an apt description for taking it in and understanding it completely. In doing so, John gets indigestion and writes, "It was sweet in my mouth as honey [but] my stomach was turned bitter." Then John, who is used as a metaphor for all of the People of God who will actually live out these events, is told that he (and they) "must prophesy again concerning many peoples and nations and tongues and kings."

Apparently, in this Second Interlude, understanding the open book of Daniel was a pleasurable, and even joyous event for the People of God who were to live at the Time of the End. But the actual living out of these events from the book of Daniel was a bitter disappointment to them and led to more "prophesying." That is, it led these people to sharing further the events described in the book of Daniel when the prophetic time came to an end.

Now look more closely. This particular puzzle piece is bigger than the first one we looked at. It reveals multiple clues in a second part, a Part B, if you will, of the Second Interlude. This Part B (Revelation 11:1–13) covers the same interlude between the Sixth and Seventh Trumpets, but the time period mentioned is the 1260 day-year prophecy of Daniel 7:25 and 12:7, repeated twice in Revelation 12. It comes to an end, after which an earthquake (like in the Sixth Seal) is mentioned again.

Now I don't want to get caught up in how we understand the 144,000 of Revelation 7 or what the earthquake of Revelation 11 may symbolize. That's not the part of the puzzle I am trying to bring into view. I want you to look at the people described who are the focus of both the First and the Second Interludes: What or who is being described in each of these interludes, why are the interludes placed between the Sixth and Seventh Seals and the Sixth and Seventh Trumpets, and why is it so important for John to share this information that he stops the narrative and inserts these interludes at these particular places?

By way of review, just to know that I'm not losing you, let's stop and look at these two puzzle pieces and review the particular time and place in history where these two interludes are described.

1. The First Interlude is between the Sixth and Seventh Seals: A people are described who appear right after the earthquake, the dark day, and the falling of the stars (all of which are historically documented between the mid–1700s and the early 1880s) and are described as occurring right before the split sky and the Second Coming. Carefully note especially the time in history of this First Interlude.

   In this First Interlude (Revelation 7) these people are described as awaiting the sealing of the Holy Spirit (verse 3) right before the anticipated release of the Four Winds (of destruction, verses 2, 3) and just as the Four Angels (of destruction) at the River Euphrates are being released (Revelation 9:15).

2. The Second Interlude is between the Sixth and Seventh Trumpets. The Loud Cry Angel (Revelation 10) says that the prophetic

times, both the 2300 days-years (historically calculated as 457 BC to AD 1844) and (as specifically stated in Revelation 11) the 1260 days-years (historically calculated as 538–1798 AD), come to an end at approximately the same time as the First Interlude comes to an end. (If you need to, compare again with Daniel 7:17, 19.) This is followed by 1) a joyous time of understanding the prophecies of Daniel and 2) a bitter experience followed immediately by further "prophetic" activity.

Look at these two puzzle pieces. Is a picture beginning to emerge?

Do you know who you are?

Maybe, maybe not.

Okay, let's look for more pieces to this particular part of the puzzle. Turn to Revelation 12, the next gap in the Slinky, the Third Interlude that John inserts in his story. John stops in his narrative of the Time of the End events (Revelation 2–11) and reviews the history of the People of God (Revelation 12) in three parts:

1. The nation of Israel giving rise to the coming of the Messiah, the birth of Christ (verses 1–5),

2. The emergence of the Christian Church who must hide in the wilderness for 1260 day-years of persecution (verses 6 and 13–16), and

3. The emergence of the offspring (the remnant) of the Woman who appear at the end of the 1260 days-year

prophecy (verse 17). This emergence of the "remnant of her seed" occurs at the same time period in history as the first two interludes that we already examined.

If the Woman is the original or "mother" Christian Church, then the "seed" of the woman is the Protestant churches that sprang from the Woman. In verse 17, only a remnant of that seed remains of the original Christian Church. This group in this Third Interlude emerges at the end of the 1260 day-years, this "remnant of the seed." Now remember that this is the same group that appeared at the same historical time as was described in the two previous interludes. This group is now described in verse 17 as those "who keep the commandments of God and hold to the testimony of Jesus," which Revelation 19:10 describes as the spirit of prophecy. Again mark carefully the time in history when this Third Interlude occurs.

Let's go for one more puzzle piece, the Fourth Interlude. Turn to Revelation 14:6–12. In Revelation 14 John pulls out the Slinky and inserts an expansion of Revelation 7. Here is described the same group who were noted in Revelation 7 as being sealed in their foreheads (Revelation 7:3) to mark that they belong to God (2 Timothy 2:19). Compare Ephesians 1:13, 14 with 2 Corinthians 1:22, if you're not sure what the seal is or who does the sealing. Revelation 14 now reveals the purpose for their sealing as 1) following "the Lamb [in testimony and in faith] wherever He goes" and 2) giving a series of three final messages about the culmination of the Eternal Gospel.

These are final messages or last messages to a dying world because "the hour of His judgment has come." These messages of this Fourth Interlude are given using the same metaphor of Sanctuary-Day-of-Atonement *judgment* language as

was used at the end of prophetic time described in Daniel 8:14 where the sanctuary is described as being "cleansed" of the sins of God's People (understood by all as a judgment scene).

These three messages are:

1. Choose to worship the God who is Creator.

2. Choose to escape from the system of worship that causes confusion and rebellion.

3. Choose to recognize the consequences of worshiping or not worshiping (having or not having a relationship with) God. Those who don't worship God are eternally lost. Those who do worship God persevere or endure. They survive and are saved because they keep the commandments of God and have their faith in Jesus (in relationship).

These three messages are delivered by and acted on by the same people group that we have been describing in the previous three Interludes just prior to the Second Coming of Jesus Christ (compare the time frame in Revelation 12:12–16 with the time frame in verse 17). Again note when in history this Fourth Interlude occurs—as the two time prophecies are coming to an end—the 1260 years and the 2300 years.

Is this part of the puzzle of Revelation solved for you? Have we finished this part of the puzzle? In each of these Interludes, which all coincide in their timing at the same time in history, the Apostle John describes the same group of people. Do you know the identity of these people? They have the following characteristics.

- They appear at the end of the 1260 day-years after the falling of the stars.

- They are awaiting the sealing of the Holy Spirit.

- They are charged with calling the large group of victors in the Time of the End.

- They go through a great disappointment in order to "prophesy" further to the whole world.

- They are the "remnant of the seed" of the Woman (original church) in the wilderness.

- They keep the commandments of God and the testimony of Jesus and/or the faith of Jesus.

- They have the gift of the Spirit of Prophecy.

- They are to give the Three Angels' Messages to the world.

Do you recognize who these people are? Do you know who *you* are? You are a member of the Seventh-day Adventist Church. You are a Seventh-day Adventist Christian.

You are not just a pretty face who shows up on Saturday morning because your friends do or because that's what you or your family have always done. Yours is not just another in a long line of denominations. Your church, the Seventh-day Adventist church, is the final denomination.

You are called out by God to deliver the last message of the eternal Gospel to a dying world, to a world that is about to be visited by the Seven Last Plagues and to witness the Second Coming of Jesus Christ.

Do you know who you are?

"*So what's the hold up?*"

Good question. I was doing a series of Bible studies on the book of Revelation with a group of people. We were going through the book, chapter by chapter, verse by verse. When we got to the end, the people who were studying with me asked, "So what's the hold up? Why hasn't all of this process continued on to its final conclusion?" I didn't know.

All the pieces are in place. The world is *right now* in those Interludes between the Sixth and Seventh Seal, the Sixth and Seventh Trumpet. Everything is poised to go forward into Revelation 15 and onward. But it's not going forward; it's on hold.

Why? So I came back to look at the Seventh Church. Specifically, I came back to look at the interval between the Sixth and Seventh Churches. I came back to look at Laodicea. Then it hit me.

Did you notice that there is an interlude between the Sixth and Seventh Seals and between the Sixth and Seventh Trumpets? Every time he gets to this spot in history—between the Sixth and Seventh—John has stopped for an interlude, a descriptive passage about the People of God who live at this point in history. Did you ask yourself, "Where is the interlude between the Sixth and Seventh Churches?"

Turn in your Bible to the beginning verses of Revelation 3, which talks about the church of Sardis. "To the angel of the church of Sardis write: He who has the seven Spirits of God and the seven stars, says this: 'I know your deeds, that you have a name that you are alive, but you are dead. Wake up!'"

This is the "wake up" call of the Holy Spirit to the People of God in the Fifth Church. This is the breath of the Spirit awakening the dead bones of Ezekiel 37. Historically, this is usually interpreted to be the Protestant Reformation of the 1500s up to and including the second Great Awakening of the 1800s. The forward movement of the People of

God, escaping from the grasp of the Jezebel element in the Thyatira Church (Revelation 2, especially verses 24–29), has begun and continues on through the increased spiritual activity and the testing time of the Sixth Church, Philadelphia (Revelation 3:7–13).

Now read the description of the Seventh Church in Revelation 3:14–15. "To the angel of the church in Laodicea write: the Amen, the faithful and true Witness, the Beginning of the creation of God says this: 'I know your deeds, that you are neither cold nor hot.'"

The forward progress under the Sixth Church of Philadelphia comes to a grinding halt. Why? Laodicea's hallmark is apathy. The people of the Church of Laodicea are totally consumed with themselves (see Revelation 3:17). The true condition of the people of the Church of Laodicea is that they don't know who they are, *or* to whom they belong, *or* what they are to do. This is the Interlude between the Sixth and Seventh Churches—the apathetic condition of Laodicea.

There is a pause in the forward progress of the People of God as Laodicea tries to figure out who she is. Like the people of Israel in the time of Elijah, like the people who stood there that day on Mt. Carmel, not saying anything in response to Elijah's question—those people and this church of Laodicea don't know to whom they belong. They don't know their true condition. They don't know what they are to do.

They don't know who they are.

And I concluded that until Laodicea understands who she is and what she is to do, the whole system, the whole forward progress of the People of God is at a standstill. We are stuck between the falling of the stars and the split in the sky. We are awaiting the sealing of the Holy Spirit. We are at the end of the Sixth Church, the Sixth Seal, the Sixth Trumpet, but the system—as outlined in the rest of the book of Revelation—is at a standstill.

The true condition of the people of the Church of Laodicea is that they don't know who they are, or to whom they belong, or what they are to do.

Of course, God will not tolerate this situation for very long. He only allowed the children of Israel to wander around in the wilderness for forty years until He brought a test—the temptations at Baal-peor—that separated those who were loyal to Him from those who were not.

It was the same at Mt. Carmel. A test was brought that revealed who was God and who was not. It also revealed who was loyal to God and who was not.

A test is coming to the world and to this group of people—the people of the Interludes. This testing time is what we in Adventism commonly refer to as the Shaking Time. (See Hebrews 12:26, 27; Haggai 2:6, 7.) According to the prophecy of Revelation 14:7 "the hour of His judgment *has* come," that testing time which began at the end of prophetic time and is increasing in intensity. For details, review the history of the children of Israel in the book of Numbers. For the logical outworking of this testing time (1 Peter 4:17, 18), please wait. It's a topic for a later conversation.

This group—once the Shaking Time has done its work—this group will move forward to deliver the three messages with vigor and with power. And under the guidance of the mighty Latter Rain Angel described in Revelation 18 they call out the large group of victors of Revelation 7.

When that's complete—then comes the Second Coming of Jesus.

Do you recognize yourself in this part of the puzzle?

Do you know who you are?

As I said, we have turned the corner from talking about Christians in general to talking about Seventh-day Adventist Christians in particular, and we are getting closer to the answers to our curiously hard question, Do you know who you are?

Actually the topic we just finished is one of those answers. It doesn't apply to other Christians unless they want to become part of God's special called-out and sent people. Yes, Christians in general are called-out and special as we noted in our discussion of being a Priest. But the Remnant has a special calling, different from other Christians, just as Elijah and John the Baptist were different from the other believers of their day (An example of one of these believers is Nathanael under the fig tree in John 1:47–48). But I am prematurely getting into our next discussion of the Remnant, so hold that thought.

The fact that you are a Seventh-day Adventist Christian with a special task for God is not about being arrogant. Being part of a church that has forgotten who she is and is wallowing in her own self-importance and self-indulgence is not something to be proud or arrogant about. Rather, it is a cause for shame, for the proverbial "sack cloth and ashes" treatment, which is an excellent, positive reason for the Seventh-day Adventist position on jewelry and other outward adornment. (See Exodus 33:4–6 as an example.)

In the opinion of the world, the Seventh-day Adventist Church has no need to be ashamed. We have the best church organizational structure in the world. Many other denominations say so. We have the largest Protestant education system in the world. We have the largest Protestant health care system in the world. But excellent as these are, they are not the reason for the existence of the Seventh-day Adventist Church. Our church exists for one reason only—to be the Remnant, to display by precept and example the messages of the Three Angels of Revelation 14. We are the Remnant who is to call out the Final Remnant—those unnumbered victors on the sea of glass in Revelation 7 who come out of the final, great tribulation.

Excellent as they are, our church structure, our education system, and our hospitals are only a means by which we are to spread the Remnant message. But we frequently pat ourselves on the back for these systems, and more. We say: "Is this not Babylon the great that I have built?" (Daniel 4:30). Or to return to our Laodicean metaphorical description of Revelation 3:17, "I am rich, and have become wealthy, and have need of nothing." But again I am digressing into a later conversation about what it means to be a Witness.

So, I'm going to grab a quick drink of water and, if you are ready, push on into our next conversation.

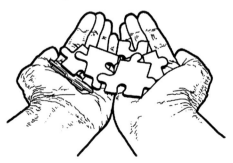

Chapter 11

Do You Know You Are Part of the Remnant?

"Behold, I am going to send you Elijah the prophet before the coming of the great and terrible day of the LORD. And he will restore the hearts of the fathers to their children and the hearts of the children to their fathers, lest I come and smite the land with a curse." Malachi 4:5, 6

Hi. Welcome back. Did you get a drink too? I did and now I'm really excited to return to our conversations because we've started down the path to getting some more answers to our curiously hard question, "Seventh-day Adventist Christian, do you know who you are?"

The Bible tells so many stories about the Remnant that our conversation could easily get entangled in multiple metaphors or extensive illustrations. But then we would lose the focus on the topic at hand. There are stories about Noah, about Abraham, about Job, about Jacob. And we find illustrations of the Remnant based on the story of Joseph and the story of David. There are prophecies of the Remnant from Isaiah to Malachi. It's obviously a hot topic in the Scriptures. And I haven't begun to mention the New Testament references. Yes, it would be easy for us to get lost in this topic.

Therefore, I want to talk with you as a Seventh-day Adventist Christian. I want to focus on the Remnant as it pertains to the Time of the End. As I reminded you in our last conversation, we are the final church of the last days. We *are* that part of the People of God especially called to deliver a last day message to the world. We *are* the Remnant of the Time of the End. Do we—do you—know what that means? Do you know who you are? We really have turned a corner in our conversations, and we are heading full steam down the road.

Next stop—the metaphor of the Remnant.

Oh, and by the way, don't forget to bring along your Bible. You must be able to check out what I tell you.

To begin, let's take time for a review. We'll look at what we have talked about so far and why it was important to discuss it prior to this juncture. I want to couch this review in terms that apply to all the "Remnants" identified in Scripture. Every Remnant follows the same path. Every Remnant endures the same experiences. Any one of the Remnants you might find in the Bible cannot function as a Remnant, cannot *be* a Remnant unless and until they have studied out, experienced, and chosen to participate in all that we have stated up to now.

1. Under the conviction of the Holy Spirit, every Remnant has undergone a most distressingly painful *change of heart* (Ezekiel 36:26, 27). As a result, the Remnant has *chosen* to live in Covenant Grace-Faith Relationship with God—the Covenant Relationship of R-G-B—the Covenant Relationship based on God and His Grace and Gifts *and* the Remnant's Faith response (Ephesians 3:14–21). They believe that God is and that God knows what He is doing. The Remnant lives the motto on U.S. coins—"In God We Trust"—in everything (Hebrews 11:6). This choice to accept a change of heart and this choice to live in Covenant Relationship with God does not make them the Remnant. It makes them true Christians. Like all true Christians in this Covenant Grace-Faith Relationship, the Remnant follow the example of their spiritual father, Abraham (Galatians 3:7, 9, 29).

2. Every Remnant has been given a *message* about the coming crisis to deliver to the people of the world,

both to those who have chosen to live in relationship with God and to those who have not so chosen. The message is always the same message: Choose to return to the Lord for He is about to return to you (Jeremiah 23:2–6). It is a call to return to the Covenant Grace-Faith Relationship. We will especially talk about this topic as it relates to the message of our Remnant Seventh-day Adventist Church in a later conversation.

The crisis does not change them into the Remnant. The crisis reveals them to be the Remnant.

3. Every Remnant is asked to personally *endure* and to *explain to others* how to endure a crisis that envelops their world. The crisis does not change them into the Remnant. The crisis reveals them to be the Remnant. This is where the Remnant is recognized as separate and distinct from other Christians. Over and above being Christian—like Noah, not only must the Remnant survive, they must address the crisis for the benefit of others (Hebrews 11:7; 2 Peter 2:5).

4. In anticipation of and in preparation for the coming crisis, every Remnant is assigned a *task* to do

that will *provide for the survival of others.* Like good Stewards and like faithful Priests, they take their assignment very seriously (Genesis 45:5–7; compare Numbers 18:1 with Exodus 28:29). We will talk more about this particular topic in later conversations.

5. Because it is a crisis and because they are ordinary people who have been asked to do an extraordinary task, every Remnant *must* function, can *only* function, in the *power of the Holy Spirit* (Zechariah 4:6). But their connection with the Holy Spirit will have to have been established *prior to the time* when they must work by His power (Matthew 25:1–4).

We have already discussed all of these points. Originally, we did not discuss them as pertaining directly to the Remnant, but they do. All of these points, in fact, come together in defining who the Remnant are, what they must do, and how they must do it. As I said earlier, these kinds of discussion topics have occupied the thoughts and discussions within the Seventh-day Adventist Church for decades, sometimes separately, sometimes jointly. We frequently speak to each other as if we understand the implications of these discussions on our identity and our mission.

If that is so, then what keeps the Seventh-day Adventist Church from *being* the Remnant of the End Time? Why are we stuck in the ignorance and apathy of Laodicea? Because, as Seventh-day Adventists, we choose not to recognize or to address one more characteristic of the Remnant. And that leads me to remind you of a parable and not one, but two short stories.

First, the parable. Look at Matthew 13:3. "Behold, a sower went out to sow." And you can read the rest of the parable, which I'm sure is familiar to you, about the three unproductive soils. According to Jesus' explanation of the parable, the soil in which the seed was sown beside the road is the hearts of those hearers who choose not to take the time to understand. The soil in which the seed was sown upon the rocky places is the hearts of those hearers who are too shallow of commitment to withstand the rigors of the Christian life. But as for the soil in which the seed was sown among the thorns, in these hearts the seed finds sufficient receptiveness and depth to grow. Please notice: These hearts, this soil, grows the Gospel seed very well. If this Christian heart can grow thorns, it can grow the seed of the Gospel.

The worry of the world and the deceitfulness of riches—are equally deadly to the Gospel seed.

Observe what happens when the Gospel seed is sown among the thorns. The thorns of the "worry of the world" rise up to choke out the Gospel and the thorns of the "deceitfulness of riches" rise up and choke out the Gospel. Both kinds of thorns—the worry of the world and the deceitfulness of riches—are equally deadly to the Gospel seed and to the hearts in which the thorns grow.

Now, for the two short stories.

First story: The day had been a long one. Elijah's eyebrows and the hair on his arms were singed by God's fire that consumed the sacrifice. Blood soaked Elijah's robe from the slaughter of the priests of Baal. Deep round, red circles marked Elijah's knees where he had knelt for hours praying for rain. Sore calluses ached on Elijah's feet from running all the way from Mt. Carmel to Jezreel, guiding the chariot of King Ahab in the driving rain that poured down in answer to Elijah's prayer. Elijah was dead tired.

But hardly had he gotten to sleep when a messenger shook him awake with the disturbing news that Jezebel would "make your life as the life of one of" the slain prophets of Baal "by tomorrow about this time." Despite the wealth of evidences of the Lord's power and protection that Elijah had witnesses that day on Mt. Carmel, he sprang up from his short repose and immediately ran for his life.

He ran in wild abandon all night and all the next day ninety miles through the kingdom of Israel and through the kingdom of Judah to the city of Beersheba in the south, where he left his servant behind. He continued running into the next night another "day's journey" until he collapsed of utter exhaustion under a juniper tree in the deserts of the Sinai Peninsula.

In his complete mental, spiritual, and physical meltdown, Elijah was afraid for his life. After being awakened and fed twice by an angel, Elijah still did not understand that the Lord was with him, but continued forty days more to Horeb, the mountain of God (that is, Sinai).

Second story: The dungeon cell was like all dungeon cells of his day—dark, damp, and cold. The underground temperature remained around fifty-five degrees Fahrenheit. It was vermin infested and minimally furnished. John the Baptist, a man of the outdoors, was now confined to a space entirely too small for a man who was used to roaming in the wilderness of Judah and Perea east of the Jordan River.

He knew he had brought this upon himself because of his public condemnation of King Herod in the dalliance with, and marriage to, his brother's wife. But John did not regret his pronouncements of sin against the king. Although he knew that his popularity with the people would

protect him temporarily, ultimately he expected to be where he was: in prison and marked for death.

But he also knew that the Messiah was now in the world. And like all good Jews, he expected the Messiah to quickly right all wrongs—vanquish the Roman legions, depose the Idumaean despot Herod, and establish the righteous reign of the Servant spoken of by David and Isaiah and the other prophets.

John had seen the dove descend and alight on Jesus. John had heard the voice of God proclaim, "This is My beloved Son, in whom I am well pleased" (Luke 3:21, 22). Hadn't he? He had been told by the Holy Spirit that this was the sign he was to watch for, the sign by which he would recognize the Messiah (John 1:32–34). Hadn't he?

Then why was his cousin Jesus not doing what the Messiah was supposed to do? Why wasn't Jesus raising up an army and fomenting a revolution? Why wasn't Jesus coming to get John out of this terrible prison?

Elijah and John the Baptist are specifically named in Scripture as supreme examples of the Remnant who are to deliver a message to a world that is about to witness the coming of the Lord. Elijah was given the privilege of publically inviting the people to choose whom they would worship—God or Baal. Then he called on God to come and defeat the wicked powers that were leading the People of God astray. Elijah had both parts of the Remnant message in his message, even though the emphasis was on the first part, to choose.

John the Baptist was given the privilege of inviting the people to choose to return to God and prepare for the coming of the Messiah. Then he baptized Jesus and set in motion the combined work of the Son, the Holy Spirit, and the Father to initiate the work of the Messiah in defeating Satan, the real enemy of the People of God. John the

Baptist had both parts of the Remnant message in his message, even though the emphasis was on the second part, He is coming.

Yet these two men were like all the others in the long line of Remnants. They were exceedingly and painfully *human*. Does this amaze you or were you expecting it? This is the characteristic that we frequently ignore to our peril: The Remnant is *not* superhuman. The Remnant is exceedingly and painfully human.

Does this sound like anyone you might know?

Do you know who you are?

L ook at 1 Kings 19:4. Do you recognize the symptoms? If you have read any magazine articles recently on Post-Traumatic Stress Disorder (PTSD), you will recognize immediately that Elijah was having an acute situational stress reaction. A panic attack. As emotionally high as he was on Mt. Carmel, was how low he crashed afterward. His focus had shifted from God to himself. He completely lost all self-confidence (which is probably okay), but he also lost all confidence in his relationship with God (which was not okay).

What restored his lost "confident expectancy," his Hope? What did he hear on the mountain after the wind, and the earthquake and the fire passed by? He heard the truth in the Word of the Lord. He was reminded that what had happened was not about him. God had a Remnant already preserved, and God still had a work for him to do. His choice to listen to the Word of the Lord restored his Hope.

Now look at Matthew 11:2, 3. John the Baptist had been so certain, so confident when he was knee deep in the Jordan River. He had known what to say to those who came for baptism. He had known what to say to the Pharisees who questioned him. He had recognized the sign of the Messiah promised him by the Holy Spirit. He had declared that Jesus was the Lamb of God who

had come to take away the sins of the world (John 1:19–29).

But now, in the cold, dark prison cell, John

Like all the others in the long line of Remnants, they were exceedingly and painfully human.

---

was no longer confident. He no longer saw in Jesus the mighty Warrior King that everyone expected the Messiah to be. After a time in solitary confinement, John was thinking, "Did I make a mistake? Did I get it wrong? Should we look for someone else?" His focus shifted from God to himself. John was despondent and depressed. It was a classic case.

What restored his lost "confident expectancy," his Hope? What did he hear in the message that his disciples brought back from Jesus? He heard the truth in the Word of the Lord in the prophecy of Isaiah 61:1 and compared it to the life experiences of Jesus. As the Holy Spirit brought to his remembrance Isaiah 62 and 63, he realized that the warrior king must also come as a servant and a shepherd and that His garments must also be stained with blood. Now John's declaration of Jesus as the "Lamb of God" began to make more sense to him, especially as the sanctuary lessons and Isaiah 53 came together in his mind. The Word of the Lord reminded him that what was happening was not about him. Events were unfolding as they should and God was still in control. His choice to listen to the Word of the Lord restored his Hope.

Elijah and John the Baptist aren't any different than the rest of God's Remnant People. Like you and me, the Remnant struggle with their humanness. Just because they are called to do the work of the Remnant doesn't make them superhuman.

In their appointed work the Remnant also have a lot to remember. Who is in charge of helping us remember? John 14:26 will clue you in as to where this conversation is going. The Remnant must remember that they have chosen to live in a Covenant R-G-B Grace-Faith Relationship. Just as it does for all Christians, this means: They must remember what Jeremiah 23:6 teaches—that it is the Lord's *righteousness* that He shares with His people, and thereby qualifies the Remnant to represent Him. They must remember what Zechariah 4:6 teaches—that it is the Lord's *power* that He shares the Remnant, and thereby makes the Remnant effective. They must remember what 1 John 4:19 teaches—that it is the Lord's *love* that he shares with the Remnant, and thereby makes the love of the Remnant possible.

Sounds like R-G-B, doesn't it?

The Remnant are Christians, to be sure, but they are also ordinary human beings who are asked to do extraordinary tasks. When they choose to listen to the promises in the Word of the Lord, it can restore their Hope.

But there are two kinds of thorns. There are two sides to our humanness, when we take our eyes off of God and focus on ourselves. On the one side is the total loss of confidence—in one's faith, one's spiritual experience, and one's relationship with God, which results in fear of rejection, despondency, and depression. So one kind of thorn is the loss of "confident expectancy," the loss of Hope in God.

As you might have suspected, I have a third short story, a story that we have discussed in previous conversations. It is the story of us—the Remnant— Seventh-day Adventist Christians. We are described as suffering from the other kind of thorns, the other side of our painfully obvious humanness, when our focus shifts to ourselves—the devastating, critical, fatal situation of Laodicea. The other side of our humanness is self-confidence. "Because you say, 'I am rich, and have become wealthy, and have need of nothing …'" This second kind of thorn, "the deceitfulness of riches," is just as effective in choking out the Gospel as is "the worry of the world," and it is just as deadly. Perhaps more so.

Be careful now. Don't assume you know what "riches" means. The Scriptures describe many types of riches. For example, Deuteronomy 7:7 tells us, "The Lord did not set His love on you nor choose you because you were more in number than any of the peoples." This describes *the riches of popularity and majority*. Being the largest group makes you rich in political and social power, which is quite handy if you are trying to be the biggest or the best in some activity or in some institutional competitiveness.

Deuteronomy 8:17 tells us that we "may say in [our] heart, 'My power and the strength of my hand made me this wealth.'" This describes *the riches of physical and/or economic power*. Either one makes you rich in social status and in the ability to get things done. Both of these kinds of power are—mistakenly—considered by many religious people to be the mark of the Lord's blessing.

And finally, look at Deuteronomy 9:4–6: "'Because of my righteousness, the Lord has brought me in to possess this land.'" This especially describes *the riches of spiritual arrogance* displayed by Laodicea in the Time of the End. Spiritual riches are especially helpful in establishing superior knowledge of the Scriptures, superior obedience to the Law, superior theological debating and eschatological parsing. There's nothing like spiritual arrogance to establish ecclesiastical exclusiveness from the world. In the deceitfulness of all their various riches, Laodicea can say, "I am rich, and have become wealthy, and have need of nothing."

What will it take, do you think, to wake up the self-confident to their need of the Covenant Grace-Faith Relationship with God?

There's nothing like spiritual arrogance to establish ecclesiastical exclusiveness from the world.

How about what got the attention of Elijah and John the Baptist? How about truth in the Word of the Lord? If so, here it is in Revelation 3:15–17. (Do you have your Bible right there beside you? Please turn there and follow along with me. This is too critical for you to take my word for this.) "I know your deeds and that you are neither cold nor hot; I would that you were cold or hot. So because you are lukewarm, and neither cold nor hot, I will spit you out of my mouth. Because you say, 'I am rich, and have become wealthy, and have need of nothing' and you do not know that you are wretched and miserable and poor and blind and naked." Do you think this will wake them up? Maybe? Maybe not?

Okay. How about a worldwide crisis? If so, Jesus described such a coming crisis in Matthew 24:15–22. You can read those verses for yourself—a desecration of the holy place, the necessity for the People of God to flee, and a great tribulation that will wipe out all life if it were not for the intervention of God. If you look around our world, you can see that these events have already begun to take place. Do you think this will wake them up?

It would seem that the thorns of despair and depression of Elijah and John the Baptist are easier to deal with than the thorns of arrogance and apathy of Laodicea. What will it take, do you think?

What would it take to get through to you?

Do you know who you are?

Let me suggest one more possible breakthrough strategy. Turn to Genesis 32:24. "Then Jacob was left alone, and a man wrestled with him until daybreak." What about a personal confrontation with God at a time when the people of Laodicea are "left alone"—when all the strength of popularity has vanished, when all the power of riches has turned to rust, when all the air has gone out of the balloon of religious superiority? At that time Laodicea will be left to face a power that she in her arrogance cannot conquer—the convicting power of the Holy Spirit (John 16:8) and the truth of the statement "and you do not know that you are wretched and miserable and poor and blind and naked."

Yes, I know. The remedy for Laodicea's problem is in Revelation 3:18–20. But will she choose to take her medicine? Will she choose to wake up and become the Remnant?

Will I? Will you?

Do you know who you are?

The truth is that the Remnant is painfully human. Like the Pogo cartoon strip of many years ago, "We have met the enemy—and he is us." Whether it's the thorns of the "worry of the world" like Elijah and John the Baptist, or whether it's the thorns of the "deceitfulness of riches" like the arrogance and apathy of Laodicea, our human hearts seem to grow these thorns even better than we grow the seed of the Gospel.

The Remnant needs to choose to accept a "new heart" before she can function as the Remnant.

It is obvious that the Remnant needs to choose to accept a "new heart" before she can function as the Remnant, before she can overcome her one quality—her humanness—that will do her in. Now you understand the importance of our previous discussions. Until the Remnant is empowered (Ephesians 3:16), until the Remnant receives her "heart transplant" (Ezekiel 36:26, 27), until the Remnant is "transformed" (Romans 12:1, 2), she will languish, she will not know who she is, and she will be unable to carry out all that we will be discussing in our coming conversations.

Obviously, I think that the confrontation with God is the final scenario that will "shake" the depressed and discouraged or arrogant and apathetic People of God awake. Why do I think so? The story of Adam, the story of Noah, the story of Abraham, the story of Jacob, the story of Job, the story of Elijah, the story of David, the story of Jonah, the story of … Shall I go on? Every story of a Remnant in Scripture comes to a confrontation with God in which the Remnant is "left alone" with God, in which the Remnant is left without any other resource but themselves, in which the Remnant must "present themselves" before God and choose to continue in a Covenant Grace-Faith Relationship with God. The Remnant must choose to believe that "He is, and that he is a rewarder of those who seek Him"—or bail out (Hebrews 11:6).

In our Seventh-day Adventist theology, we call this "the shaking time," so previously I used that word "shake" on purpose. I believe what Peter said: "For it is time for judgment to begin with the household of God" (1 Peter 4:17). Or as it says in Hebrews 12:27, "And this expression, 'yet once more,' denotes the removing of those things which can be shaken, as of created things, in order that those things which cannot be shaken may remain." I believe that every member of the Remnant will be faced with this situation of being "left alone" with God and will be asked to choose.

Of course, I do not know exactly what the Holy Spirit will do—with you or me—or how He will do it. But I do know that the plans of God call for the Remnant to appear and to function (Revelation 12:17). I do know that the promise of Zechariah 4:6 will be fulfilled: "not by might, nor by power, but by My Spirit, says the Lord of Hosts." I do know that the promise of Philippians 1:6 will be fulfilled: "For I am confident of this very thing, that He who began a good work in you will perfect it until the day of Christ Jesus."

The only question remaining is—do you know what choice you will make? Do you know who you are?

Are you surprised at where this conversation ended up? When we talk about the Remnant, we frequently mention the specific details of who, what, when. But we hardly ever mention "how." And "how" is the most important because without the power of the Holy Spirit, nothing happens, nothing at all.

With the throb of Zechariah 4:6 in our bones, let's begin to define the knowledge base, the message, and the mission of the Remnant—specifically, the People of God at the Time of the End. I'm ready for our next conversation if you are.

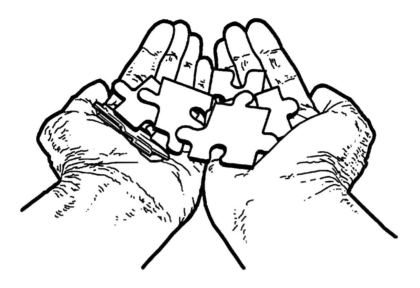

Chapter 12

Do You Know You Are to Restore the Long-lost Teachings of the Bible?

"And those from among you will rebuild the ancient ruins; you will raise up the age-old foundations; and you will be called the repairer of the breach, the restorer of the streets in which to dwell." Isaiah 58:12

If you are keeping track, during our last two conversations we turned the corner into that third division of discussions that I outlined for you when we began meeting like this. (That was a long time ago, wasn't it?) If you remember, I described this third section as Last Day Events scenarios.

I said then that if these divisions don't really mean much to you, you can ignore them. Nevertheless, with our last two conversations, we have arrived at this juncture. We are Seventh-day Adventist Christians. We have chosen to accept that we are the painfully human Remnant of the Time of the End. We need to know: What are we to say? What are we to do? How are we to act? But

first, before we get to those questions, and we will, we need to find another answer to that curiously hard question: Do you know who you are?

I want to go through some history with you, a history of "the church" and a history of *our* church. In the process I want to explore more closely "who we are" in the context of our church heritage. Yes, I know, history can be dry and boring. But, I will make it as interesting and engaging as I can, and surprise you with a "mystery" guest in the process. So, if you're willing, follow along with me on this exploratory *adventure* in history—and self-recognition.

I will begin this conversation with another question. What is a Protestant? Or let's say it this way: What is a Protest-ant?

Does this man's face look familiar? Do you remember who he is? I'm sure that you immediately recognized Martin Luther. In 1517 he nailed a list of ninety-five theses or beliefs to the church door, principles on which he took issue with the Mother Church. Call to mind that at this time there was only one Christian church recognized in Europe. And remember also that in 1521 at the Diet of Worms Luther's teachings were condemned as heresy and the people propagating his teachings as heretics, allowing them to be persecuted and even put to death.

In 1526 at the Diet of Speyer the German princes decided that each ruler could decide which religion would be upheld in his own territory. Essentially, this put on hold the edicts of persecution and death from Worms.

In 1529 the Second Diet of Speyer reversed this decision, deciding rather that the Holy Roman Empire would force all rulers to recognize the Mother Church and abide by its edicts. In response, several German Princes "protested." They "spoke for" the right of their subjects to hold to their own religion, which is the meaning of "pro-test." "Pro" is Latin for "for" or "in favor of" and "test" is Latin for "to speak up or about" from which we get the word "testify." The German Princes "spoke up in favor of" allowing those they represented to follow their conscience in religious matters and against the coercive edicts of the Mother Church.

At that meeting the German Princes "protested." At the Second Diet of Speyer in 1529, for the first time, the word "Protestant" was used to designate those who spoke for the right to hold to their own religion and who spoke against the errors being taught by the Mother Church.

What were the errors that Luther and the other Reformers were protesting? This list contains the major errors as Luther and others came to understand them. (Bible Study Alert: review Daniel 8:11, 12 for a concise summary of these issues in metaphorical form.)

Doctrine	Mother Church replaced with
Christ as Lord	Head of the Church as Lord
Cross as Salvation	Church liturgy as salvation Mass/Sacraments/ Indulgences/ Pilgrimages
Ten Commandments	Church tradition and edicts
Great Controversy	Church supremacy on earth
Hope of the Resurrection	Angry God/Hell and Purgatory
Heavenly Sanctuary	Forgiveness by clergy on Earth
Holy Spirit	Church Authority as Infallible
Jesus as High Priest	Elevation of Saints/ Mariology

As you can see, they had good reason for protesting. They had good reason for calling it the "Reformation." They were protesting to reform the only church they had ever known, the Mother Church in Rome. In the process, these reformers established what Protest-ant Christians have rec-ognized as the basic tenets of Protestantism.

Peter Waldo and the Waldensians gave us an appreciation of the study of the Bible as the only guide to a Christian's life. Jon Huss gave us the importance of obedience to the Commandments of God as outlined in the Scriptures. Luther gave us Justification by Faith in the atoning sacrifice of Jesus Christ on the cross. Calvin gave us an understanding of personal growth in sanctifica-tion. The Anabaptists gave us baptism as an out-ward expression of an inner personal decision. John and Charles Wesley and the Methodists gave us an appreciation of personal choice and duty in practical holiness.

As Seventh-day Adventist Christians, we share these values and Scriptural insights with Protes-tants of all denominations. As we said in our sec-ond conversation, we agree with other Christians that these teachings—these doctrines—are bibli-cal. We Seventh-day Adventists are Christians.

But as we have also said in our previous con-versations, we Seventh-day Adventists are more than Christians. We are Christians at the Time of the End. We are Christians at a time when several more biblical teachings, which were lost sight of by the Mother Church, become especially import-ant in more clearly defining the issues of the Great Controversy at the Time of the End.

In Christendom, Seventh-day Adventists are unique in teaching and adhering to these long-lost teachings of the Scriptures. Not that any one of these teachings is unique to us. Many other Protestant groups teach one or more of these doc-trines. But no other group simultaneously pro-claims all of these vital teachings that Adventist scholarship gradually rediscovered as the Adven-tists grew into their role of those who must pro-claim the last message of God's grace to a dying world.

This is the topic that I want to discuss with you. I call it the Seven "Ss" that characterize the unique understanding and message of the Sev-enth-day Adventist Church.

One time my brother-in-law (an elder in his Lutheran congregation) visited our church at a time when our Sabbath School was discussing the failure of our forerunners, the Millerites (and many others), to accurately predict the Second Coming of Jesus in 1844. Later, as we ate lunch, he asked why our church focused so much on what seemed to him to be a terribly trying time for our denomination and by our own admission was a "Great Disappointment." It was an interesting question. Why *are* we so taken with our histori-cal past? With the way our understanding of Bible truth has unfolded in the history of our church?

We are interested in our past because the unfolding history of the Seventh-day Adven-tist Church helps us to remember the important teachings of the Bible for two significant pur-poses. First, these teachings help us keep Jesus at the center of our spiritual lives, and second, these teachings will play a very significant part in the closing moments of earth's history.

Let me quickly outline the Seven "Ss" that, for the most part, define Seventh-day Adventist Christians as a distinct denomination. They are:

1. Second Coming of Jesus Christ

2. Sanctuary

3. Spirit of Prophecy

4. State of the Dead

5. Sabbath

6. Seraphim (Three Angels)

7. Salvation by Faith

I will introduce each one of these teachings in their historical Adventist context. Then we can discuss briefly why we care about them: first, how Jesus is at the center of each teaching, and second, how each teaching will have a major impact in last day events.

So let's begin with the Second Coming of Jesus. Do you recognize this man? Of course you do. He's almost as familiar to Seventh-day Adventists as Luther is to Lutherans. In 1825 William Miller was a farmer in Low Hampton, New York, a sometime agnostic, a sometime Deist, but always a skeptic. How-

ever, through his personal experiences in the War of 1812 and his own Bible study, he discovered Jesus Christ as his personal Savior. Then with his Cruden's Concordance and his Bible he began to search the Scriptures to discover biblical truth for himself. When he discovered Daniel 8:14, "Unto two thousand and three hundred days; then shall the sanctuary be cleansed" (KJV), it changed his life.

Allow me to paraphrase what Miller wrote in *Wm. Miller's Apology and Defence*: Imagine my surprise and consternation when I discovered in these same scriptures that our Lord would soon be returning to this earth. Daniel 8:14—'unto two thousand and three hundred days; then shall the sanctuary be cleansed.' I was delighted. But my conscience said, 'What of the ones who don't know? Go and tell it to the world.' And this message and the telling of it—changed my life

and the lives of those who followed after me (pp. 11–15).

Those of us who know our Adventist history know that William Miller and those who followed him experienced a Great Disappointment when Jesus did not come back on October 22, 1844, as they thought He would.

And it is still the one theological question that Seventh-day Adventists do not have an answer for: Why has Jesus not yet returned? Like Noah who preached for 120 years that a flood was coming, Seventh-day Adventists have preached that Jesus is coming again for more than 170 years, as of 2013. And like Noah, we have been the target of scoffers who say: "Where is the promise of His coming? For ever since the fathers fell asleep, all continues just as it was from the beginning of creation" (2 Peter 3:4).

What does it matter, you say? It matters a great deal. Jesus promised He would come again. He promised in John 14:3, "And if I go and prepare a place for you *I will come again*, and receive you to Myself, that where I am, there you may be also" (italics supplied).

The faithfulness and truthfulness of God and His promises hang in the balance until Jesus comes.

In fact, every twenty-fifth verse of the New Testament describes the Second Coming. And we aren't just talking about the physical phenomena in the sun, moon, and stars. The resurrection of the dead is promised when Jesus comes. Our change from mortality to immortality is promised when Jesus comes. The end of pain and suffering and death is promised when Jesus comes. The righting of all wrongs is promised when Jesus comes. The end of sin is promised when Jesus comes. The faithfulness and truthfulness of God and His promises hang in the balance *until* Jesus comes.

To say it plainly, Jesus promised: "I will come again." Unlike others at the Time of the End, Seventh-day Adventists are not scoffers. Neither do Seventh-day Adventists propound fanciful theories about whether He is coming or how He is coming. Seventh-day Adventists believe the Scriptures. If Jesus says He is coming, then He is coming!

And that is the significance of this teaching in the scenario of the Time of the End events. We believe the promises of God, and we will hold to them until He fulfills them. Because when He fulfills this promise—when He comes again—this will confirm and validate all other promises, those for the Time of the End and those concerning all that will follow His Second Coming. Seventh-day Adventists are "looking for the blessed hope and the appearing of the glory of our great God and Savior, Christ Jesus" (Titus 2:13). We are still Adventists.

Here is our second teaching—the Sanctuary. Our next historical figure is Hiram Edson, a farmer from Port Gibson, New York, and a follower of William Miller. He was part of the group that was waiting for Jesus to return on October 22, 1844, part of that group which was waiting for the "sanctuary to be cleansed" (Daniel 8:14). Their thinking, which was in line with all of Protestant Christendom at the time, was that the earth was the sanctuary and that it would be cleansed by the fire that accompanied the Second Coming of Jesus. Yes, he was part of that group who suffered such great disappointment.

Again, let's let him tell it in his own words. He wrote: "But as the clock tolled twelve midnight,

our fondest hopes and expectations were blasted, and such a spirit of weeping came over us as I never experienced before. We wept and wept until the day dawn" (Edson, untitled manuscript).

Apparently after weeping for a goodly portion of the night, he possessed clearer thinking with the coming of daylight. As his confidence recovered, he led some of his friends to the barn for prayer. When they knew that the Spirit would answer their prayer for more light, they went to the house for breakfast. He continues his story: "Afterward O.R.L. Crosier and I went across the cornfield to encourage some of my Advent neighbors. I was stopped about midway of the field. Heaven seemed open to my view, and I saw distinctly and clearly, that instead of Our High Priest coming out of the Most Holy of the Heavenly Sanctuary to come to this earth, that He for the first time entered the second apartment of that sanctuary; and that He had work to perform in the Most Holy before coming to this earth" (Ibid.)

This was it—the cornfield vision we've all heard about. This was the insight the disappointed believers needed. And it is the insight we need today.

There is so much to understand here in the

symbolism of the Old Testament sanctuary and all that it illustrates: the outer court and the altar of burnt offering, the laver, the first apartment of the sanctuary and its furniture, the second apartment and its furniture. Previously, we touched on some of this in our conversation about being a ministering Priest. Do you remember? (If you don't, you could review our conversation of Chapter 8.) But we will talk about these things when we get to our conversation about the Sanctuary.

For now, look at Hebrews 8:1, 2: "Now the main point in what has been said is this: we have such a high priest, who has taken His seat at the right hand of the throne of the Majesty in the heavens, a minister in the sanctuary and in the true tabernacle, which the Lord pitched, not man."

Whatever activity is symbolized in the Sanctuary, you will find Jesus at the center of that activity.

For now, let's concentrate on Jesus. Whatever is going on in the heavenly sanctuary, whatever activity is symbolized in the Sanctuary, you will find Jesus at the center of that activity. Check out what gifts Jesus is giving *from* the Sanctuary and you will know what activities Jesus is doing *in* the Sanctuary. Remember that the enemy of souls wants to negate what Jesus is doing, so Jesus has to constantly reaffirm with us and defend for us our choice to accept His gifts, as well as work with us in our gifts, as part of the Covenant Grace-Faith Relationship (Zechariah 3:1–7). (If you are not certain what these gifts are, review our conversation of Chapter 4.) Just know that Jesus is at the center of all this activity.

As for the Time of the End significance of the Sanctuary—the end result of the Day of Atonement ritual in the Old Testament sanctuary was the cleansing of the sins of the children of Israel. The end result of the activity of Jesus as High Priest in the heavenly Sanctuary is the cleansing of the horrid, deadly awfulness of sin from the Saints, the People of God. The symbolism of the Sanctuary guarantees that there will be an end to sin. (I will say more about this in a later conversation in Chapter 13.) I am—and I hope you are—exceedingly glad that a time is coming when there will be no more temptation, no more suffering, no more sin. Jesus will put an end to sin.

Third on our list of teachings is the Spirit of Prophecy.

Here is a face I know is familiar to you: Joseph Bates, sea captain, quiet reformer, spiritual intellectual giant, one of the three most influential people who started the Seventh-day Adventist Church—and a non-believer in Ellen White as a prophet.

It's true. Two years after the Great Disappointment, when James and Ellen White were at a meeting where she went into vision, Joseph Bates was there watching, skeptical and unbelieving.

He understood that she was quite sincere. He had studied her work and found that nothing she said was contrary to the Word of God, but he was not convinced. He thought that the visions might be manifestations of her ill health and weak bodily condition. Then … well, let's hear the story from John Loughborough, an eyewitness at the time. He wrote: "One evening, in the presence of Brother Bates, who was yet undecided in regard to these manifestations, Mrs. White, while in vision, began to talk about the stars, giving a glowing description of the rosy-tinted belts which she saw across the surface of some planet, and added, 'I see four moons.'

"'Oh,' said Brother Bates, 'she is viewing Jupiter'" (*The Great Second Advent Movement: Its Rise and Progress*, p. 258).

When Ellen White came out of vision, Brother Bates questioned her closely and discovered that she knew absolutely nothing about astronomy, which her husband, James, confirmed. Joseph Bates was convinced.

He wrote about Ellen White: "I can now confidently speak for myself. I believe the work is of God, and is given to comfort and strengthen his 'scattered,' 'torn,' and 'peeled people,' since the closing up of our work … in October, 1844. I confess that I have received light and instruction on many passages that I could not before clearly understand. I believe her to be a self-sacrificing, honest, willing child of God" (Ibid., p. 264).

Now where is Jesus in this Spirit of Prophecy gift to the Seventh-day Adventist Church? Do you remember those gifts of the Spirit that we mentioned earlier? This is one of them. Look at Joel 2:28. I know you have your Bible close at hand when we have these conversations. "And it will come about after this that I will pour out My Spirit on all mankind; and your sons and daughters will prophesy, Your old men will dream dreams, Your young men will see visions."

Jesus said He would send the Holy Spirit and that the Spirit would bring gifts—including the gift of prophecy. Yes, Jesus is very much at the center of the Gift of Prophecy, just as He is with all the spiritual gifts.

Now, what impact does this teaching have in last day events? A prophet is someone who speaks for God. In the last days God will still need to speak. In the last days the church will be going through very difficult times. Like a ship approaching an unfamiliar harbor, the church will need a harbor pilot. When that happened in the past, God sent a prophet. For the church of the Time of the End, this has already happened in the person of Ellen G. White.

And remember: We aren't home yet; uncharted waters lie ahead. Rest assured that when we need it again, God will communicate with His people—through the Holy Spirit who is in charge of the spiritual gift of prophecy. Remember 1 Corinthians 1:27: "But God has chosen the foolish things of the world to shame the wise, and God has chosen the weak things of the world to shame the things which are strong …"

Teaching number four is the State of the Dead. Do you know this man? Yes, this is James White. If James White were to speak to us today, he would say that in his day the Scriptural teaching about the condition of humans after they are dead was generally understood and agreed to by many members of many denominations. For him in his day, this was not a new teaching. From the beginning of the Protestant Reformation, many Lutherans, Puritans, Episcopalians, Methodists, and Baptists read and took the words of Ecclesiastes 9:5 at face value. It says: "For the living know they will die; but the dead do not know anything, nor have they any longer a reward, for their memory is forgotten. Indeed their love, their hate, and their zeal have already perished, and they no longer have a share in all that is done under the sun."

Prior to joining forces with the Millerite movement, James White and Joseph Bates both belonged to the Conditional Christian Connection Church. Can you guess what the word Conditional stood for? The conditional state of humans in relation to immortality—that is, humans are mortal; they go to sleep when they die. If they wake up in the resurrection of the righteous (Revelation 20:4–6), they are given immortality. If they wake up in the resurrection of the wicked (Revelation 20:5, 12–15), they are annihilated (see John 5:29; Revelation 20:15).

No one had to teach this doctrine to the Adventists; it was already commonly believed. It wasn't until the middle 1800s that going directly to heaven or hell when you die became popular among mainstream Protestants, along with spiritualism. The teaching about the State of the Dead seemed like a no-brainer in 1844.

Today when we introduce this Scriptural teaching during evangelistic meetings, it is just the opposite. Very few believe this Bible teaching today. Most people believe that when you die you go directly to heaven or hell. They do not understand that what they believe is exactly the opposite of the teaching of Jesus.

Do you remember what Jesus said about this particular teaching? Good. I thought you might know, but look anyway at John 11:11. What does Jesus say? "Our friend Lazarus has fallen asleep; but I go, that I may awaken him out of sleep." Because Lazarus was "sleeping" the disciples thought he was feeling better and would quickly recover. "So said to them plainly, 'Lazarus is dead'" (John 11:14). Jesus taught what Adventists believe. The State of the Dead is—the dead are "asleep." Or as another Scripture says, "The living know they will die, but the dead do not know anything" (Ecclesiastes 9:5).

And today, as we move forward in the Time of the End, few seem to understand the importance of this teaching. "Why do you Adventists care about that?" Do you know why we care?

Here's why. Satan wants us to believe that we are as gods, that we will not surely die (Genesis 3:4, 5). If, at death, we go straight to heaven or hell, then there is no resurrection, there is no sin, there is no judgment, there is no sanctuary, and there is no final end to sin and to Satan.

But there's a larger issue here. If we continue in some kind of conscious state after death, especially if the living think that the dead have gone to heaven to be with God, then they can also expect that the dead would try to communicate with them here on earth.

Here Satan uses his most deceptive plan—spiritualism. In the Time of the End, Satan will be disguised as an angel of light (see 2 Corinthians 11:14) and, "the one whose coming is in accord with the activity of Satan, with all power and signs and false wonders, and with all the deception of wickedness for those who perish, because they did not receive the love of the truth so as to be saved" (2 Thessalonians 2:9, 10).

During the final events of earth's history, God will speak. But God will not speak through dead people.

As I said in discussing the Spirit of Prophecy previously, during the final events of earth's history, God will speak. But God will not speak through dead people, which is to say, God will not speak through the spirits of demons. It may not look like it right now, but for Seventh-day Adventists in the Time of the End, the State of the Dead is an extremely important teaching.

Teaching number five is the seventh-day Sabbath.

You might not recognize this man, but I do. He looks exactly like my friend Douglas whom I told you about in a previous conversation. But this isn't my friend, of course. This is John Nevins Andrews, a brilliant preacher and writer who worked himself to death in Europe. He was our first official overseas missionary *and* a Sabbath scholar.

The first official Sabbath tract was written and published by Joseph Bates. But the first definitive, scholarly study commissioned by the Seventh-day Adventist Church was written by Andrews.

I will not belabor this teaching. Suffice it to say that we are not the only Protestants to become aware of this teaching of the Bible. And as every Adventist knows, the Sabbath along with the Second Coming is the very definition of who we are—Seventh-day Adventists.

But let me ask you this question. Where is Jesus in the Sabbath? Turn in your handy Bible to Mark 2:27, 28. Here you read that "the Son of Man is Lord even of the Sabbath." What does that mean? Look at the preceding verse. "The Sabbath was made for man, and not man for the Sabbath."

The Sabbath is supposed to be a gift. It was made for us. The Lord God, the Creator of heaven and earth set aside a special time to meet with His special creatures—just like I make time for my grandson, Braeden—our milk-and-stories time. The Creator of the universe wants to spend time … with *you*. The personal, intimate Covenant Grace-Faith Relationship He has with *you* is at the very center of the Sabbath. I will leave it to you to look up all the scriptures about the Sabbath in your concordance and study them in that light.

We've been examining each of these teachings with a focus on Jesus and on the Time of the End. What about the Sabbath in the Time of the End?

Every monarch and every country has a symbol: a coat of arms, a flag that symbolizes that ruling entity. This flag needs to be unique in order to be recognized as standing for one and only one entity—like the flag of Jamaica, or the flag of India, or the flag of the United States.

For God, the symbol of His sovereignty, the symbol of His right to be worshiped as the Lord God Creator, is a slice of time, unique in its configuration. This slice of time is not demarcated by the sun or the moon or the stars or the earth—it is defined simply by His right as Creator and Lord to declare it to be so, every seventh day. I leave it to you, in your study of the Sabbath, which I suggested earlier (and that I hope you are going to undertake, maybe for the first time), to discover how the Sabbath symbolizes all the various parts of God's Covenant Grace-Faith Relationship with us.

When Jesus returns to this earth, He will be flying His flag.

For now just know: The Sabbath is the flag of God. When Jesus returns to this earth, He will be flying His flag. Satan wants to take God's place as the ruler of the universe and wants the people of the earth to worship him, instead of God (see Isaiah 14:12–14). He has already attempted to replace God's flag with a flag of his own devising (Daniel 7:25).

But believe me: when Jesus returns to this earth, He returns as Lord of the Sabbath, and He will be flying His flag.

Do you remember the pictures of those countries that were liberated from tyranny by American troops and how the people welcomed those troops by waving American flags? When Jesus returns, the people who belong to Him and who are waiting to be liberated on this earth will be waving His flag.

Now for teaching number six—the Seraphim (the Three Angels).

Do you know who this man is? Very good. His name was Uriah Smith. As a young man he and his sister Annie lived and worked with James White, helping him to put out his small paper, the *Advent Review and Sabbath Herald*. He grew up in the White home, hearing the early history of the Adventist message from Ellen White and Joseph Bates and from other early Adventist pioneers who visited regularly. Uriah Smith became the editor of the *Review*, remaining so for fifty years, and wrote many scholarly works, including *Daniel and the Revelation* (a book that I cut my Adventist teeth on). He knew and loved the Adventist message and understood the Messages to be delivered by the People of God at the Time of the End.

URIAH SMITH

Do you remember our earlier conversation in Chapter 10 (for those who are experiencing these conversations as a book) about those people and those messages? Good for you. The book of Revelation highlights a people who "keep the commandments of God and their faith in Jesus" (Revelation 14:12). These People of God, who are to function as *evangels* (that's the Greek word *euangelos*), are given three final messages to share with the world in the Time of the End (see Revelation 14:6–12).

I don't propose to explore those messages in depth now, for we'll examine them in a later conversation. Instead let me ask: What relationship does Jesus have with these Three Angels and their messages?

To answer this question let me remind you of one of the ways we described the People of God in the Time of the End. Look at Revelation 10:9, 10. "And He said to me, 'Take it [the little book of verse 2], and eat it; … I … ate it …and it was in my mouth sweet as honey; and when I had eaten it, my stomach was made bitter.'" Do you recognize this experience and who these people are? That's right! This is a description of the People of God at the time of the Great Disappointment of 1844. Seventh-day Adventists, because of their October 1844 experience, especially identify with this description, but it applies to many other Christians of that time as well.

Also please notice in Revelation 10:11 the instructions given to these people. These people have a work to do, a prophecy to give—those messages found in Revelation 14:6–13.

But did you notice who gave the prophecy to them? Who personally delivered this specific task to them? Can you identify the Strong Angel of Revelation 10?

Let's do a little comparative Bible study. Look at the description of the Strong Angel in Revelation 10:1, 2—"clothed with a cloud, and the rainbow was upon his head, and his face was like the sun, and his feet like pillars of fire." Do you recognize this Strong Angel who stands with his right foot on the sea and his left foot on the land?

Look at Revelation 1:13. John the Revelator turned when he heard a voice speaking to him. He saw in the middle of the lamp stands "one like a son of man." In verse 15 John continues his description: "His feet were like burnished bronze when it has been caused to glow in a furnace." Verse 16 says, "His face was like the sun." Everything is here except the rainbow. Ah, to see the rainbow, we have to go to Ezekiel 1:26–28. I'll wait while you look at that one on your own. (Dum-dum-dee-dum-dum) There, did you see the rainbow?

Ezekiel was describing God on His Throne. John was describing Jesus in the lamp stands. And both descriptions coincide with the Strong Angel that stands on the land and the sea.

Do you get the picture?

The Strong Angel on the land and the sea is Jesus Christ Himself. He is the one who says to these people who have gone through the Great Disappointment: "Here, this is your assignment. Go tell them. You must prophesy again. Give them the Three Angels' Messages." In fact, in Revelation 14:4 just before they get their assignment, these People of God are described as "… the ones who follow the Lamb wherever He goes." Jesus is at the center of the Three Angels' Messages and their proclamation.

But what about the Three Angels and the Time of the End? Let me sample for you some of these messages. In Revelation 14:7 the First Angel says: "Because the hour of His judgment has come." The opening of the judgment is described in Daniel 7:9, 10: "I kept looking until thrones were set up, and the Ancient of Days took His seat … the court sat and the books were opened." Verses 13 and 14 further describe the judgment in the coming of Jesus in His Day of Atonement role as High Priest (a Time of the End event): "I kept looking in the night visions, and behold, … one like the Son of Man was coming, and he came up to the Ancient of Days and was presented before Him." Closely behind these scenes, the Seven Last Plagues, judgments of God, come in the last hour of earth's history as described in Revelation 16.

In Revelation 14:8 the Second Angel says: "Fallen, Fallen is Babylon …" The fall of Babylon is described in more detail in Revelation 18 and is immediately followed by the Second Coming of Jesus in Revelation 19.

In Revelation 14:9 the Third Angel says: "If anyone worships the beast or his image … he will also drink of the wine of the wrath of God … in full strength." The only time God's wrath is given in full strength is at the end of the world, again in the Seven Last Plagues of Revelation 15 and 16.

To miss the Three Angels' Messages is to miss the last appeal from God to a dying world. While time lasts, "as long as it is still called 'Today'" (Hebrews 3:13), it is the time to respond to the everlasting gospel and the Three Angels. I leave it to you to determine if the Seraphim (the Three Angels) have any relevance to the end times.

Now for teaching number seven—Salvation by Faith.

This time I have two men as illustrations. Both came into prominence during the struggle at the 1888 meeting of the General Conference of Seventh-day Adventists: Alonzo T. Jones, editor of *The Sign of the Times* at Pacific Press, and Ellet J. Waggoner, MD, both from California. They became notorious because they wanted the Seventh-day Adventist denomination to see more of Jesus and less of the Law when it came to Salvation. This issue has come to be known as Righteousness by Faith.

In a nutshell, this issue is set forth in these two Scriptures:

- "And the testimony is this, that God has given us eternal life, and this life is in His Son. He who has the Son has life; he who does not have the Son of God does not have the life" (1 John 5:11, 12).

- "For by grace you have been saved through faith; and that not of your-selves, it is the gift of God; not as a result of works, that no one may boast" (Ephesians 2:8, 9).

As for Jesus being at the center of this teaching, we have been discussing this concept since our early conversations. It may seem obvious to us that the Gift of God—Salvation by Faith—has its beginning and its end in the person of Jesus Christ. This gift—and our choosing to accept it by faith—is what saves us, and not anything we have done, or are doing, or will ever do. It seems obvious to us because we are on this side of 1888. But this wasn't obvious to those Seventh-day Adventists who were struggling with this issue at that time.

And, as you may know, this issue is not dead. We, each and every one of us from time to time, think that somehow there must be something we can do to earn or to deserve or to arrange for or to guarantee our own salvation. And there isn't. Salvation is such a big problem—so much bigger than any of us—that only God can solve it. As we just read in Ephesians 2:8, all we can do is believe it and accept it—and it is ours. Jesus is at the center of it all.

What about the Time of the End? Why is this issue, this teaching so important in the end times?

Martin Luther was climbing the *Scala Sancta* (the Holy Stairs) in the Lateran Palace in Rome on his knees when he heard the voice of God tell

him: "The righteous shall live by their faith" (cf. Habakkuk 2:4 and Romans 1:17). Martin Luther came to understand that this teaching was at the heart of the Reformation, at the heart of all other teachings. And it will be at the heart of all other issues at the Time of the End. At that time the righteous are identified in Revelation 7:14 as those who "come out of the great tribulation" and "have washed their robes and made them white in the blood of the Lamb."

In the Time of the End every kind of theology known to man (see Colossians 2:8) will be running rampant in the world. At the core of every one of them will be the idea that we don't need a Savior. Every philosophy known to man will be trying to devise a way to avoid accepting Jesus as a personal Savior, trying to find an excuse for not needing a Savior: sin and behavior don't matter—or—I can overcome sin by my good behavior—or—I can rewrite the rules and not call it sin anymore and say that I have never sinned.

The bottom line, especially in the Time of the End, is that the adversary of souls does not want you to know that you need a Savior. He does not want you to know that Jesus is available to you with the simple sinner's prayer of repentance (see Luke 18:13), "God, be merciful to me, a sinner." "I accept Your gift of the death of Jesus Christ as a substitute for my death and the righteousness of Jesus Christ as my own righteousness" (see 2 Corinthians 5:21).

In the Time of the End?

We are living in the Time of the End. Therefore, make sure you don't finish this conversation (or put down this book) today without knowing and accepting for yourself that Jesus died for you.

This is not complex theology. It's as simple as the child's song. Sing it with me.

"Jesus loves me this I know
For the Bible tells me so.
Little ones to Him belong.
They are weak but He is strong.

Yes, Jesus loves me.
Yes, Jesus loves me.
Yes, Jesus loves me.
The Bible tells me so."

Understand that in the face of the big problem of Sin, *you* are a little one. This is not a song for little kids. This is *your* song. It is now the Time of the End. You are the little one staring into the face of such a big problem. Become a little one. Let your faith be like a little one and sing this song for all you're worth—and mean it. Not surprisingly, this is one of the simpler answers to our curiously hard question: Do you know who you are?

Now for the surprise, the "mystery" guest. There is one more "S"—a mysterious "S" that "is an eighth and is part of the seven." (Borrowed without shame from Revelation 17:11.) Actually, this eighth "S" underlies all the teachings of the Scriptures—for it is the Scriptures themselves—or as the Protestants said it, *Sola Scriptura.*

There were several Latin phrases that were the battle cry of Protestants.

Sola Scriptura	Only Scripture
Sola Gracia	Only Grace
Sola Fida	Only Faith
Solo Christos	Only Christ

But Seventh-day Adventists have a struggle with the first phrase, only Scripture. They put great credence in the writings of Ellen G. White, some going so far as to read her writings and ignoring Scripture. Therefore, let me ask Ellen G. White to address this teaching in her own words.

In our time there … is need of a return to the great Protestant principle - the Bible, and the Bible only as the rule of faith and duty. (*The Great Controversy*, p. 205)

The Lord desires you to study your Bibles. He has not given any additional light to take the place of His Word. (*Letter* 130, 1901)

In the Scriptures God has set forth practical lessons to govern the life and conduct of all, but though He has given minute particulars in regard to our character, conversation, and conduct, yet in a large measure, His lessons are disregarded and ignored.

God has, in that Word, promised to give visions in the "last days"; not for a new rule of faith, not as a new revelation, but for the comfort of His people, and to set before us the plain lessons of His word, to correct those who err from the Bible truth, that the right way may be pointed out. (*Early Writings*, p. 78; *Testimonies for the Church*, vol. 5, p. 665)

The Spirit was not given—nor can it ever be bestowed—to supersede the Bible; for the Scriptures explicitly state that the

Word of God is the standard by which all teaching and experience must be tested. Through the Scriptures the Holy Spirit speaks to the mind, and impresses truth upon the heart. (*The Great Controversy*, Introduction, p. vii; *The Desire of Ages*, p. 671)

But I do not ask you to take my words. I exalt the precious Word before you today. Lay Sister White to one side. Do not repeat what I have said, saying, "Sister White said this," and "Sister White said that." Do not quote my words again as long as you live until you can obey the Bible. Find out what the Lord God of Israel says, and then do what He commands. (*Manuscript 43*, 1901—from an address to church leaders given the night before the opening of the General Conference session of 1901)

The Bible, and the Bible alone is to be our creed, the sole bond of union. God's Word is infallible. Let us lift up the banner on which is inscribed, "the Bible, our rule of faith and discipline." (*The Review and Herald*, December 15, 1885)

So there you have it. The seven "Ss" that set us apart from the rest of Protestantism. None of them is unique to us. But to hold all of them collectively—at the same time—is very unique. No other denomination holds to all seven—plus the eighth—as valid teachings of the Scripture.

These seven—and the eighth—center themselves in Jesus. These seven—and the eighth—will become extremely important in the Time of the End.

Seventh-day Adventists are people of the Book.

Please remember: Seventh-day Adventists are people of the Book. "Here is the perseverance of the saints. Here are they that keep the commandments of God [They are to be students of the Book] and their faith in Jesus." For Seventh-day Adventist Christians, their very lives are to be consumed with the relationship they have with Jesus (Revelation 14:12).

May you and I live up to our precious heritage is my prayer.

And so with our last two conversations and now this one, we are fully engaged in, and have embarked on, the third and final leg of our exploratory journey, seeking the answer to our question, "Seventh-day Adventist Christian, do you know who you are?" Throughout this particular conversation, I have promised you a discussion of several topics that are vital to our understanding of who we are as Seventh-day Adventist Christians, especially in the Time of the End. So if you're ready, let's get to it.

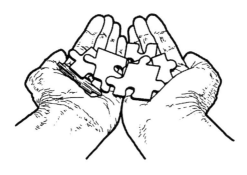

Chapter 13

Do You Know You Are to Live in the Sanctuary Message?

"For this reason I bow my knees before the Father …that He would grant you, according to the riches of His glory, to be strengthened with power through His Spirit in the inner man, so that Christ may dwell in your hearts through faith … that you may be filled up to all the fullness of God." Ephesians 3:14–19

[T]rumpet Fanfare] "Ladies and gentlemen—and children of all ages—give me your attention, please! You have already enjoyed the always entertaining Dandy Dogs and Ponies in Ring #1, and the mysterious Oriental Elephants in Ring #3! But now! Direct your attention to Ring #2, the center ring, as we present—the amazing—the startling—the astounding …"

This was always my favorite part of the circus, the ringmaster and his flowery introductions. I loved to hear his effervescent language. I loved how it built my excitement in anticipation of what was coming—something unknown, perhaps

frightening, but surely mysteriously wonderful. I'm feeling that way about the topic we are going to discuss now.

All through our conversations I've been putting off one particular topic, telling you that we will discuss it at a later time. I've been promising you a further discussion of Becoming Like, of the third level of the R-G-B Grace-Faith Relationship, of the results—both *internal* and *external*—of allowing God to change you and me. Well, at last the time has come. We have discussed the topics in Ring #1—the Gift of Jesus and our Faith as we *choose* to receive Him. We have discussed the topics in Ring #3—the Gift of the Holy Spirit as He grows our Hope ("confident expectation") in our more intimate Christian walk with Jesus as by Faith we *choose* to give Him permission to empower us.

Therefore, if you will—ladies and gentlemen—let me direct your attention to the center ring, and be sure to bring your Bible. You can't identify your performers—or check out your ringmaster—without a program.

When we took the guided tour of the wilderness Sanctuary, you'll remember that we left the tour group while it was in the first apartment. That was in Chapter 8. Because you are a Seventh-day Adventist Christian, I assume that you are familiar with the Sanctuary's second apartment—the Most Holy Place—which held the ark of the covenant. I assume that you know about the two angels looking down on the mercy seat and about the contents of the ark: the Ten Commandment tablets, the pot of manna, and Aaron's rod that budded. We assume that we already know the theological significance of these things, yes? Well, do you?

And while we're at it, let me ask you some further questions about the Sanctuary. Let's look (in your ever-present Bible) at Hebrews 8:1, 2. "Now the main point in what has been said is this: we have such a high priest, who has taken His seat at the right of the throne of the Majesty in the heavens, a ministry in the sanctuary, and in the true tabernacle, which the Lord pitched, not man." Protestants have understood for a long time that Jesus is functioning as our High Priest "in the true tabernacle," that is, "into heaven itself" (see Hebrews 9:24).

But we, as twenty-first century human beings, struggle with the concept of a literal sanctuary in a literal heaven. We wonder what it was that Moses *really* saw when he made "a copy and a shadow of the heavenly things" (Hebrews 8:5). Therefore, we frequently speak in metaphorical clichés. We often say that Jesus is interceding for us in the heavenly Sanctuary but don't really understand what we mean by that phrase.

What *is* He actually doing in there? What does a High Priest do, not just in the second apartment, but in the entire sanctuary? What does that mean exactly? How is He dealing with our sins—where *are* our sins exactly and what is He doing with them? What is He doing to "cleanse the sanctuary"? How does all of this relate to the Gospel of the Covenant Grace-Faith Relationship? What is the "sanctuary message"? Do you understand the significance of the "sanctuary message" for the twenty-first century Seventh-day Adventist Christian—and for the world? Especially now that we are living in the Time of the End? At the time of the Judgment?

Do you know who you are?

Let's start with something familiar: Hiram Edson's cornfield vision. As we noted in our last conversation, the Millerites of New England and the Midwest were devastated when Jesus did not return on October 22, 1844, as were several million people who, during that same time period, had heard the imminent Second Advent being preached in England, France, Italy, Scandinavia, throughout the Middle East, the Indian subcontinent, and the rest of Asia by preachers other than the Millerites. Of them all, the Millerites were probably more intense, more exacting in their date calculations, and—therefore—more disappointed. Although we just read it in our last conversation, let's hear again what Hiram Edson wrote as he later described the experience of the morning after.

"Afterward O.R.L. Crosier and I went across the cornfield to encourage some of my Advent neighbors. I was stopped about midway of the field. Heaven seemed open to my view, and I saw distinctly and clearly, that instead of Our High

Priest coming out of the Most Holy of the Heavenly Sanctuary to come to this earth, that He for the first time entered the second apartment of that sanctuary; and that He had work to perform in the Most Holy before coming to this earth" (Edson, untitled manuscript).

For the Millerite believers in 1844, this was what they needed: an explanation of what happened, what they got right and what they got wrong. They had calculated the timing of the event quite accurately, as had Luther and the Reformers. From the 1500s onward many theologians (i.e.; Luther and Calvin of the 1500s, Joseph Mede in the 1600s, Isaac Newton in the 1700s) knew and taught that something was going to happen around 1840. What the Millerites got wrong was not the timing, but the event itself, because they had adopted the popular Protestant misunderstanding that the sanctuary was the earth. Therefore, in their minds, the "cleansing of the sanctuary" (see Daniel 8:14) meant the cleansing of the earth by fire at the Second Coming of Jesus (see 2 Peter 3:7).

For the Millerite believers, the cornfield vision of Hiram Edson clarified that just as the High Priest had a work of atonement to do on the yearly Day of Atonement in the second apartment (as described in Leviticus 16:33), so also Jesus our High Priest had a work of atonement to do in the heavenly second apartment on the 2300 day-year Day of Atonement identified in Daniel 8:14 and described in Hebrews 9:23. "Therefore, it was necessary for the copies of these things in the heavens to be cleansed …"

While this explanation solved their dilemma at that time, they had a difficult time following the thread of their new understanding forward into the whole truth of the second apartment ministry. And we, too, must move forward in our more complete understanding and appreciation of the second apartment ministry. Why must we, you

ask? Because the author of Hebrews tells us that we must.

"Since therefore, brethren, we have confidence to enter the holy place by the blood of Jesus, by a new and living way which he inaugurated for us through the veil, that is, His flesh … [this hope we have as an anchor of the soul, both sure and steadfast and one which enters within the veil, where Jesus has entered as a forerunner for us (Hebrews 6:19–20)] let us draw near …" (Hebrews 10:19–22).

Let us draw near—to the Veil—"because the hour of His judgment has come" (Revelation 14:7). Let us draw near to the Veil.

I'm sure you understand that everything about the wilderness Sanctuary was very real, while at the same time symbolic.

The very real courtyard with its curtains symbolized that even in the midst of the very real, very human encampment of the children of Israel, God wanted a sacred spot in order to do what He's always wanted to do, in order that He "may dwell among them" (Exodus 25:8). This has been His goal from before Eden and it will be His concluding triumph in the earth made new. "Behold, the tabernacle of God is among men, and He shall dwell among them, and they shall be His people, and God Himself shall be among them" (Revelation 21:3).

The very real altar of burnt offering symbolized the Gift of Jesus:

1. Described symbolically by John the Baptist as "behold, the Lamb of God who takes away the sin of the world!" (John 1:29).

2. Described graphically by Jesus: "The Son of man did not come to be served, but to serve, and to give His

life a ransom for many" (Matthew 20:28).

3. Explained theologically by Paul, saying, "For all have sinned and fall short of the glory of God, being justified as a gift by His grace through the redemption which is in Christ Jesus … for a demonstration … of His (God's) righteousness at the present time, that he might be just and the justifier of the one who has faith in Jesus" (Romans 3:24, 26).

4. Explained resultantly by Paul: "He [God] made Him [Jesus] … to be sin on our behalf, … so that we might become the righteousness of God in Him" (2 Corinthians 5:21).

What does this mean for you and me in actuality—since we aren't bringing a lamb to an actual altar, since Jesus has already been sacrificed for us? We bring the same thing that the sinner at the wilderness Sanctuary brought. We bring the very core of our being, the place where we *choose*. We bring our heart (see Romans 10:9).

> *We bring the same thing that the sinner at the wilderness Sanctuary brought. We bring the very core of our being. We bring our heart.*

This is not a ritual such as circumcision or baptism; this is submission of our will to the will of God—in faith. Yes, the outward ritual follows: circumcision for the Jew, baptism for the Chris-

tian. However, as both the Old Testament (Deuteronomy 30:6) and the New Testament (Romans 2:29) confirm, we must first choose inwardly; we must bring our heart to God.

That's the symbolism of the altar of burnt offering that was very real in the wilderness Sanctuary, and is equally real in the heavenly Sanctuary. Where Jesus now is in the heavenly Sanctuary "at the right hand of the throne of the majesty in the heavens" (Hebrews 8:1), is grace and forgiveness, submission and faith. Here at this altar of burnt offering we may "draw near with confidence … that we may receive mercy and may find grace to help in time of need" (Hebrews 4:16).

Please notice what I am saying about this point because Seventh-day Adventists sometimes give a mixed message about this topic. We want seekers to know that they can come to Jesus (at the altar of burnt offering), but we want our own believers to understand that Jesus has moved on in His ministry in the heavenly Sanctuary. The function of the altar of burnt offering is still in operation in the heavenly Sanctuary even in the Time of the End for those who have never surrendered their heart and might yet choose to do so.

Even though Jesus has moved on in his duties as High Priest in the Sanctuary, the functions of the altar of burnt offering continue to apply to those who have lived in an intensely intimate relationship with Jesus but have "missed the mark" in some of their heart choices. Even these people—including you and me—must from time to time reconfirm their *choice* of the Gift of Jesus and the Cross: inwardly in their hearts (1 Corinthians 15:31), outwardly in ritualistic form in the Ordinance of Humility or the foot washing. That's why it's called the "daily" sacrifice.

(Bible Study Alert: discover for yourself what the Hebrew word *tamid* means and how it is used in Exodus (how frequently the *tamid* was sacrificed and why) and in the rest of the Bible. Start with Exodus 29:38–39, then look at Numbers 28:3,

4, then add Daniel 8:11, 12. Now look at Hebrews 9:12 and Revelation 4:6 and consider the meaning of *tamid* for the sinner of today.)

We talked about this early on in our conversations. This is the first level of the Covenant Grace-Faith Relationship. This is "Receiving From" of R-G-B. And this is Sanctuary, the very real heavenly Sanctuary.

We also talked about the laver and the first apartment of the wilderness Sanctuary in our conversation of Chapter 8—about being a ministering priest. Do you remember? We learned that we are washed and purified (in baptism and at foot washing—at the laver) to function as ministering priests of the first apartment of the heavenly Sanctuary just as certainly as did the priests of the wilderness Sanctuary amidst the furniture in that first apartment. We study the Word and learn about Jesus at the lampstand. We are empowered by our Holy Spirit giftedness to minister and intimately experience the face-to-face ministry of Jesus at the Table of the Bread of the Presence—literally "of the Face." We intercede for others and for ourselves, having "much incense"—the righteousness of Christ—"add[ed] to the prayers of all the saints upon the golden altar which was before the throne" at the altar of incense (Revelation 8:3).

All of these acts of "divine worship" (Hebrews 9:6) are organized and empowered by the Holy Spirit—when we *choose* to give Him permission and to abide in "confident expectation" (Hope) by Faith that "what He had promised, He was able also to perform" (Romans 4:21).

And Jesus? What is He actually doing? Besides His function related to the altar of burnt offering in heaven, Jesus is quite busy continuing the functions of the first apartment of the heavenly Sanctuary. He is breathlessly monitoring our activities as ministering priests and sending the Holy Spirit

in His name to us—every time we ask (see Luke 11:13; John 14:16, 17).

Don't forget we have an "adversary, the devil, [who] prowls about like a roaring lion, seeking someone to devour" (1 Peter 5:8). We have an enemy, "the accuser of our brethren ... who accuses them before God day and night" (Revelation 12:10). Jesus has to constantly confront our adversary with His blood on our behalf and defend our right to ask and His right to send the Holy Spirit (see Zechariah 3:1–5).

I know that you remember this very well. You and I both stopped at this point in our conversation to pray and to reconsecrate ourselves to this more intimate abiding process. This is the Second Level of the Grace-Faith Relationship. This is the "Growing In" of R-G-B. Just as certainly as you and I are conversing here together, it is a certainty in the heavenly Sanctuary.

Also remember that Jesus as High Priest is still functioning in this way, especially today in the time of the judgment. Just like the altar of burnt offering, the functions of the first apartment are still validly working and very much needed today.

Which brings us back to the Veil. Did you notice that I've approached the Veil at least twice already without actually going there? Why do you suppose that is?

Do you remember a scene from *The Lion, the Witch, and the Wardrobe*—the first book in C. S. Lewis's Chronicles of Narnia series—where Susan is about to meet Aslan for the first time?

> "Aslan is a lion—the Lion, the great Lion."
>
> "Ooh," said Susan. "I'd thought he was a man. Is he—quite safe? I shall feel rather nervous about meeting a lion"...
>
> "Safe?" said Mr Beaver... "Who said anything about safe? 'Course he isn't safe. But he's good. He's the King, I tell you."

When I approach the Veil, I feel just like Susan. I feel rather nervous, actually more than nervous. I'm like everyone else whoever was about to meet God. I'm deathly afraid. Why?

What was the symbolism of the Veil in the wilderness Sanctuary, which separated the first apartment from the second apartment? What separates us from God? Isaiah 59:2 tells us, "But your iniquities have made a separation between you and your God." What happens to those who are sinful in the presence of a holy God? Isaiah 33:11–14 says, "You have conceived chaff, you will give birth to stubble; My breath will consume you like a fire. And the peoples will be burned to lime, like cut thorns which are burned in the fire. Sinners in Zion are terrified; trembling has seized the godless. 'Who among us can live with the consuming fire? Who among us can live with the continual burning?'"

This is one of the most frightening scriptures I know. No wonder the sinners in Zion are terrified. No wonder so many people are deathly afraid as they approach the Veil.

I want you to pay very close attention right here. If you are trying to multi-task and watch television, or mend a backpack, or knit, or cook, stop! Put it down. Pay attention. I have come to the critical part that you must understand in order to be part of the People of God in the Time of the End.

What else do you see on it? Spots? Lots of spots on the Veil?

Stand here with me and look at the Veil. Note all the rich blue and purple and scarlet and see how it's covered with the figures of angels (see Exodus 26:31). What else do you see on it? Spots? Lots of spots on the Veil? Now look behind you at the horns of the altar of incense. You will see more spots there—red stains, dark brown. And if we were to go out to the altar of burnt offering, you would see more dark brown stains on the horns of that altar. Very real stains and spots.

I want you to look at Leviticus 4:6. The priest is making a sin offering for the sin that he himself has committed. "… and the priest shall dip his finger in the blood, and sprinkle some of the blood seven times before the Lord, in front of the veil of the sanctuary." Now look at verses 17 and 18. (This sin offering is for a sin of the whole congregation.) "… and the priest shall dip his finger in the blood, and sprinkle it seven times before the Lord, in front of the veil. And he shall put some of the blood on the horns of the altar which is before the Lord in the tent of meeting." Now look at verse 34. (This applies to a sin either of a leader or of the common people.) "And the priest is to take some of the blood of the sin offering with his finger and put it on the horns of the altar of burnt offering; and all the rest of its blood he shall pour out at the base of the altar." Are you getting the picture?

Look at one more place, Leviticus 6:25, 26. "This is the law of the sin offering … the priest who offers it for sin shall eat it." And Numbers 18:1 says, "So the Lord said to Aaron, 'You and your sons and your father's household with you shall bear the guilt in connection with the sanctuary; and you and your sons with you shall bear the guilt in connection with your priesthood.'"

Do you understand where your sins are, all the sins that have been forgiven you?

What has God allowed to happen with all the sins for which the People of God have asked forgiveness, all the transgressions and iniquities that were heaped upon the Savior, our Lamb of God? Did you see them there—all those spots?

They have been transferred to the heavenly Sanctuary—to the altar of burnt offering, the altar of incense, and the Veil—and the High Priest Himself. Jesus Christ is the sin offering, the Sanctuary, and the High Priest. He has released you and me from the overpowering burden of carrying the weight of our sins. It's His job as High Priest in the heavenly Sanctuary to carry them. Intercession is not a soft job for the faint of heart. The Veil represents the contaminating sin that has been transferred from the People of God to the heavenly Sanctuary.

The Veil also represents something else. Did you see it there in Hebrews 10:20? "… by a new and living way which He inaugurated for us through the veil, that is, His flesh …"

The humanity of Jesus is the Veil He wore while here on earth to cover His divinity so that the disciples and others could be in His presence without being burned by "the consuming fire" of the Almighty God. The Veil is a protection for us while we are ministering priests, allowing us to work alongside God the Son and to be empowered by God the Holy Spirit without being consumed. And the Veil—the humanity of Jesus Christ—continues to be our protection as He represents you and me before "the throne of the Majesty in the heavens" when He presents us in the final judgment. Because He is our Elder Brother, "the first-born among many brethren," and because by Faith we are not "ashamed of [Him]" before the world, "He is not ashamed to call [us] brethren" before the Father (Romans 8:29; Luke 9:26; Hebrews 2:11).

But the Veil will not always remain in place. For just as the Veil in the temple was torn in two at the time of Jesus' crucifixion, Jesus intends to remove this protective Veil of separation between God and His people at the End of Time. Jesus intends "to present you faultless before the presence of His glory with exceeding joy" (Jude 24, KJV).

How is that possible? Is this some kind of magic act? No!

Since the day we chose to give our heart to the Lord, since we chose by Faith to accept His first Gift of Jesus, since we chose to abide "in Hope by the power of the Holy Spirit" (Romans 15:13), Jesus—as our High Priest, our Advocate, our Elder Brother (choose the metaphor you like best)—has steadily been moving us forward by the power of the Holy Spirit in the cleansing process. He has been changing our thoughts and actions *externally* in ministry even as He has been changing our hearts *internally* by the repetition of the choices we are making in Him.

The process of "cleansing" is very practical and very real. Jesus is very aware that these very real changes in His people are part and parcel of "Receiving From" and "Growing In." Jesus is very confident that what He is doing is effective and all sufficient so that He can "appear the second time for salvation without [being concerned about our] sin, to those who eagerly await Him" (Hebrews 9:28).

But now "the hour of His judgment has come" (Revelation 14:7). Now the final determination must be made as to "who is able to stand?" (Revelation 6:17). The time has come to examine the wedding garments. (Bible Study Alert: Examine the application of this parable in Matthew 22:11–14 on your own at some future time.) The time has come to determine who will receive the reward that Jesus will bring with Him at His Second Coming (Revelation 22:12).

The very real Day of Atonement ritual that was carried out in the wilderness Sanctuary must now be carried out in stark reality in the heavenly Sanctuary. The sins of the People of God are still there—in the heavenly Sanctuary. They still separate the People of God from their God. These sins must be moved out of the way. Only Jesus Christ, the High Priest can do this. You and I can only watch—by faith. And this faith is now critical. How confident are *you* in Jesus?

Do you believe that He is able to do this?

Do you know who you are?

1.   Do you truly believe that *for you* Jesus is all of those things in the ark of the covenant:

    a)   The Son of God and the very image of the invisible God (the character of God as reflected in the Ten Commandments)

    b)   The compassionate caring God "who will supply all your needs" (the manna)

    c)   The God who has all power and "authority … in heaven and on earth" (Aaron's rod)? (I'm betting you know where the Scripture references for these articles are found.)

2.   Do you truly believe that Jesus Christ can "bring [His] blood inside the veil … and sprinkle it on the mercy seat … and make atonement for the holy place … and for the tent of meeting … and for the altar that is before the Lord … , because of the impurities of the sons of Israel … and because of their transgressions …" which are attached to the heavenly Sanctuary? (Leviticus 16:15–18). Do you believe that the substitutionary sacrifice of Jesus is sufficient to cover, carry, and remove *your* sins?

3.   Do you truly believe that Jesus Christ is able to remove those impurities from the heavenly

Sanctuary and to "lay hold of the dragon, the serpent of old, who is the devil and Satan" and "bind" him in "the abyss" with the chains of those sins for which he was the root cause? (see Revelation 20:2).

4.   Do you truly believe that Jesus is God and that He is a rewarder of those who diligently seek Him? (Hebrews 11:6).

At this point—at the third level—it's not about what you have promised or what you have done or even what you have become. It's about His spotlessness, His faithfulness, His righteousness in representing us in the second apartment. To be sure, you and I have a serious self-examination to perform and a critical heart work to do during this Day of Atonement time to enter into the Covenant Grace-Faith Relationship, to Receive From, to Grow In, and to Become Like Jesus. But while Jesus is in the second apartment representing us, we must cling to our Faith—in Him and what He can do. Not what we can do.

Never forget: Our confidence in *Him* allows us to "draw near with a sincere *heart* in full assurance of *faith*, having our hearts sprinkled *clean* from an evil conscience and our bodies washed with pure water. Let us hold fast the confession of our *hope* without wavering, for He who promises is *faithful*" (Hebrews 10:22, 23). Jesus intends to "present to Himself the church in all her glory having no spot or wrinkle or any such thing; but that she should be holy and blameless" (Ephesians 5:27).

This has been very intense, I know. I've been holding my breath for about the last five minutes. These issues affect me just as much as they affect you. So let me step back for a moment, catch my breath, literally, and remember something. In a previous conversation I promised you some startling conclusions. So let me suggest these three for your consideration:

1. "The hour of His judgment has come." This is not a future event. The judgment and the revelation as to who is, and who is not, in a Covenant Grace-Faith Relationship with God is going on right now in the heavenly Sanctuary, the heavenly court and throne room, and has been since the beginning of the Heavenly Day of Atonement in 1844 (see Daniel 8:14). Although these decisions will not be revealed until Jesus comes again, you and I are already telling everyone how we stand in the judgment.

Jesus explained to Nicodemus the very simple way that He has of knowing whether someone is saved or lost. And it's quite simple really. The final judgment is the answer to this question: Are you moving toward the Light or away from the Light? (Read John 3:18–21 for a more complete understanding.)

Are you moving toward the Light or away from the Light?

Here's the Question: Will you be part of the first resurrection or the second resurrection as Jesus described them in John 5:29? Answer: Are you moving toward Jesus or away from Jesus?

2. Jesus has the ability—and is willing—to take away the *punishment* of sin, the *power* of sin, and finally the *presence* of sin from our hearts. He can redeem our hearts, change our hearts, and cleanse our hearts. It is true that at His Second Coming the People of God will receive some physical changes—immortality and imperishability. But these are side issues and pale in importance when compared with what He can and will do for our hearts. It is what Jesus does for our hearts in the second apartment of the heavenly Sanctuary that is all important—the final removal of the *presence* of sin— that propensity to sin that began in Genesis 3 and has dogged humanity since then.

3. "Who is able to stand?" This is the very real and frightening question lamented by those who call for the rocks to fall on them when Jesus comes (see Revelation 6:17). What's the answer? You need to know this one if you're going to stand at the Second Coming.

Do you know who you are? At this juncture, you very definitely need to know who you are. Isaiah 33:15, 16 gives some very practical and pointed answers to the question, but Psalm 24:4 says it succinctly: "He who has clean hands and a pure heart." Psalm 15:2 adds, "He who walks with integrity, and works righteousness, and speaks truth in his heart."

Question: How will the angels and other heavenly beings recognize these People of God who are able to stand?

The answer is found in the verses of Revelation that immediately follow the question in Revelation 6:17. "And I saw another angel having the seal of the living God … saying, 'Do not harm the earth … until we have sealed the bond servants of our God on their foreheads'" (Revelation 7:2, 3).

Question: How will the people of the world recognize these People of God who are able to stand?

The answer is in the companion verses of Revelation 14:4, "These are the ones who follow the Lamb wherever He goes."

For me personally, this will not happen unless I am in a Covenant Grace-Faith Relationship with God. Only as I accept His Gifts by Faith, abide in His Hope by Faith, and become a partaker of the divine nature by Faith can I hope to stand when "all those things which can be shaken" will be shaken (Hebrews 12:27). Only by Faith will you and I be able to stand—by living in the Covenant Grace-Faith Relationship all the way through the Sanctuary message. Only by learning to live by Faith in the first two levels of the Grace-Faith Relationship are we prepared to live by faith in the third level.

A re you one of those people who likes large theological words? Then let me suggest one for your consideration: glorification. God has something He would like you to do for Him. He would like you to live in such a way that "they may see your good works and glorify your Father which is in heaven" (Matthew 5:16). In fact, we will discuss four of these life activities in our last four conversations.

But for now, do you know what it means to "give Him glory?" (Revelation 14:7). The word glory means "to cause to shine forth." In paintings of the holy family during the Middle Ages, "glory" is the halo around the heads of the holy family. It made them "shine forth" so that you could distinguish them from the rest of the people in the picture. In the same way, your good works make God "shine forth."

As you might expect in the Covenant Grace-Faith Relationship, "shining forth" is a two-way street. When the People of God bring glory to God, He causes them to "shine forth" (Exodus 34:29, 30; 2 Corinthians 3:18). That's why we use the word "glorification" for the third level of the Grace-Faith Relationship. And it's in this "glorification," this "shining forth," that the People of God can so powerfully deliver the Three Angels' Messages. But that's the topic for our next conversation.

Do you think the world would like to see a people who are actually living as if they have "their faith in Jesus"?

W hat do you think? Do you think the world would like to hear that God has a plan to draw them close to Him? Do you think the world would like to see a people who are actually living as if they have "their faith in Jesus" (Revelation 14:12) and as such, God is drawing them close to Him, radically changing their hearts so that they are partakers of the divine nature and are "Becoming Like" Him?

Yes, I think so, too.

This is part of the task of the Remnant, to so live that people of the world are drawn to want to experience this for themselves. And this is another part of the answer to our curiously hard question, Seventh-day Adventist Christian, do you know who you are?

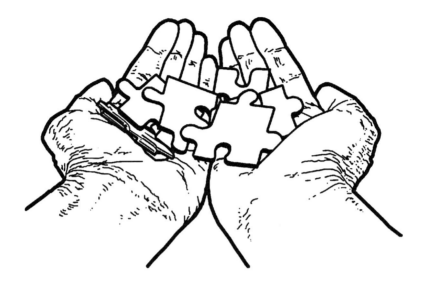

Chapter 14

Do You Know You Have the Last Message to be Given to the World?

"Though He slay me, yet will I trust Him." Job 13:15 KJV

Hi, again. I decided not to go anywhere. I've been waiting right here since our last conversation. Emotionally, I'm a bit overwhelmed with the necessity—and the consequences—of each of the topics we've discussed from the very beginning of our dialogs. Further, I'm contemplating today's conversation. While it's not our most important one, it brings all the others together. With this conversation we reach the climax of the question I've asked so many times, Seventh-day Adventist Christian, do you know who you are?

We've worked our way from the very basics of being a Christian, through the intensity of a more intimate relationship to God, to the realization that in the Time of the End God has raised up a unique group of people—Seventh-day Adventists. God has empowered them to "prophesy again" (Revelation 10:11), to deliver His loving message for the final time—the messages of the Three Angels found in Revelation 14:6–12. As the visible beginnings of the Remnant, like Elijah and John the Baptist, the Seventh-day Adventist Church is to call out the larger invisible part of the Remnant, those in the world who desperately want to enter into a Covenant Grace-Faith Relationship with Him.

While waiting for you, I've been reviewing all the points we have discussed: from knowing we are Beloved Saints, living in a Covenant Grace-Faith Relationship, being ministering Priests and Stewards, to grasping the concept of abiding in the empowering embrace of the Holy Spirit, to understanding the unique calling and role—and responsibility—of the Seventh-day Adventist

Church in its painfully human weakness to deliver God's Time of the End message. This is why I led you through all of those conversations and why I repeatedly asked my curiously hard question—so that we could finally reach this point, and begin to know who we are.

I've been wanting to bring focus and clarity to these topics for some time. For so long I've wanted to ask every Seventh-day Adventist that I have ever met, "Do you know who you are?"

Let me say at the outset that I want to keep this conversation as simple as I can. I'll try to avoid metaphorical words and long, complex phrases. I think it's important that we speak now in clear, unambiguous words. This topic is too important to do otherwise.

And instead of beginning as I usually do with a story, I'm going to save my story until later. I think it will fit better there anyway. This is another of those conversations that begins with Bible study. Dig out your Bible—I know you brought it—and patiently follow me through the pages. What I bring to you will be worth it.

I think I need to begin by asking another question: What are the Three Angels' Messages all about? Let's begin by reading them all the way through. Turn to Revelation 14:6. And while you're finding the passage, let me remind you one more time that I'm not trying to impress you with my Bible knowledge when I ask you to read Scripture with me or when I put the reference in parentheses for you to think about or study on your own. God has given us great wisdom in His Word. He has provided a vast treasure house that we need to explore and understand. When I ask you to bring your Bible to our discussion, I want you to know that it's God's words and God's ideas that I'm interested in exploring with you, and not my own.

Revelation 14:6–12 says, "And I saw another angel flying in midheaven, having an eternal gospel to preach to those who live on the earth, and to every nation and tribe and tongue and people; and he said with a loud voice, 'Fear God, and give Him glory because the hour of His judgment has come; and worship Him who made the heaven and the earth and sea and springs of waters.'

"And another angel, a second one, followed, saying, 'Fallen, fallen is Babylon the great, she who has made all the nations drink of the wine of the passion of her immorality.' And another angel, a third one, followed them, saying with a loud voice, 'If anyone worships the beast and his image, and receives a mark on his forehead or upon his hand, he also will drink of the wine of the wrath of God, which is mixed in full strength in the cup of His anger; and he will be tormented with fire and brimstone in the presence of the holy angels and in the presence of the Lamb. And the smoke of their torment goes up forever and ever and they have no rest day or night, those who worship the beast and his image and whoever receives the mark of his name.'

"Here is the perseverance of the saints who keep the commandments of God and their faith in Jesus."

It's not my intention to completely unpack and explore all of the exegetical nuances that lie in these three messages. I'm sure you've heard dozens of sermons and evangelistic presentations on these verses that attempt to do that very thing. Instead, I want to discuss the essence of these three messages in the context of our previous discussions and the over-arching concept of the Covenant Grace-Faith Relationship—the messages that the beloved and saintly, priestly, Spirit-empowered, painfully human Seventh-day Adventist Church, as God's Three Angels of the Time of the End, must share with the world. (I know. I'm being redundant, and may seem overly dramatic. It's just that the thought of humans having to carry such a powerful, critical message for God at the Time of the End is overwhelming. At least it is to me.)

Look at Revelation 14:6, 7 in your Bible or from the quotation I just read to you. (The verses I quoted above, for those who are reading this as a chapter instead of hearing it as a conversation). What's in the message of the First Angel? What do you see?

The Millerites of the 1840s saw the gospel, the obedience (in giving God glory), and the judgment. And with their understanding of the 2300 days of Daniel 8:14 and the cleansing of the sanctuary, the judgment meant the imminent Second Coming of Jesus. What more do *you* see, especially in light of your understanding of the Covenant Grace-Faith Relationship?

The First Angel's Message is an acknowledgement, by Faith, of the Creator God of the Covenant Grace-Faith Relationship.

The First Angel's Message is the fulfillment of the commandment and the promise in Hebrews 11:6, "And without faith it is impossible to please Him, for he who comes to God must believe [1] that He is and [2] that he is a rewarder of those who ["diligently" from KJV] seek Him." The First Angel's Message is an acknowledgement, by Faith, of the Creator God of the Covenant Grace-Faith Relationship. This is the God who is and who is able to give gifts that function. This is the God who, through His Holy Spirit, is in charge of my

life. This is the God who can reconcile me to Himself and remove ("cleanse" is the metaphorical word) the separation of sin—which is the positive side of the judgment, not the frightful side. (Did you notice the three levels?)

What confirmation and assurance can I give you about the truth of this First Angel's Message? Look at the last part of verse seven. God is worthy to be believed, He is worthy to be worshiped because He is the Creator God. I'm amazed at how many basic Bible teachings are incorporated in this First Angel's Message. I can't begin to count all of the gifts of God that we are "Receiving From" Him, wrapped up in the whole of the First Angel's Message, symbolized by the Sabbath, and validated in God's creatorship.

I see you framing a question in your mind. Why give the First Angel's Message to the world? Because the people of the world must be aroused to the existence and the sovereignty of the Creator God. They must be enabled to see their true separated condition from Him and to acknowledge the choices facing them. The People of God do not deliver this First Angel's Message to the people of the world by hammering them with guilt, nor deriding their lifestyle, nor shaming them with isolation. This is a call to a relationship and must be done by love—which we will talk about in our last four conversations.

Now look at the Second Angel's Message in Revelation 14:8 (either in your Bible or above). What do you think? What's the meaning of the Second Angel's Message?

The Adventist Millerites were recognized for their unswerving devotion to the concept of the impending second advent of Jesus. Many of the churches of their time believed in one of the teachings about Revelation 20:2, which came out of the Counter-Reformation. They were either premillennialists (believing that Jesus had already come, in people's hearts) or postmillennialists (believing that Jesus would not come until *after* a 1000 years of prosperity and righteousness). Therefore, the churches to which the Adventist Millerites belonged disfellowshiped them when they wouldn't keep quiet about their beliefs in the literal, soon coming of Jesus. Their refusal to accept a basic biblical teaching of Scripture confirmed for the Millerites that "Babylon had fallen." They believed that the Christian world was being deceived and led astray and would suffer the consequences of that deception.

Further, the Millerites also read Revelation 18:1–8, which described for them the depth of the deception and the cataclysm of the consequences of being part of Babylon. They took seriously the call from heaven in verse four—"Come out of her, my people"—and were more than ready to be separated from Babylon.

But what more do *you* see, especially in terms of the Covenant Grace-Faith Relationship? Is this only a "come out" command or is there also an "entering in" option as well? What choices are implied?

Look closely at the Second Angel's Message, and you will see that there are two choices. Either you can choose a pretense of a relationship with God, seeking what *you're passionate* about, what looks good for *you to possess*, and what will improve the *power of your* situation. (Bible Study Alert: Compare Genesis 3:6 with 1 John 2:16 for a description of the "love of the world.") Or you can choose to *abide* in and "Grow In" a Covenant Grace-Faith Relationship based on what you can *compassionately* do for others, what you can *mercifully* share with others, and how you can *humbly* serve your God in ministry. (Bible Study Alert: Compare Micah 6:8 with Philippians 2:1–4, which describes the mind of Christ. These two Bible studies should remind you of some-

thing we talked about in Chapter 6. This is why I talked about these concepts early on, because they become essential to our understanding and to the carrying out of our work as Seventh-day Adventists in the Time of the End.)

The seventh-day Sabbath is a symbol of the Covenant Grace-Faith Relationship. As the First Angel explained: Standing in awe of God and giving glory to God in the judgment is to worship God because He is the Creator. Once this is understood, any other day of worship becomes a symbol of independence from, and rebellion toward, God.

Having said this, please understand that under the Second Angel's Message, choosing to worship on Sabbath instead of on Sunday does not make you a Seventh-day Adventist or one of the People of God any more than standing in the dugout makes you a baseball player. While the day of worship is symbolic of the kind of relationship you have chosen, the day is *not* the relationship itself, neither is having your name registered on the membership roles. This fact highlights two more thoughts:

1. This second message is not just for the world; this message is for you and me. "Choose for yourselves today whom you will serve …" (Joshua 24:15) should make us consider and repent from our complacent Laodicean tendencies.

2. The choice that you and I make will separate us into one of two groups: either the group that embraces and receives a lie and a delusion (2 Thessalonians 2:9–12) or the group that embraces the Covenant Grace-Faith Relationship with all of its Gifts, empowerment, and reconciliation.

Now look at the Third Angel's Message in Revelation 14:9–12. Do you see what the Millerites saw? This one is easy, right?

Yes, the consequences of each of the two choices. Movement toward or away from the Light defines the members of each group. (We explored this judgment concept in our last conversation from John 3:19–21. Review that now, if you need to.) The contrast between the two groups will be stark and plain for all to see. The choice of each individual *internally* in his heart will be acted out *externally* in his behavior.

Those who move toward the Light are "Becoming Like" their Father. They are "sealed … on their foreheads" with "the name of My God, and the name of the city of My God … , and My new name" (Revelation 3:12). Their compassionate behavior toward their fellow man and their faith in God demonstrate the results of their sealed empowerment by the mighty Angel of Revelation 18. (I'll let you investigate this Angel's identity and His work on your own. Compare Romans 4:11 and 2:29 with Ezekiel 36:26, 27; Ephesians 1:13, 14 with Revelation 7:3; and Joel 2:28 with Revelation 18:1.) "Here is the perseverance of the saints who keep the commandments of God and their faith in Jesus" (Revelation 14:12).

Those who move away from the Light share a different experience. For convenience, because of coercion, or out of genuine commitment, "they worship the dragon" and his minions (Revelation 13:4). They are marked "on their right hand or on their forehead" (Revelation 13:16) by intolerance and persecution of the People of God, indifference toward their fellow man and independence from God. They are tormented and tortured by the deluding influences of Babylon (compare Revelation 17:4, 6 with 2 Thessalonians 2:9, 10). "And it set him aflame all around, yet he did not recognize it; and it burned him, but he paid no attention" (Isaiah 42:25).

They have no reconciliation and, as a result, they "have no rest day and night" (Revelation 14:11). "Was it not the Lord against whom [they] have sinned, and in whose ways they were not willing to walk, and whose laws they did not obey?" (Isaiah 42:24). "Therefore, I have brought fire from the midst of you; it has consumed you" (Ezekiel 28:18). In their rebellion, they are consumed by the fires they have lit themselves.

Just as crisis reveals character, intensity determines resolve and confirms character choices. In the Time of the End the crisis is so intense that the choice and the character become permanent.

As we noted in an earlier conversation, crisis does not change character. Crisis reveals character. Just as crisis reveals character, intensity determines resolve and confirms character choices. In the Time of the End the crisis is so intense that the choice and the character become permanent.

I'm sure you noticed that in Revelation 14:9–11 God has a lot more to say to those who choose not to live in a Grace-Faith Relationship with Him than to those who do. The description of those who make the negative choice, why they make it, and the consequences of making it are complex, horrendous, and sad. It's not that they are destroyed in the cleansing fires of the judgment. It's that they miss out on the forever Covenant Grace-Faith Relationship with God. But frankly, I don't want to focus on the negative choice so I'm going to leave that discussion to someone else. I want to focus on the People of God, their positive choice, and their assignment—the Three Angels' Messages.

Given all that you and I have been discussing—the life-altering choices we have made, our discovery of the abiding presence of the Holy Spirit who changes us internally and externally, our embrace of reconciliation with the Father— given all of that, delivering these three messages ought to be duck soup. All you need is a duck and some water. All we need is our own personal assignments and the command, "Go ye into all the world."

Right? What's so hard about this?

The problem is, it's not duck soup. It's frog soup. Do you remember the question: How do you boil a live frog? The answer: Place the frog in a pan of cold water and slowly, slowly turn up the heat so that the frog doesn't notice the increasing warmth. How do you lull the People of God into complacency, putting them to sleep (see Matthew 25:5) concerning their loyalty, their source of power, and their task at the Time of the End?

Answer: Slowly, slowly turn up the heat.

We hear that the Three Angel's Messages will be given to the world in the time of "a great tribulation, such as has not occurred since the beginning of the world until now, nor ever shall be" (Matthew 24:21). We answer, "Really, Jesus? What about the flood of Noah? What about the fall of the Western Roman Empire or the destruction of the native cultures of the New World by the invading European powers, or World War II of the 1940s? What about the economic meltdown of the world in the 1930s? What about the natural disasters of the Ice Ages, the Lisbon earthquake of 1755, the 1883 Krakatoa volcanic eruption, or the tsunamis of recent times? What about the religious intolerance of the Inquisition or the Crusades or the Holocaust? Is it going to be worse than these?"

And Jesus answers, "Yes, because the powerful deceptions of 'Babylon' will make it seem not so bad." (Compare 2 Thessalonians 2:10 with Revelation 13:14.) The reason is twofold. First, we tend to see our own time as the worst or the best of times and don't see the broader scope of history, and second, because we are able to survive in our own time we tend to think that it's not so bad after all. The truth is the proclamation of the Three Angel's Messages will be extremely difficult.

In fact, we have a hard time imagining "a great tribulation, such as has not occurred since the beginning of the world until now, or ever shall be" (Matthew 24:21). Maybe we can't imagine what the final People of God will live through and work in because the canvas on which the picture is painted is too big—and impersonal. So let's make it personal; just as scary, just as devastating, just as totally consuming, but very personal.

Let's see if I can sneak up on you with a story. I can't do it as easily now as I did when we first started our conversations, so maybe I'll distract you with a question. Did you notice that for the Third Angel's Message I only asked if you saw what the Millerites saw? I didn't ask, "What more do *you* see?" Well, did you see it? Did it all come together for you as I had hoped at the beginning of this conversation?

Open your Bible to the book of Job. If ever there was a "tribulation, such as [had] not occurred since the beginning," and on a very personal level, it happened to Job. He lost his stock, his wealth, his children, his community standing, and his health—all in a very short span of time. Job was left penniless, helpless, childless, without human support, and without an understanding of what God was doing to him. "Have I sinned? What have I done to You, O watcher of men? Why have You set me as Your target, so that I am a burden to myself?" (Job 7:20).

Can you imagine a greater "tribulation, such as has not occurred" on a personal level? Can you imagine such severe physical, mental, social, emotional, and spiritual loss all at the same time? Neither can I. My mind shudders at the visual of Job sitting on his ash pile, scraping at his scabbed-over wounds until they bled, and praying out his heart to God, asking why, and getting no answer.

Yet in spite of Job's apparently hopeless situation, he refused to give up his faith and his hope. "Though He slay me, I will hope in Him" (Job 13:15). "But he knows the way that I take; when He has tried me, I shall come forth as gold" (Job 23:10). "And as for me, I know that my Redeemer lives, and at the last He will take His stand on the earth. Even after my skin is destroyed, yet from my flesh I shall see God; whom I myself shall behold, and whom my eyes shall see and not another. My heart faints within me!" (Job 19:25–27).

This is the story I promised you, the story of Job—not the patience of Job, but the faith of Job. In the face of the worst calamities that the enemy could throw at him, Job's faith stood like a rock.

The greatest crisis for the People of God will be the crisis of relationship. They will be struggling under the same duress as Job.

Just so, the People of God must stand at the Time of the End by their Faith. "Here is the perseverance of the saints who keep the commandments of God and their faith in Jesus" (Revelation 14:12). Keep in mind that with all of the terrible crises that will be raging in the world, the greatest crisis for the People of God will be the crisis of relationship. They will be struggling under the same duress as Job.

Every support of an earthly nature will be gone. Schools and hospitals will be closed. Churches will be shuttered. Church conferences and unions will be shut down. You don't think so? Whom do you think will be the first high profile targets of a crack down on those who refuse to "worship the beast" and his image? (Revelation 13:12–15). Pastors, teachers, evangelists, and church administrators will be the first ones to be removed.

Just as Job's wife and friends were of no help to him, some members of the Seventh-day Church will be the worst offenders in criticizing, persecuting, and attempting to lure away those who have chosen the path of faith. Of course, this will not happen all at once. Like the heat under the frog, the deception and the persecution will happen gradually and seem perfectly appropriate for the times.

In the end, the last message to the world will not be given in great evangelistic meetings, nor through the witness of hospital or school systems, nor through the neighborhood ministries of churches. In the end, the Three Angels' Messages will be seen in the very practical lives of individuals as they obediently honor—in unshakeable Faith—their Covenant Grace-Faith Relationship with God. Like Job, the People of God in the Time of the End will not give up their faith or their hope.

"What will this actually look like?" you ask. I've asked myself the same question and I'm going to share my answers with you in our last four conversations. But for now, try to put yourself in the place of these People of God in the Time of the End. Use the precepts of the Covenant Grace-Faith Relationship that are burning in your heart, build on the basic skeletal framework of the Three Angels' Messages, and try to express the basic thought processes that will be going through your mind as you consider how you are to survive in the Time of the End. Go ahead; give it a try.

Did you try to express yourself in three concepts? Okay, now let me try.

First Angel. I choose to acknowledge the Creator God as my Savior, Lord, and Master. While the world might estimate my value and my place in society by my physical prowess or by my intellectual, social, or my economic standing (Zechariah 4:6), God estimates my value by the love He has bestowed on me. From Him I choose to "receive" Jesus (He of the highest rank) who died for me. Therefore, my value is the highest possible because the love shown me was the highest possible (1 John 4:9, 10). Despite whatever my present circumstances are and whatever the world might think, this is my value and my place in the universe—near to the heart of God (Ephesians 2:4–6).

Second Angel. I choose to abandon the values of the world and to abide in Jesus and His values—and to "grow" by the Spirit to serve the Creator God. I know that my place of service is not based on my value but on my gifting by the Holy Spirit (1 Corinthians 12:7, 11). Whatever He gifts me, wherever He assigns me, however He empowers me, I will gladly demonstrate His love by serving others (Matthew 22:29). I realize that my choice will separate me from others—perhaps my friends, perhaps my family—who have not the made the choice I have (Revelation 18:4). Nevertheless, I will love and serve them also and demonstrate to them the Covenant Grace-Faith Relationship that they can have, if they so choose (2 Corinthians 5:20).

Third Angel. Because the Creator God loves me, I choose to return His love by obedience from the heart, by worshiping Him from an overflowing heart that He has filled with His love (Romans 6:16, 17). I choose to "keep" and hold precious His commandments, which describe His character and the character He wants to re-create in me (see Genesis 1:26a). Because He loved me first and I have chosen to love Him in return

In the midst of devastating chaos, this will be the positive lifestyle of Seventh-day Adventist Christians, living for all the world to behold in the messages of all three angels— an inspiring, engaging, practical life of Righteousness by Faith.

(1 John 4:19), I choose to "become like" Him by "partak[ing] of the divine nature" that He creates within me and demonstrates through me (2 Peter 1:4).

This is my Covenant with the Creator God. In Faith, I so choose.

There, now do you see it? This is the Third Angel's Message in its fullness, beyond the Millerite view of consequences. When it all comes together, in the midst of devastating chaos, this will be the positive lifestyle of Seventh-day Adventist Christians, living for all the world to behold in the messages of all three angels—an inspiring, engaging, practical life of Righteousness by Faith. This life will be so distinct, so obvious that no one will mistake these people for any other than the People of God. This life will proclaim volumes about God and the life that is possible in Him to the People of the World who are living in a totally different and rebellious paradigm.

Some will see the contrast and will want to leave the chaos and to share in the peace, the reconciliation, and the Covenant that the People of God have. These desperately searching People of the World will be drawn to them and to God, making up the final Remnant, "a great multitude, which no one could count" (Revelation 7:9). Others who have rejected the Creator God as their Lord will reject the example of the People of God and persecute them to the uttermost.

"And the dragon was enraged with the woman, and went off to make war with the rest of her offspring, who keep the commandments of God and hold to the testimony of Jesus." "Here is the perseverance of the saint who keep the commandments of God [who reflect His character] and their [unswerving] faith in Jesus" (Revelation 12:17; 14:12).

I have led you through all of these conversations to bring you to this point. When it all comes together, I want you, a Seventh-day Adventist Christian, to know "who you are," to make the choices and to experience the empowerment of "who you are," so that when the final crisis comes, you will be prepared to live the life of "who you are" before the world.

Now, Seventh-day Adventist Christian, do you know who you are?

I asked you earlier, "What will this actually look like?"

What will the People of God actually be doing during this time while the dragon and his minions are "deceiv[ing] those who dwell on the earth," "mak[ing them] to worship the first beast … and make an image to the beast," and "caus[ing] as many as do not worship the image of the beast to be killed?" (Revelation 13:12–15). And you answered, "They will be giving the Three Angels' Messages."

But what will that look like exactly? In our last four conversations I want to explore the very practical work of the People of God—specifically, the focus of the Seventh-day Adventist Church—during the Time of the End. I am hoping you will soon discover that this is not a work to be done in the future only. We are living *now* in the Time of the End. Because we live in the Covenant Grace-Faith Relationship, we are "created in Christ Jesus for good works, which God has prepared beforehand that we should walk in them" (Ephesians 2:10). It's time for us to get to work. See you at our next conversation.

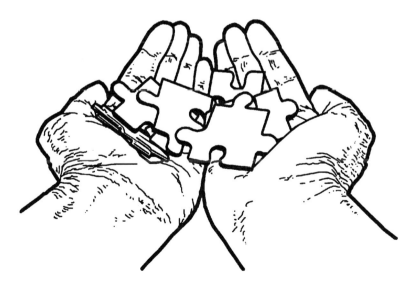

Chapter 15

Do You Know You Have a Mission—
To Make Disciples?

"For I have chosen him, in order that he may command his children and his household after him to keep the way of the Lord by doing righteousness and justice; in order that the Lord may bring upon Abraham what He has spoken about him." Genesis 18:19

*T*ake a seat here next to me. I know. I'm talking *in a whisper because the professor is already at the lectern. I asked you to meet me in this classroom today because I wanted you to hear someone explain what our next conversation is about. Oh, listen. He's ready to speak.*

Welcome to Administration 321: Long Range Planning. I'm delighted that so many of you in the administrative track have chosen to take this course. It is one of the areas that is sorely lacking in today's business world. So many in administration are so busy in their get-everything-done-now world that they forget to think about *what* it is they

are going to do, *how* they are going to do it, and *why* they are going to do it—long-term planning.

So today we will start on the most basic of levels. I want to start where I know some of you are already comfortable and knowledgeable, and I'm going to assume that you know nothing at all about planning.

Let me write this simple model on the white board: Why, What, How.

Why: Why do you—and your colleagues, assuming you have colleagues who are helping you with your enterprise—want to do this thing that you are setting out to do? What is it that you and your colleagues so firmly believe, hold in common, and have faith in that makes you think you could all work together in this common task?

To say it simply, what is your common value set? What values do you share with each other? Okay, that's the "why" question.

What: What is it that you are going to do? What enterprise are you about to undertake? Describe it in as few words as possible, as simply as possible, so that it can be perfectly clear to everyone.

To say it simply, what is your mission? Some don't like the over use of that word, so let's ask, what is the main task you have set for yourselves? That's the "what" question.

How: How will you accomplish this task? What specific steps will you take to get where you want to go? Write them down. Number them in logical order. Make sure they flow from one to the next and that they focus on accomplishing the task. This is your blueprint for every plan and every program that you will come up with to accomplish your task.

Remember, if it has nothing to do with the task, that is, the mission, if it does not get you to where you are trying to go, if it sidetracks you from your goal, don't do it. It's not part of the "how."

To say it simply, list three or four consecutive, focused steps that you and your colleagues will take together—that means you all have to agree on these steps—that will get you to where you want to go. That's the "how" question.

This is the beginning of any long-range business plan. If you don't know the principles that make up your value set, if you don't know the task you are trying to accomplish, and if you don't have a focused plan for accomplishing this task, everything you do will be, at best, just busy work, and at worst, a disastrous waste of time and resources.

Okay. Let's sneak out the back way. You've heard the part I wanted you to hear. We'll talk more when we get back to our comfortable chairs.

That class is focused on training young, soon-to-be executives on how to do long-range planning. In the days that follow the professor will present more specifics and will assign lots of practical work involving SWOT charts and various Rates of Return. I know because I took that class. But it was the introduction that I wanted you to hear, the basics laid out on the first day of class—the Why, the What, and the How.

And I wanted you to hear that presentation because …?

Now we have come to the practical, how-to of our discussion for our organization—the Seventh-day Adventist Church, God's visible Remnant at the Time of the End. Do you know the Why and the What and the How?

Why: Do you know the common values that bind our church together so that we can work together to accomplish our task? What: Do you know what the task is that the Remnant is supposed to accomplish? How: Do you know the plan—that we must all agree on—which has been put in place to accomplish our task?

Yes, I'm giving you a test. We've been through a lot of conversations together, enough for you to begin to assemble some answers to these questions. What is the "why" for the Seventh-day Adventist Church? What are the values that we all hold in common? Think back over the first five or six discussions—about being a Beloved Saint, about being in a Covenant Grace-Faith Relationship, about the biblical teachings that not only make us a Christian, but also make us Seventh-day Adventists. We, as a church, have codified these basic values, gleaning them from Scripture. We call them our 28 Fundament Beliefs. They embody the values that we, as a church, hold in common and form the basis for our ability to function cooperatively together.

Now don't be confused. These 28 Fundamental Beliefs are not the "why." However, they are our best attempt so far to write in human language what we understand our values to be. They could have been written more simply as Micah 6:8 or Jeremiah 24:7 or Matthew 22:37–40. But the 28 Fundamental Beliefs give a few more details to help us understand more clearly, and explain to others, what we believe, which is a good thing.

Okay, that's the "why."

But what about the "what" and the "how"? That's what I want to spend our last four conversations talking about.

So let's begin with the "what." What do you think is our task as a church, as the Remnant, whether at the local church level or on a worldwide level? If you were to take a poll of Seventh-day Adventists from around the world, what answers do you think you would get? Go ahead, tell me and I'll write them down.

To witness. Okay, got that. *Evangelism.* Probably so. *Uphold the Standards.* I can imagine that coming from some quarters. *Make friends for Jesus.* Yes, I can hear some saying that, too. *Preach and Teach.* Yes, very practical, probably as a "how" rather than a "what," but I'll write it down. *Growing the body.* That could be taken in several different ways.

As you can see from the short list that you and I have compiled, lots of different approaches would be suggested, lots of contenders would be advanced for the "what" as our main mission. But which one is the "main" mission, the "what" of our task.

Let me tell you a story. (You knew this was coming.)

Abram was the youngest son of a wealthy family who lived in the large seaside city of Ur. (Before the sediment of the Tigris and Euphrates Rivers pushed the delta out so far, Ur was a seaside city.) Each day as he returned from the marketplace, Abram had to pass by the sellers of idols and magical amulets. He had to pass by the temples dedicated to the various gods of the land. He was glad to be going home to the quiet place where he communed with his God.

Abram was the youngest son of a family who worshiped the old God, the original God, the God whom people didn't believe in anymore. Hundreds of years previously, when languages were confused and people were dispersed throughout the world, the old God was forgotten or rejected—or the people just drifted into indifference toward Him. He seemed irrelevant or not very friendly. Whatever the reason, almost no one worshiped the old God.

But Abram's family believed in the old God, the God of Adam, the God of Enoch, the God of Noah and the flood. They held to the belief that is described in Hebrews 11:6. They believed that God was who He said He was and they believed He could do what He said He could do.

It had been a long time since anything remarkable had come from God. But Abram had a close relationship with God. He was always glad to go home—away from the market of Ur, away from the idols and the temples, and away from the irreverence of the people—to his quiet place with God.

On this particular day, as Abram settled into his quiet place and began to pray, he heard a Voice. It was comforting, because it was a Voice he recognized. This was the Voice that spoke to him in his mind whenever he and God were in conversation. But today it was startling—because Abram had never heard the Voice speak aloud before.

Genesis 12:1–3 records what the Voice said: "Go forth from your country and from your relatives and from your father's house to the land which I will show you; And I will make you a great nation, and I will bless you, and make your name great; and so you shall be a blessing. And I will bless those who bless you, and the one who curses you, I will curse. And in you all the families of the earth shall be blessed."

I won't take the time to tell all that happened as a result of this conversation:

- the great upheaval that Abram created in his family when he told them what he was going to do;

- the discussions he had with his wife about where they were going and whether his nephew, Lot, should go with them;

- the consequent journey to Haran where Abram's father died;

- the changing of Abram's name to Abraham;

- the long wait for Abraham before his son, Isaac, was born.

The details are not important to our conversation today. What *is* important for us to note are three things:

1. Genesis 15:6 says that "Abraham believed God." Why is that so important? Read on in the same verse. "And it was reckoned to him as righteousness." There's no "prove yourself first" or "I have to see it before I will trust you" with God. Romans 4:21 says that Abraham was "fully assured that what God had promised, He was also able to perform." And God said, "That's good enough for Me." God and Abraham were developing a Covenant Grace-Faith Relationship based on Abraham's trust in God and God's ability to do what He said He would do.

2. The task given to Abraham was *not* Abraham's idea. This was God's idea. Abraham was called to his task, but God assigned the task to Abraham. What was this great and wonderful task? Look at Genesis 12:2: "And I will make you a great nation." Abraham was to raise up a family. I'm watching the disappointed, questioning look in your eyes. Everybody has a family! So, why was that such a big deal? But this was not to be just any family.

Look at Genesis 18:19. I know, I've stopped telling you to turn to this or that scripture, but this one is important. Turn to Genesis 18:19 and read with me: "For I have chosen him [Abraham], in order that he may command his children and his household after him to keep the way of the Lord by doing righteousness and justice, in order that the Lord may bring upon Abraham what He has spoken about him."

Trusting God is righteousness according to God's definition.

Abraham's task was to raise up a family that was just like himself. These family members were to trust God in the same way that Abraham trusted God. Did you see that part about "doing righteousness and justice"? (I'm hoping that you remember what "righteousness and justice" are from our earlier conversations about the Covenant Grace-Faith Relationship. Do you? If not, go back and review Chapters 4, 5, and 6, especially Chapter 6 where we discussed the two value sets of the heart in terms of Micah 6:8.) What is God's definition of righteousness, specifically from Genesis 15:6 in my first point? Trusting God *is* righteousness according to God's definition. And Abraham was to raise up a family that did the same thing that he did—trusted God.

3.   Abraham went about his task with laserlike precision. He was focused. Everything he did was focused on his main task, raising up a family that trusted God. From building altars wherever he went, to circumcising males of his household, to searching for and rescuing his nephew Lot, to fathering Ishmael by Hagar, to laughing at God about fathering a child by his old wife (yes, Abraham laughed, too, Genesis 17:17), to believing that God would raise up Isaac even after Isaac was sacrificed (see Hebrews 11:17–19), to Abraham, everything was about raising up this family that was to bless the whole world. Everything he did or thought about was focused on this one main task. This was his "obedience from the heart" (Romans 6:17) that we discussed many conversations ago.

I'm sure you don't agree with all of the ways he went about doing it; for example, lying to Pharaoh about Sarah being his wife and similarly lying to Abimelech, especially just at the time God had promised to make Sarah a mother. But Abraham was focused on his task. He was to make a family who would, by trusting in God:

- follow after Abraham,

- do as Abraham did, and

- carry on when Abraham was gone.

What do we call those whom *we* train to trust in God to:

- follow after us,

- do as we do, and

- carry on when we are gone?

What are they called in Genesis 18:19? They are called children and household. They are *family*. What did Jesus call them? Look at Mark 3:34, 35: "And looking about on those who were sitting around Him, He said, 'Behold, My mother and My brothers! For whoever does the will of God, he is My brother and sister and mother.'"

Jesus also called His followers *family*.

But by what other designation does He call them? John 13:35 says, "By this shall all men know that you are My *disciples*, if you have love for one another" (italics supplied). Jesus called these followers His *disciples*.

I have much more to say about the "how" of being a disciple in our next conversation. Right now, I want to focus on today's topic, which is, the main task of the Remnant at the Time of the End. That main task is described in Matthew 28:19, which says, "Go therefore and ..." (Are you following along in your Bible? I want you to see this for yourself. What does it say?)

In Greek the word is *matheteuo*. The KJV Bible tries to define the word rather than just say what the word means. In most other translations the word is translated as "make disciples." The main task of the church is to *make disciples*.

What is a disciple? Look at John 13:15: "For I gave you an example that you also should as I did to you." Just as with Abraham and his family, a disciple of Jesus is one who trusts in Him and:

- follows after Him,

- does what He does,

- and carries on when He is gone.

And Jesus says: "Go therefore and make disciples of all nations."

Making disciples is the main task of the Remnant, the Seventh-day Adventist Church and specifically your local church. Bible scholars for centuries have called this the Great Commission. This is task Number 1. Actually this is the only task God has given to His church. We are to make disciples.

We are to function in the likeness of Abraham:

1. The same as Abraham, we are to believe that God is who He says He is and can do what He says He can do (see Romans 4:21; Hebrews 11:6; cf. Ephesians 2:9). We are to enter into Covenant—the Grace-Faith Relationship—with God based on our trust in Him and on His ability to function, not on our ability to function.

2. The same as Abraham, we are called by God to our Great Commission, not some other commission, not a commission of our own devising, not a commission that we think is more culturally relevant or more politically correct or more socially needful. We are to accept the commission given to us by God (Matthew 28:19, 20).

3. The same as Abraham, we are to focus on our commission, on our assigned task with laserlike intensity, calling God's people out of the confusion of Babylon and into Revelation 14:12 which tells us, "Here is the perseverance of the saints who keep the commandments of God and their faith in Jesus."

Making disciples is the main task of the Remnant.

Dr. David Paulson was a dear friend of and a respected physician for Ellen White. At one time he was closely associated with the Battle Creek Sanitarium, teaching medical students in clinics in Ann Arbor, Michigan, and Chicago, Illinois.

In conjunction with his clinics, Dr. Paulson wanted to use his students to open and manage homes for pregnant prostitutes in the heart of downtown Chicago, to help them and instruct them in a better way of life. Dr. Paulson's heart went out to all who were suffering as a result of sin in the world.

When I heard the story for the first time, I thought, "Wow, what a wonderful idea." I thought of Jesus and the woman found in adultery in John 8. How like Jesus to want to help those who had been led astray and had gotten caught up in a life from which they could not escape.

But Dr. Paulson wanted to know what the Lord thought of doing this kind of work. So he wrote to Ellen White to describe what he was planning to do. By the inspiration of the Holy Spirit, Ellen White responded—don't do it. She reminded him that the medical work is important but the gospel work is more important. She said to remember that the focus of the main task is to present the gospel. The social work of helping the down and out was to be commended and was a wonderful work, but the social work was not the main task. The social work was not to consume the major portion of the time and resources of the people. The gospel must go into areas where they had not yet heard the Three Angels' Message. The medical work, especially centered in the heart of large cities, was not to dominate and become the main focus.

Jesus was in a similar situation (Mark 1:32 and onwards) when, after healing Peter's mother-in-law and after the sun went down on the Sabbath, almost the entire city flocked to Him to be healed. In the morning when Jesus had gone out to pray, His disciples came looking for Him. "And they found Him; and said to Him, 'Everyone is looking for you.' He said to them, 'Let us go somewhere else to the towns nearby, so that I may preach there also; for that is what I came for'" (Mark 1:36, 37).

Are you surprised at what the Lord's messenger told Dr. Paulson and what Jesus told His disciples? I was. Yet it happens all the time in our local churches and in our higher organizations. We plan evangelism efforts and ministry meetings. We organize social events and seminars. But do we know what the main task is? Do we know the purpose for having a particular church in a par-ticular location? Do we know the purpose of the Seventh-day Adventist Church?

Do we know who we are?

All of these activities are wonderful, helpful, reaching outward to those who don't know Jesus and inward to encourage and train the saints. But these activities are the "how," they are not the "what." They are not the main task. The purpose of these activities is to move us forward toward the main task of "making disciples," not dominate it or overshadow it. During our visit to the business school class, we learned that as wonderful and as helpful as they are, these activities are just busy work, unless we first know what our purpose is. We must be focused on the business that Jesus assigned to us.

Like Abraham, we must:

- trust God,

- understand what the main task is, and

- focus on it, like a laser, to the exclusion of all others.

And what is this task? Making disciples who, trusting God as we do:

- follow after Jesus,

- do what He did, and

- carry on in our place when we are gone.

The "what" of making disciples must be at the heart and center of all our plans. Identifying and focusing on the "what" must dominate all other considerations. Every planned activity (and they should be planned) must focus—like a laser—on accomplishing the main task of making disciples.

If perpetuating our favorite activity becomes more important than the main task, or if our activity consumes resources without helping to accomplish the main task, we should stop doing it, no matter how time honored or treasured or helpful it is.

Without making disciples, all of our favorite activities—good as they are—are just so much busy work at the least, and at the worst, are a waste of time and resources.

As we learned from the professor, the "what" must come before and determine the "how." Without making disciples, all of our favorite activities—good as they are—are just so much busy work at the least, and at the worst, are a waste of time and resources.

This was a hard lesson for me to contemplate and to carry out. Over the years I have had my favorite church activities: Christmas and Easter dramas, regularly scheduled social events, evangelistic efforts, yearly activities "that we always do." But like the bronze serpent in the wilderness, these activities stopped contributing to the main purpose of making disciples and became an end in themselves. They were no longer useful and had to be dropped. Not easy for a person like me who treasures good times and the joy of a successful activity.

Remember: the main purpose of the main purpose—is to *be the main purpose*.

At this point, I'm watching a questioning look across your face. I'm suspicious that you want to ask, "Then should I be giving Bible studies on Tuesdays and Thursdays and inviting people to prayer meetings on Wednesdays? Can I live out my Covenant Grace-Faith Relationship with God by selling tractors for a living or do I need to quit my job and become a Bible worker?"

While these may be honest, well-meaning and sincere questions coming from a desire to serve the Lord, they miss the point of this discussion. I have been telling you about the "what," the major task. These are questions about the "how," the plans that will implement the "what."

I'll save a more detailed answer to this very appropriate question until later, but for now I'll say, in the context of our discussion for today, look at the life of Abraham, his occupations and his various points of encounter with others.

It doesn't matter so much "how" you serve the Lord or in what capacity you serve the Lord. Besides drawing you closer—which is always God's hidden agenda (see Jeremiah 24:7), do you remember the purpose of your service for the Lord? The answer to the "what" question is (envelope, please) to *make disciples. Always* remember: Whatever you do and to whomever you speak in whatever capacity you currently occupy (teacher, plumber, product manager, shopper, airplane seat occupant, dog walker), your main purpose, your underlying role is to make disciples. There ought to be a big billboard in the back of your mind that you can see from anywhere in the room saying, Don't ever forget that your overarching, foundational, all-encompassing life task is making disciples.

How about now—do you have a clearer picture? Do you know who you are?

Now that we know what the main purpose is—to make disciples, let's ask: What does a disciple actually do? This is the topic of our next conversation, to which, if you are ready, we shall proceed.

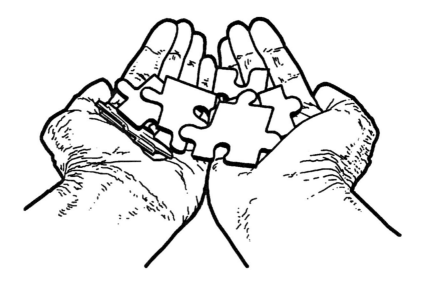

Chapter 16

Do You Know You Are to be a Witness?

"You are My witnesses," declares the LORD, "and My servant whom I have chosen, so that you may know and believe Me and understand that I am He. Before Me there was no God formed, and there will be none after Me." Isaiah 43:10

Hi, again. Come join me. I see you've brought your Bible. Good for you. I've got a cup of something warm to drink. You can have one, too, if you like. It's over there on the counter. Then come, sit next to me.

I've been thinking about our last conversation. I asked you the question: "Do you know what a disciple actually does?" And I've been thinking about disciples, especially disciples in the Time of the End, because that's where we are in our series of conversations. We're now talking about what the Remnant—specifically the visible Remnant, the Seventh-day Adventist Church—does in the Time of the End.

Turn to Matthew 24:1, 2. "Jesus came out from the temple and was going away when His disciples came up to point out the temple build-ings to Him. But He said to them, 'Do you not see all these things? Truly I say to you, not one stone here will be left upon another, which will not be torn down.'"

Here we see the disciples in their own Time of the End. They are thinking in terms of the popular beliefs of the day about the Messiah and the Temple and how the Messiah will drive out the Romans and re-establish His kingdom. Jesus is leading them up to one of His favorite study places on the Mount of Olives. As they see the magnificent buildings on the Temple Mount off to their left, they express their thoughts aloud about the Time of the End.

At Jesus' response His disciples are shocked into silence. Jesus has just told them that the tem-ple would be destroyed. How could such a thing happen? When will it happen? What kind of cataclysmic event will it take to destroy the temple? An earthquake? A war and a siege? An internal political and religious betrayal? They are silent as they climb slowly up the mountainside, occasionally glancing furtively at the Temple and then at each other.

When they arrive at their favorite study spot where they can see out over the city, they sit quietly on the ground around Him, still a little abashed by their ignorance and false assumptions. But their curiosity overcomes their embarrassment, and they ask Him, "Tell us, when will these things happen, and what will be the sign of Your coming, and of the end of the age?" (verse 3).

As you can see, Jesus has their attention focused, not on their presuppositions, but on what He has to tell them. I'm going to let you read what He says to them on your own. It's there in Matthew 24:4–14. Go ahead, read it to yourself. And I'll read it silently, too.

How much of what you've just read has already taken place? Jesus told them that all of these things would take place before He comes. From your perspective, from where you stand in the stream of time, how many of them have already happened?

O ne day as I turned into the driveway from retrieving my grandson Braeden from school, he and I saw little orange flags marching across our lawn. A surveyor's tripod stood guard at one end of the line of little orange flags and at the other end was a large hole in the yard. I took Braeden to the tripod.

"Look down the line of flags, Braeden. How many of them do you see?"

"Five flags, Papa."

"Let's walk down the row of flags and see what we can find."

We started walking. "Keep looking at the flags." We continued following the flags. "Whoa, what is this? What did we find?"

"The water meter box, Papa."

We had indeed come to the meter box in the ground, but the flags went on. We followed the line of flags until we came to the hole.

"What do you think is in the ground, Braeden? Look at the flags, how they march in a line right over the water meter box. What do you think is in the hole?"

He looked in the hole. "A pipe, Papa."

"What do you think is in the pipe?"

"Water."

According to Matthew 24:14, there is only one more flag to go.

Like Braeden and the orange flags, throughout our discussions you and I have been following our own set of flags. We know where we stand. Just as Jesus explained to the disciples, we can see the events behind us and we can see the events still to come. We know what's in the pipe. We know where we are.

In the Seventh-day Adventist Church, this overview of events behind us and before us, the events that you've just read in the Gospel of Matthew, collectively we call them the Great Controversy. We can see—by looking at all the flags that we have passed and the very few flags yet to come—that the Seventh-day Adventist Church is an end-time church. In fact, according to Matthew 24:14, there is only one more flag to go. All of the other events that Jesus described have already happened. Only verse 14 is yet to be fulfilled. I could show you the same thing in Revelation 12.

All of the verses have happened. Only verse 17 is yet to be fulfilled.

Why am I telling you this little story about Braeden and the flags—when I'm supposed to be talking with you about what a disciple actually does? Because I want you to be impressed that the time is short. We don't have any fooling around time. Everything we discuss, everything we undertake as a church of the Time of the End is as serious as a heart attack. We must pay attention—to who we are and what we are to do. There's only one flag to go.

With that little aside, let's return to my question. What does a disciple do—exactly? Are you a disciple? How do you *make* a disciple?

This is the place where I usually tell you a story to illustrate my main point. And right here, I need a story about a disciple in the making, but where to find one? Where would you look for such a story? What Bible character would you pick? Would you pick an obvious story from the disciples of Jesus: Peter, John, or Matthew? Maybe you would pick Paul. I personally like the story of David. Or I could highlight Timothy or Dorcas or Luke.

But each one of these people could be seen as having some advantage, some relationship with someone who gave them a leg up, something going for them. Because of their "obvious" advantage, you might decide that this person or that person can't really be a model of a disciple for you to follow.

So I'm going to choose a person with *no* advantages and *no* possibility of being a disciple. I'll choose the wild man of Gadara, the one we usually call the Demoniac, because you and I can both relate. At some time or another both of us have felt like or have been a "wild" person.

Do you remember him, this wild man of Gadara? Read with me in Mark 5:1–5. Yes, open your Bible to Mark 5 as we will be working right here for a while.

"They came to the other side of the sea, into the country of the Gerasenes. When He [Jesus] got out of the boat, immediately a man from the tombs with an unclean spirit met Him, and he had his dwelling among the tombs. And no one was able to bind him anymore, even with a chain; because he had often been bound with shackles and chains, and the chains had been torn apart by him and the shackles broken in pieces, and no one was strong enough to subdue him. Constantly, night and day, he was screaming among the tombs and in the mountains, and gashing himself with stones."

Can you, in your wildest dream, imagine anyone less qualified to be a disciple? If this wild man of Gadara could become a disciple, do you think *you* could become a disciple? Do you know who you are?

By the way, do you remember what a disciple is? In our last conversation, I described Abraham and what he was like. Do you remember? Yes, of course, you do.

- Abraham believed God.

- Abraham was assigned his task by God.

- Abraham focused on his task.

And then I said that Abraham was in the business of making disciples, people who would follow him, do as he did, and carry on when he was gone.

Let's watch how Jesus interacts with this wild man from Gadara. Let's see if Jesus goes about making disciples in the same way as Abraham did, especially with someone as unutterably unqualified as is this man. And let's see if Jesus will tell us what a disciple does.

Imagine now that you are with Jesus and the disciples. You have just gotten out of the boat when this wild, hairy, naked man comes rushing out of the rocks near the beach. He is growling, screaming, spitting. His dirty fingernails claw the air, just waiting to tear into your flesh. At least that is what it seems to you.

What do you do? What is your first reaction? What would any self-respecting, practical, superstitious fisherman do and say?

"Get back in the boat!" you shout as you leap into it. "Someone push us off! We're outta here! Come on, push! Push!"

Wait a minute! Where's Jesus? He's not in the boat. Where is He? You and the other disciples look back at the beach. Jesus is still standing there. The wild man is on his knees in front of Jesus, and they are having a conversation. And you want the answer to only one question. *Why* is Jesus still standing there?

When you are in trouble, Jesus never abandons you. Remember Matthew 28:20, "And I am with you always, even to the end of the world." Jesus recognizes a brother who is in trouble, a brother who cannot even speak for himself. The demons inside of him have taken control of his speech and his actions. But the man is crying out for help. And Jesus knows it. Jesus is not going anywhere until this man is free to choose.

Can you relate to this man's pain—his physical pain, his mental pain, or his spiritual pain? Have you ever felt like this man, trapped in such agony, such desperation? There is no way out. You are totally surrounded. Do you feel like this now?

Jesus does not leave him. Jesus helps him. Jesus frees him! The demons are gone and the man is in charge of his own mind again.

Here is my point: Do you think this man now has a relationship with Jesus? Do you think this man feels any emotional attachment to Jesus? Would the words "thankful" or "grateful" be strong enough to express how this man feels right now?

Following is not about behavior; following is about belief.

And how does Jesus feel about this man? Is the word "love" sufficient to describe how Jesus feels about him?

Jesus and this man have established Covenant with each other. In this encounter they have exchanged friendship and bonds that are closer than blood relationships. Like Abraham, this man believes. You'd better believe it: This man believes in Jesus.

And like the disciples that Abraham was making, this man will now follow Jesus—to the ends of the earth, if necessary. Wherever Jesus goes, this man wants to go too. Following is not about behavior; following is about belief. Hear me again: Following is not about behavior; following is about belief.

You see, what Abraham *was* and what he asked his disciples to *do* is one and the same thing. The two descriptions are parallel. Abraham believed in God *and* he wanted his disciples to follow him—and also believe in God.

First of all, a disciple believes and follows. Carefully think about the implications of this. Only follow someone in whom you believe. Therefore, cautious logic says, be very careful in whom you believe and whom you follow. Remember Jesus' admonition about false christs and false prophets. Remember the old joke about what it says on the dollar bill: "In God we trust," everyone else is suspect. There is really only one Person who is safe enough for that kind of loyalty.

Therefore, if you're defining what a disciple is or if you're trying to make a disciple:

1. A disciple believes in God and follows Him.

Notice the corollary: The disciple you are making should not believe in *you*. The disciple should believe in God and follow Him. The disciple may not know this at the outset and only come to learn it later, but you should know it at the outset with all your heart. No big heads, please.

And a second corollary comes to mind. In order to make a disciple for Christ, *you* have to believe in God and want to follow Him yourself. I'll pause a moment and let you ponder that thought. (Combine Acts 2:38 with 1 Corinthians 2:10–12, then ask yourself, am I able to share spiritual things unless the Holy Spirit is working through me? And when is it that I receive the Holy Spirit? If you're not sure, check Chapter 6.)

2. A disciple accepts his task from Jesus.

Now let's see what Jesus will do next. Read Mark 5:18, 19 with me. "As He [Jesus] was getting into the boat, the man who had been demon-possessed was imploring Him that he might accompany Him. And He did not let him, but He said to him, 'Go home to your people and report to them what great things the Lord has done for you, and how He had mercy on you.'"

This man desperately wants to follow Jesus. And Jesus says, "No." As if that is not crushing enough, Jesus then says to him, "Go home to your people and give your testimony about the mercy God has shown to you."

Do you know who these people are to whom he has to witness? Of course you do! They are the same people whom you have been assigned to witness to. Some people will love this wild man now saved—just like some people will love you and will hear your testimony gladly. And how will they treat him? Actually, how will they treat you? They will take you in and love you and feed you and hear you tell your story over and over again.

Some people will hate this man—just like some people will hate you for the pain you have put them through. These people are not so anxious to forgive and are not so anxious to hear of the wild man's healing—or of your healing. They are not so anxious to hear you tell that your pain has been cured, when theirs has not. How will they treat him—or you? You know, don't you? Because you have already experienced their hot, angry words and their rejection. You've had the door slammed in your face by these people.

Some people will be jealous of this man's experience—just as some will be jealous of your experience. They will not be hot in their rejection for it's not fueled by pain. No, jealousy is much more subtle, much more insidious. It simmers; it doesn't boil. They will nibble away at your reputation. They will suggest that your healing isn't complete; your repentance isn't genuine, especially the first time you stumble. And you will stumble.

They will suggest that your healing isn't complete; your repentance isn't genuine, especially the first time you stumble. And you will stumble.

And there are those people who will ignore him—and will ignore you and your witness. They just don't care. These folk are sometimes harder to deal with emotionally than those who are angry. People who are angry at you at least recognize your existence. They relate to you and later may even turn to love you. But those who don't care, don't even know you exist, they dismiss your witness as silly, irrelevant, nonsensical, or irrational.

Jesus assigned to this wild man his task. "Go and tell your people," He told this wild man, just as Jesus tells you and me, "Do just what I do. Go and tell your people."

Now, what was it that Jesus was sent to do? "The Spirit of the Lord is upon Me, because He anointed Me to preach the gospel to the poor. He has sent Me to proclaim release to the captives, and recovery of sight to the blind, to set free those who are oppressed, to proclaim the favorable year of the Lord" (Luke 4:18, 19).

Jesus says to us, just as He said to the wild man, "Do what I do."

Just as Abraham received his task, we receive our task.

Just as Abraham asked his disciples to do what he did, Jesus asks us to do what He did.

A disciple does what Jesus did. He goes and tells his people; he goes and sets them free.

> 3.   A disciple is focused on his task and carries on after Jesus is gone.

Does this totally unqualified wild man do it? "And he went away and began to proclaim in Decapolis what great things Jesus had done for him; and everyone was amazed" (Mark 5:20).

You mean he is actually going to go home and face the angry, hateful people, and the simpering, jealous people, and the dismissive, ignoring people?

Yes, he is and he does.

He goes home and he tells everyone—those who love him and those who hate him and those who are jealous of him and those who ignore him. Like Abraham, this man is focused. Like a good disciple should do, this man carries on after Jesus is gone.

Was he left *alone* to carry on by himself? We are *never* left alone! "I will ask the Father, and He will give you another Helper, that He may be with you forever; that is the Spirit of truth, whom the world cannot receive, because it does not see Him or know Him, but you know Him because He abides with you and will be in you. I will not leave you as orphans; I will come to you" (John 14:16–18). We are *never* left alone. Don't even consider the thought.

And as it said in the scripture we just read: "Everyone marveled." They marveled that God could change such an unqualified man into a disciple. They marveled that God would even consider using such a person. But He did.

My son Christopher (yes, the one who is a great chef and who wondered why his mother was "keeping" all of her cookbooks) is a lawyer, a public defender in Florida. Every day he calls on people to tell what they have seen and heard and experienced. He has to list their names on the docket of the court before he can call them to testify—just as God needs your name on His docket before He can call on you to testify. (It's the reason for public baptism, to get your name on the public docket.)

Christopher has to list these people under a particular heading. Can you guess what that heading might be—those people who are there to tell what they have seen and heard and experienced? They are listed under the heading of "witnesses." In the wild man of Gadara, Jesus has just created a "witness," a disciple (follower) who will tell all that he has seen and heard and experienced. There is no more powerful witness.

How about you? Would God consider using you? Is God calling you to be a disciple and a witness? Do you know who you are?

We know that the church's purpose is to make disciples. Are you making your disciple? You can start where Jesus told his disciples to start in Acts

1:8: "And you shall be My witnesses both in Jerusalem, and in all Judea and in Samaria, and to the remotest part of the earth." You can start at home and gradually reach out.

But I want to get back to my original question: "What is a disciple? What does a disciple do, exactly?"

A disciple is one who:

- Believes in God *and* follows him.

- Accepts his assignment *and* does what Jesus does.

- Focuses on his task *and* carries on after Jesus is gone.

This is what it means to be a Witness. This is what we are called to *do* as a church. And it is what we are called to *be* as a Christian, a Disciple and a Witness.

Witness is something you are, not just something you do

Witness is something you are, not just something you do—on occasion, when the church has organized a witnessing campaign, on a Sabbath afternoon. Witness is the way you live your life, every moment of every day. You are the Witness as to what God, when He is given permission, can do for, in, and through a human being.

And I am drawn to this question: Is Jesus calling *you* to be a Disciple and a Witness? I know. I'm sorry. I'm hammering on this like you might not have been listening. But it's so crucial because so many of us don't know who we are, don't know what Jesus has called us to be and to do.

It begins with that first very curious, very intimate, very personal question. It's the question that is put to so many people throughout the Bible. Do you know who you are and what you are called to be and to do?

From Noah: "Now if you will build this ark and get in this ark, I will establish My covenant with you—and bring you through this flood alive" (see Genesis 6:13–21). Noah answered the question for himself (do you know who you are and what you are called to do?), became a carpenter and a boat builder, and invited others to follow him into the ark.

From Joshua: "Choose you this day whom you will serve" (Joshua 24:15). Joshua chose for himself, became a general and a spiritual leader, and called others to follow him around Jericho and into the Promised Land.

From Elijah: "Why hesitate between two opinions? If God is God, then serve Him. If Baal is god, then serve him" (1 Kings 18:21). Elijah answered this question for himself, became a prophet, and called others to follow him in the worship of the one, true Creator God. (Yes, some are not called to be generals or carpenters. They are called to be prophets. Some, but not all.)

From David in the Psalms as quoted in Hebrews: "Today if you hear His voice, do not harden your hearts" (Hebrews 4:7). Many times David chose to answer that call for himself, became Judah and Israel's king, and called others to follow him in building the nation God intended they should build.

And from Jesus Himself: "Behold I stand at the door and knock" (Revelation 3:20).

After all of our time together, I still don't know you well enough to assume anything, so I will ask this question of you. Have you ever previously responded to that question, ever answered that call to be a disciple? Have you heard the convicting voice of the Holy Spirit calling you to take that first step: To believe in God and follow Him, to make Covenant with God, and commit your life to follow Him as a disciple?

Or maybe—I don't know—maybe you made this commitment some time ago, but the worries and riches and pleasures of life rose up and choked the life out of that commitment. And today you are hearing the voice of Jesus calling you to renew that commitment "today, while it is called today." This would be a good time—while the conviction is upon you again—to re-establish that Covenant relationship with God.

I know that this is a radical commitment to ask of you. But this is what the Holy Spirit has been preparing you for through all of our conversations. As Seventh-day Adventist Christians, we know with certainty that the metaphor of the Sanctuary calls us to be ministering Priests as we share with people all three wonderful promises of the Three Angels. We know that the consequence of choosing to Receive from, Grow in, and Become like Jesus (R-G-B) is to be part of that persevering group of whom it is said, "The saints of the Most High shall take the kingdom and possess the kingdom forever" (Daniel 7:18).

We know that in the abiding power of the Holy Spirit we are called to deliver this confident

---

The purpose of a disciple is to witness.

Witness of the Remnant to "every nation, tribe, tongue, and people" (Revelation 14:6). In whatever walk of life God has called us—carpenter, general, prophet, or king—however the Holy Spirit has gifted us, we are called to share the Covenant of the Grace-Faith Relationship with the people.

The word "Christian" means a follower of Christ, a disciple. The purpose of a disciple is to witness.

When my children were away at college, I had a hard time getting them to commit to visiting my wife and me at Christmas. I called them and said, "Are you coming this year for Christmas?"

And they answered, "Well, I don't know. Maybe."

"What do you mean, maybe? Are you coming or not?"

"Well, I don't know what else might be happening. I don't know what other offers I might get."

Commitment is hard when you think there might be a better deal just down the road. Let me assure you: There is no better deal. This is Covenant with the living, Creator God of the universe. This is the ultimate deal. Now is the time to make such a commitment, especially as the time is short. We are living in the Time of the End.

Wow! That got a little intense. But that's the way it is as we approach the end of the Time of the End. You might not think so, but it only gets more intense as we discuss what we, as Seventh-day Adventist Christians, are actually doing in the Time of the End and why—which is the topic of our next discussion.

I see that your cup is empty. If you want to refill it, please help yourself. Then we can proceed, if you're ready.

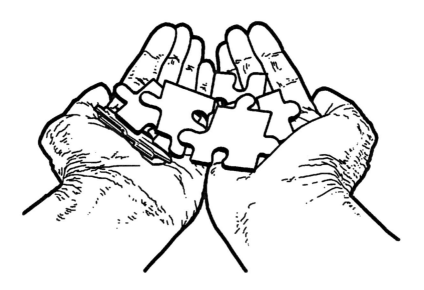

Chapter 17

Do You Know You Are One of the Sheep?

"Therefore watch; for you do not know what hour your Lord comes." Matthew 24:42

Welcome. I see you didn't take long to return. So I assume that you're ready to ask the question put to John the Baptist by many penitents who came to him: "What must I *do*?" (see Luke 3:10–14). I think *you* have wanted to ask this question for some time now. So many Christians want to start at this point. Like the penitents with John the Baptist or the rich, young ruler with Jesus, they want to know "how" to live. But we must first have in place the "why" and the "what" before we can address the "how." Well, all the pieces are now in place, and we're ready to talk about what to *do*. But, please don't be disappointed if it's not exactly what you'd hoped for.

From the beginning the topics that we've discussed have prepared us for an answer based on principles and not on rigid rules. So let's proceed with the idea that we are looking for principles, not rules. And like the disciples, let's go to the source. Let's ask Jesus what we should *do*.

Let me take you back to where we left Jesus with His disciples in Matthew 24:3. "And as He was sitting on the Mt. of Olives, the disciples came to Him privately, saying, 'Tell us, when will these things be, and what will be the sign of Your coming, and of the end of the age?'"

This is a rather common question, actually. In today's world, so many people want to know when the end of the age will be—though most won't say it in so many words. I'm sure you've seen many articles in weekly news magazines about the end of the world. And any number of movies and TV shows are about angels and Armageddon. We see scientists of many different religious persuasions—and some with no religious belief at all—

who are asking: "What's up with the increasing earthquakes? The increasingly severe hurricanes? The rising sea levels?"

From all of these reactions I know that it's not just the Evangelicals or the Seventh-day Adventists who are interested in what's going on. Lots of people want to know, "When is the end of the age?" I suspect that's one of the reasons we Seventh-day Adventist Christians want to understand the books of Daniel and Revelation, to discover "when is the end of the age?"

As we saw at the beginning of our last conversation, in Matthew 24 Jesus shared numerous events with His disciples that introduced the Time of the End, and He said, "But that is not yet the end." Then He gave the one sign that will introduce the end of the age. Do you remember what it was?

Turn in your ever-ready Bible to Matthew 24:14: "This gospel of the kingdom shall be preached in the whole world as a testimony to all the nations, *and then the end will come*" (italics supplied).

Jesus followed this announcement with predictions of several scary events of the Time of the End, followed by several counterfeit attempts to deceive the very elect, followed by the Second Coming and the resurrection (Matthew 24:14–35).

Was that the end of His sermon? Check out the rest of Matthew 24 and 25. Now what do you think—was that the end of His sermon? I agree. No, it was not. He had much more to say. Jesus told several stories, gave several examples, and related three parables—all having one message: "Watch! Stay Alert! Pay Attention! The 'end of the age' is coming, and you just might want to be prepared for it when it happens."

When we lived in Milton-Freewater, Oregon—just across the state line from Walla

Walla, Washington, we had a roof fire. It was cold that day, and we had a fire in our wood stove. What we didn't know was that the strong wind was pushing the embers from our stove fire down onto and in under the wood shakes on our roof.

We had no warning at all. When John, our oldest son, went to the barn to retrieve a hammer, he looked up at the roof and saw a soft glow. He came into the house, wondering aloud (fortunately) if we had a light on in the attic. He could see a glow coming from the roof, he said. It was such a minimal sign, a passing comment easily ignored.

"No, the light in the attic isn't on."

"What do you suppose it is?"

We went out to look. Suddenly the glow on the roof went from being an item of passing interest to being an item that had our all-consuming attention.

What one item is to have our all-consuming attention as Seventh-day Adventists Christians, do you think?

At this Time of the End, in this age of increasing chaos in the world, what one item is to have our all-consuming attention as Seventh-day Adventists Christians, do you think? Take a look at the words and the ideas that Jesus presented to His disciples in Matthew 24:6–12 and compare them to our world. Is it wars in Afghanistan or Sudan? *Earthquakes* in Japan or Chile? *Famine* in Somalia? Is it the *tribulation* of Christians in Uzbekistan or in Vietnam? Is it a *falling away* in Australia or in the United States? What about *false prophets* in supermarket tabloids? *Lawlessness* in the Catholic Church or in the Seventh-day Adventist Church?

All of these ideas are mentioned by Jesus. And then He says: "… but the end is not yet. You're getting close. But the end is not yet."

Let's keep looking at Matthew 24 and review the long series of events that Jesus mentioned from verse 15 and onward. Are these to consume our interest? What about the *abomination of desolation* in verse 15? Is that it? What about the *great tribulation* in verse 21? The *false christs and prophets* in verses 23 and 24? The *false signs and wonders* in verse 24? How about the *false second coming* in verse 26? Should that consume our time and interest? How about the signs in the *sun, moon, and stars* in verse 29? You and I know many people from our home churches who are concerned about these very important signs of the Time of the End.

But what's the *one* event that is to be the all-consuming event to the Remnant, something that they should be *doing*? Especially when they know that (like John the Baptist or Elijah) they are the *visible* Remnant, functioning in and by the power of the same Holy Spirit who enlivened Elijah and John the Baptist, and are to call out the *invisible* Remnant?

"This gospel of the kingdom shall be preached in the whole world as a testimony to all the nations, and *then* the end will come."

You would think that with all this activity and all these signs, the coming of the end of the world would be obvious to everyone, but apparently not. Jesus mentions three groups who don't get it.

Look at Matthew 24:38, 39, which describes the first group of people who are consumed with life: parties, dinners, marriages—fellowship. Not only do they not see it coming, they don't even *know* that it's coming. These are the Unknowing. They don't know the *event* and they aren't watching.

Now look at Matthew 24:43. Here is the second group, described as a headman, a householder who is responsible for his house and all who are in it. He's not watching and his house is broken into. These are the Unwatchful. They don't know when to *watch*. They don't know the *timing* of the event, and they aren't watching.

Check out the last group in Matthew 24:45 and 48. This third group is described as those who aren't *expecting* something to happen, illustrated by two slaves—one who is faithful and sensible and one who is evil. The faithful slave is watching and he's ready; he's expecting his master to come. And some time soon. But the evil slave doesn't *expect* the master so soon and is acting out when his master returns unexpectedly. These are the Unexpectant. They don't know the *immediacy* of the event or the exact timing of the master's return.

To all of these groups—and to you and me, and to the Seventh-day Adventist Church— Jesus says: "Watch, you don't know the event. Be Alert, you'll miss the timing. Pay Attention, you aren't expecting."

Have you ever seen the YouTube video (it's yesterday's video now, but it illustrates this point beautifully) of the young lady in the mall who was so busy texting that she fell into a fountain in the center of the mall? She didn't seem to *know* that the fountain was there. She certainly wasn't *watching* where she was going. If she knew about the fountain, she didn't *expect* it to be there so soon. Just shows you how easily this can happen to anyone.

Are you *watching*? Are you *expecting*? Do you *know* who you are?

I just have to ask you: What do you think about us? What are we—as Seventh-day Adventists— consumed with in the external world? Is it possible that we are so concerned about the wars, the natural disasters, the downturn in the economy, the politics in the United States—or in the church—that we don't know what to watch for? Is it possible we are so focused on the abomination, attempting to avoid the false christs and the fake signs and wonders that we've forgotten what event we *should* be watching for?

Is this the way, if possible, to mislead the "very elect"?

And if not consumed with the world, what are we consumed with internally, in the church? Have we become so consumed with life—family, work, and even church fellowship—that we don't *know* what the coming *event* is? Have we become so attentive to maintaining the organizational structure—schools, hospitals, conference offices, and meetings—that we have become *inattentive* to the nearness of the *time*? Or, in the opposite extreme, have we haughtily assumed the prerogatives of the Master, judgmentally abusing those whom we are to love and serve as stewards, not realizing the *immediacy* of His *expected* return?

What was it that Jesus said we are to be *doing*? What event should alert us that the end is near? "This gospel of the kingdom shall be preached in the whole world as a testimony to all the nations, and then the end will come."

Two significant words stand out in Jesus' statement: *world* and *gospel*. We recently moved from a large costal megalopolis to a small mountain town. Walking any street in either of these two settings, you will observe radically different people groups and the kinds of *worlds* they each represent. In the same way many *gospels* are being offered to each of these people groups: the social gospel, the economic gospel, the health gospel, the marital happiness gospel. What world and what gospel do you think Jesus had in mind for His disciples—and for us, His Remnant at the Time of the End?

Jesus described the *world* of His disciples in Acts 1:8, "But you shall receive power when the Holy Spirit has come upon you; and you shall be My witnesses both in Jerusalem, and in all Judea and Samaria, and even to the remotest part of the earth." Jerusalem, Judea, and Samaria were certainly the world for Peter and John. But it's not the world where most of us live.

So let's rewrite this description for your local world. "But you shall be My witnesses both in your local neighborhood, and in your home church and your county, and even out into the whole viewing area of your local television station."

Our world is our immediate surroundings; our world is our neighborhood.

Do you understand? What Jesus told His disciples, He is telling you and me: The whole world begins here; the Holy Spirit's power begins to work right here—first. The Holy Spirit can handle the world, but He wants us to be involved with our neighbors, in the neighborhood of our churches, in our town or in our county. Our world is our immediate surroundings; our world is our neighborhood.

If that is the world to which we have been called, what about the gospel? Of all the gospels available, which gospel did Jesus specifically design for us to share with "the whole world," or at least our part of the world? Jesus used three parables to tell His disciples—and us—which gospel: the parables of the Ten Virgins, the Talents, and the Sheep and the Goats.

Turn to Matthew 25:1–13 right now and read it through. I know you know the story, but read it through again so that I can discuss it with you. All done? Good, let's look at this first parable of the gospel, the Parable of the Ten Virgins.

You saw, didn't you, that all ten virgins *know* that the bridegroom is coming; all are *expecting* Him. But, all are tired of *watching* and all have fallen asleep. When they are suddenly awakened by the coming of the Bridegroom and must lead the procession to the bridal house (check Revelation 14:6 to see how this is done), all of the virgins discover something about themselves. While they are trimming their lamps, they find that only half of the virgins have extra oil for their lamps. (The oil is symbolic of the Holy Spirit. If you're not sure of this, look at Zechariah 4:1–6.) The lamps (see Matthew 5:16 to see what "lamp" means) of these "wise" virgins are powered by the oil. They are Spirit-driven.

Half of the virgins do *not* have oil for their "lamps." They have to scramble around, looking for a source of power and end up being self-driven. Spirit-driven versus self-driven: When it comes to the gospel, the difference is crucial. The gospel is Spirit-given and Spirit-driven.

Look at Ezekiel 37, a story I know you're familiar with. In this chapter God tells Ezekiel about Israel (the People of God) who are to deliver the gospel to the world, but in the vision, Ezekiel sees them as a valley of dry bones. Ezekiel is told to prophecy (speak for God), and as he does, the bones come together, the muscles and organs appear on them. Skin covers them and they stand up. But there is no breath in them. Like the virgins, they are asleep and not even breathing.

In verse 9, God tells Ezekiel to "prophecy to the breath [*rauch* = spirit, breath] … [to] breathe on these slain, that they come to life." When Ezekiel does so, "the breath came into them and they came to life and stood on their feet, an exceedingly great army."

Now look at verse 11 where God explains the vision: "Son of man, these bones are the whole house of Israel. Behold, they say, 'Our bones are dried up and our hope has perished. We are completely cut off.'" But in verse 12 God says to them: "Behold, I will open your graves and cause you to come up out of your graves." What does God mean by this "resurrection," this "coming to life?" (If you remember our conversation in Chapter 6, you know already.) In verse 14, God through Ezekiel says to the exiles in Babylon—and to us—who are not physically dead but are spiritually and emotionally dead: "I will put my Spirit within you and you will come to life" (cf. Romans 8:11).

Without the oil of the Spirit, we are just dry bones; we are virgins without oil. Our lamps are dark.

The gospel is Spirit-*given* and Spirit-*driven*. Without the oil of the Spirit, we are just dry bones; we are virgins without oil. Our lamps are dark. We have no power to share the gospel.

The gospel of Jesus is the *Spirit-given* and *Spirit-driven* gospel.

Turn back to Matthew 25:14–30 and read the second gospel parable, the Parable of the Talents. (Go ahead. I'll wait.)

Here Jesus tells His second parable about a well-to-do master who went on a journey and entrusted his possessions to his three servants. One received five pieces of silver, one received two pieces of silver, and one received one piece of silver. They weren't all given the same amount, but each was given according to his ability. All *knew* the master, all received, and all knew what was *expected*. (For a self-study of what the Master—that is, Jesus—expected of them, study for yourself John 13:15, 34; 14:12 and Luke 17:10, the Steward mindset.)

The first two servants believed the master to be kind, but just. Therefore, they acted according to Hebrews 11:6. Do you remember what it says there? (If not, check our definition of Hope in Chapters 4–6, especially Chapter 6.) "And without faith it is impossible to please Him, for he who comes to God must believe that He is, and that He is a rewarder of those who seek Him."

These two servants knew that, while their master expected a return on His money, He was a kind and just master. They had faith in His character and joy in His service. They had the Steward mentality (Chapter 9); they wanted to please him. By their faith in the master, they connected to the master, and as a result they were fruitful.

The evil servant had a different attitude toward the master. "I knew you to be a hard man … and I was afraid" (Matthew 25:24, 25). What did the evil servant's words reveal about his feelings for the master? Does he love and trust the master or is he afraid of the master and a bit angry at having to live under such a severe and strained relationship? The evil servant acted out of fear and anger, and as a result, he was unfruitful.

Again, the difference is crucial. Compare the attitude of the servants toward the master: *faith* vs. *fear*; and the result, *fruitful* vs. *unfruitful*.

We learned in the first parable that the delivery of the gospel begins with the Holy Spirit. According to the second parable, when the Spirit comes, He brings gifts. But these gifts do not function until they are connected by faith in Jesus to the power of the Spirit (Ephesians 3:16,17).

When the attitude is faith in Jesus, then the power of the Holy Spirit flows and the result is fruitfulness (John 15:5). When the attitude is fear, there is no connection to the Spirit. Where there is no Spirit, there is no power. Where there is no Spirit, there is no fruit.

> *When the attitude is fear, there is no connection to the Spirit. Where there is no Spirit, there is no power. Where there is no Spirit, there is no fruit.*

Jesus' gospel is faith-based in the power of the Holy Spirit. The result is fruitfulness—in the lives of those who hear the gospel *and* (please, notice) in the inner life of the one who delivers the gospel. Remember what Jesus says in Matthew 7:20, "By their fruits you shall know them." The internal faith of the Christian isn't always evident to outside observers, but the fruitfulness is. Our second parable says that the gospel that Jesus intends for us to deliver is the *faith-based* and *fruitful* gospel.

Now read Jesus' third gospel parable in Matthew 25:31–46, the Parable of the Sheep and the Goats. I'll wait … have you finished? Good, let's review now. Here we see all the nations gathered before the Son of Man when He comes in His glory and sits on His throne. Like a shepherd, He divides them into two groups, the Sheep on the right hand and the Goats on the left hand.

These two groups wonder why Jesus knows how to divide them. They all seem to acknowledge Him. They all gather around Him, acting as if they know Him and belong to Him. But Jesus is not interested in their current actions. Instead, He is interested in their actions before His arrival.

What is the difference between the Sheep and the Goats? How does Jesus divide them? What criteria does He use?

Interestingly, Jesus has previously described how He will divide them in Matthew 7:21. "Not everyone who says to me, 'Lord, Lord' will enter the kingdom of heaven." The criterion for division is *not* who acknowledged Him as Lord. Likewise, Jesus said, "Many will say to Me on that day, 'did we not prophecy in Your name, and in Your name cast out demons, and in Your name perform many miracles?'" Both groups actually did these things—in His name. So the criterion for division into the Sheep and Goats is *not* the actual actions they might have performed.

No. The criterion Jesus uses is: To whom and for what reason did you do these actions? "And if you love those who love you, what credit is that to you? For even sinners love those who love them. And if you do good to those who do good to you, what credit is that to you? For even sinners do the same" (Luke 6:32–34). But Jesus says, " … to the extent that you did it unto one of these my brothers of Mine, even the least of them, you did it to Me" (Matthew 25:40). Jesus is focused on their motives and their actions taken toward "the least of them."

Did you notice that *neither* group—neither the Sheep nor the Goats—seems to know that Jesus identifies most strongly with "the least of them." The Sheep certainly don't understand it; but to the Sheep, it doesn't matter. They are others-focused. They just take care of everyone—out of love.

The Goats don't understand this categorization, "the least of them," either. They do care for some; but the Goats are self-focused. They claim that they do miracles for the Lord and that they take care of some—those they know, those who offer a reward, those by which they can gain recognition or power. But for whatever reason, they aren't interested in taking care of the "least of them."

No, neither group seems to know that Jesus identified most strongly with "the least of them," those with whom they were not acquainted, those who could give no reward, those who had no access to power.

Jesus' gospel is others-focused in love. To the Sheep, who are others-focused, it doesn't matter. They just loved. The Goats, who are self-focused, ask: "What's in it for me? What reward might be coming to me?" Whom they serve and why: It makes all the difference to Jesus. Jesus' gospel is *others-focused in love*—with no thought of recognition or reward.

And finally, do you remember Jesus' original instructions in Acts 1:8? "But you shall receive power when the Holy Spirit has come upon you; and you shall be My *witnesses*" (italics supplied). Do you remember the end-time event that totally consumes the Remnant (Matthew 24:14)? "And this gospel of the kingdom shall be preached in the whole world for a *witness* …?" (italics supplied).

Jesus' gospel is given by *Witnesses.*

To summarize all three parables, Jesus' gospel is: Spiritual, powered by the Holy Spirit; Fruitful, based on faith in Jesus; Loving, others-focused and Witness-delivered.

"And this gospel of the kingdom shall be preached in all the world for a witness unto all nations; and then shall the end come" (Matthew 24:14).

What I am about to say may seem trite or grandiose or unnecessarily alarming to you. Nevertheless, it is true. Did you catch the timing of these parables? Do you understand that when the Virgins are leading the "gospel" band at the Master's *coming*, when the Master has *come* to settle accounts with His Servants who received the silver to invest, when the Lord has *come* to separate [read: judge] His Sheep and Goats, when "this gospel shall be preached … to the whole world," this flurry of activity marks the "end of the age" just before the Second Coming of Jesus and is all-consuming for the Remnant? Here's the startling, perhaps alarming statement: Do you understand that this has already begun in the Seventh-day Adventist Church?

As Jesus said, "Today this scripture has been fulfilled in your hearing" (Luke 4:21). Already, some are in close relationship with Jesus. Already, some are receiving power from the Holy Spirit. They are Spirit-driven; they are faith-based and fruitful; they are lovingly focusing on others, especially "the least of them."

Are you missing it? Are you watching? Are you interested? Do you know who you are? Even more importantly, do you know how you can participate in this Spirit-given and Spirit-driven, faith-based, others-focused, witness-delivered gospel to your part of the world?

"Now when they heard this, they were pierced to the heart, and said to Peter … 'What shall we *do*?'" (Acts 2:37, italics supplied.) Ah, yes, here is our question, with which we began this conversation: "What shall we *do*?"

Peter answered, "Repent, and let each of you be baptized in the name of Jesus Christ for the forgiveness of your sins; and you shall receive the gift of the Holy Spirit" (Acts 2:38). From the beginning of our discussions so many conversations ago, I began as I did because the answer to "Do you know *who* you are?" and "Do you know *what* to do?" is "repent, be baptized, and receive the Holy Spirit."

Has the Holy Spirit pierced you to the heart? Do you know what to *do*? I pray that you do. Carefully consider all that you and I have discussed

from the beginning before answering. Review Chapters 4–6 if you aren't sure.

Revival and reformation without repentance is just fanaticism, an excitement that will die out without effect.

In a recent Wednesday night prayer meeting, my group was reading a powerful book, *Revive Us Again*, by Mark Finley that describes exactly what we have been discussing. But please notice: Before revival and reformation comes repentance. The three R's of coming into the Covenant Grace-Faith Relationship are repentance, revival, and reformation. They have to happen in that order. Revival and reformation without repentance is just fanaticism, an excitement that will die out without effect.

Repentance ("coming to Jesus" as the old preachers like to say) is the door through which we enter on the way to revival and reformation. Revival means exactly what it says, "bring back to life," which only the Holy Spirit can do. (Remember Ezekiel 37:14?) Reformation (the process of re-forming or as Romans 12:2 says, "transforming") is to "partake of the divine nature" (2 Peter 1:4). Again, this is not something we can do under our own power. If this sounds like R-G-B, I can assure you that it is absolutely intentional—on God's part.

From the time Sin entered the world, God has had one purpose, one unrelenting, driving, all-consuming purpose—which is true 24/7. Please read this Scripture and notice the numbers used in the reference. "I will give them a heart to know Me, for I am the LORD; and they will be

My people, and I will be their God, for they will return to Me with their whole heart" (Jeremiah *24:7*). Every Gift we have discussed—and more gifts that we haven't discussed—all lead to the same final conclusive gift: the Covenant Grace-Faith Relationship.

Aren't you thankful that God has given you this Gift in order that you might live? Would you like to share this Good News (read, Gospel) that God wants to live in a Covenant Grace-Faith Relationship with those whom He created—with the world?

"And this gospel of the kingdom shall be preached in all the world for a witness unto all nations; and then shall the end come" (Matthew 24:14). Do you want to be a part of it? The gospel to the whole world *has already started* in your part of Jerusalem—in your home church, in your neighborhood, in your city and your county, out into the viewing area of your local news station, and even into the remotest parts of the earth. And you can be part of it—as you are connected to others who are covenanted with the Father, and the Son, and the Holy Spirit.

Do you know what to look for?

Are you watching?

Do you know who you are?

I hope you are beginning to realize that if you want to know what you are supposed to *do*, do not examine a checklist of potential places or church offices in which to serve the Lord. Rather begin at the beginning of the Covenant Grace-Faith Relationship. Ask first:

1. Did I choose to accept the Gift of Receiving Jesus as my Savior?

2. Did I choose to accept the Gift of Growing with the Holy Spirit as my guide:

    With what spiritual gifts? To be enhanced by what training, in what setting?

    To serve in fellowship with whom, those with complementary spiritual gifts?

    To be empowered according to His agenda and plans?

3. Did I choose to accept the Gift of character development (read: Fruits of the Spirit), Becoming like my heavenly Father?

As you can see, the intention of the Covenant Grace-Faith Relationship is to change *you*. Yes, the practical work gets done, the world is warned, the everlasting gospel is preached, the people are made aware of the choices they must make and the consequences of those choices. To be sure, the work of "preach[ing] the everlasting gospel to every nation, tongue" is done in numerous ways. But the first target of God's Grace is *you*.

But the first target of God's Grace is you.

But as I warned you, the answer to the penitent's question, "What must I do?" does not have a "how" answer, but a "who and why" answer. Not what you were expecting, I would guess. This is why I spent so much time at the very beginning of our conversations developing the "why" of the Covenant Grace-Faith Relationship. Until you know the "why," the "what," and the "who," you will waste a lot of time trying to find the "how" of the Seventh-day Adventist Christian life. In the Time of the End, we don't have any time to waste.

Next up: So what *are* we supposed to be *doing*?

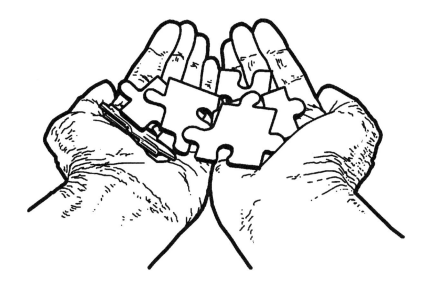

Chapter 18

Do You Know You Are to Build an Ark—
a Refuge of Safety?

"By faith Noah, being warned by God about things not yet seen, in reverence prepared an ark for the salvation of his household, by which he condemned the world, and became an heir of the righteousness which is according to faith." Hebrews 11:7

Welcome back. During our last several conversations I mentioned a concept that I didn't fully explain, the "visible" Remnant. Let me expand on it for you now because it will lead us into our topic for this conversation.

God has always *had a "visible" Remnant.*

God has *always* had a "visible" Remnant. These are the People of God whom He calls to speak to the world, to draw out from the world the "invisible" Remnant who do not realize that they are part of the People of God, but when they are called, they will respond to God's messages.

If you know your Bible history, you can probably name those who have been part of the "visible" Remnant. They're a veritable *Who's Who* of God's brightest and best. They have arisen in every generation, and when they have spoken, some who had not known the true God responded.

You might think of Noah as he preached and built the ark or Abraham as he witnessed to his neighbors, the ancestors of the prominent nations of the Middle East. You might think of Elijah on Mt. Carmel and certainly of John the Baptist at the River Jordan. If you expand your sights beyond the Scriptures, you might think of Martin Luther at the doors of the Wittenberg Church or John Wesley in England or Joseph Wolfe in Africa and the Middle East or William Miller in New England. (These folk are well worth knowing about, and the Internet is an easy place to search them out.) Whenever these members of the visible Remnant and others like them have called, some "who dwell on the earth" have responded.

In the Time of the End, God also has a people who are called to speak for God. These are the "visible" Remnant who are to call out the people from the world—the invisible Remnant—who will respond.

In a previous conversation (Chapter 10, for those who have a hard time imagining that this is a conversation and not a book), we talked about the People of God at the Time of the End. Only they didn't sound at all like Elijah or John the Baptist or Martin Luther. We found that the Bible describes these people as self-satisfied and believing that they are "in need of nothing" (Revelation 3:17). These people actually have a name, a moniker of notoriety. Do you remember their name? Yes, of course, Laodicea.

The disaster is that Laodicea has a message from God to bear to the world—in fact, three messages according to Revelation 14:6–12. But Laodicea doesn't seem to know who she is. Laodicea doesn't seem to know that she stands at the Time of the End as the last in the long line of the "visible" Remnant.

Some time ago we talked about what it is that Laodicea needs in order to discover and fulfill her role as the Remnant. We won't go over it again, but you can review it for yourself in Revelation 3:18 and John 10:27. (If those Scriptures aren't enough to jog your memory, review Chapters 10, 11, and 17.)

In our very early conversations we outlined the gift of reconciliation that God has given to us (Chapters 4–6). In our later conversations (Chapters 15–17) we discussed the ministry of reconciliation that God has given to the People of God in the Time of the End. Its purpose is to lead the people of the world ("those who dwell on the earth," Revelation 13:8, 14, or "every nation and tribe and tongue and people," Revelation 7:9; 14:6) back to a relationship with God. Then we outlined how this ministry will benefit those who *receive* it and how it will benefit those who *give* it. Again I will let you review this ministry and what sharing it does for you. You'll find it in 2 Corinthians 5:18–20 and Ephesians 4:12–16.

Now for the last part—what I promised you in our last conversation—what we *do*. I know, it seems like we've already been *doing* a lot. And we have. We've been establishing our Covenant Grace-Faith Relationship with God. We've been actively accepting the three Gifts of God (and the complex of additional gifts that go with them). By the abiding power of the Holy Spirit, we've been acting the part of Priests, studying our instruction manual (the Word of God), participating with other gifted people in ministry, and praying intercessory prayers for others. We've been living the lives of Stewards and Disciples, demonstrating our Witness—through our lives and our ministry—that we know the joy of living in the Covenant Grace-Faith Relationship, which is the reality of the third message of the Three Angels' Messages (Revelation 14:12, 13) that we proclaim as the visible Remnant. Both Seventh-day Adventists as well as other Christians call this "righteousness by faith" (Habakkuk 2:4; Romans 1:17).

But now comes the capstone, the particular activity that will consume the People of God—the visible Remnant—in the Time of the End. It's a task that we don't usually think about. Nevertheless, it's a critical activity that *must* be done. The task is to build an Ark, a Refuge of Safety.

Go with me to a hillside covered with lush foliage. It's a beautiful sunny day, like so many of the days since God created the world. The world we see *is* the world that God originally created, with beautiful large trees, verdant vines rich with brightly colored fruits stretching over vast areas. Look! In every direction, as far as your eyes can see, the world is filled with beauty. Although sin has reigned in this world for almost 1500 years, you can see the stamp of God's creative power from Eden. It's still there in the plants and animals—and the people.

This particular hillside is relatively open and looks down on a large city full of beautifully crafted houses. In your mind's eye, can you see them down there below us? They are decorated with gold and jewels and sparkle in the sunlight.

The people of this world have built houses such as these everywhere. They have a passion to compete with each other, driven to outdo one another in creativity and personal wealth. The marvelous architecture of these houses reveals the intellectual strength of these people. However, the beautiful designs mask the violence and bloodshed, the cruelty to animals and people, and other horrible acts that are regularly planned in these houses and take place in this beautiful world—the world God originally designed to be a paradise.

It's unusually quiet and peaceful up here on this hill right now because it's still early morning—before the scoffers arrive. For you see, on this beautiful hill is where Noah is building a large boat, far from any body of water. You can see it just over there to your right. It's hard to miss at 450 feet long, 75 feet wide, and 45 feet high.

From this hill Noah has been preaching for 120 years. Noah has been saying that God is going to destroy this world. Noah has been telling people that the unthinkable—and heretofore unknowable—is going to happen: Water is going to fall from the sky.

You might ask: "Why would God do such a thing?" The people of Noah's day certainly are asking that same question: "Why *would* God do such a thing?"

Noah has been telling these highly intelligent people that the world has fallen under the destructive spell of Sin. He cries out that the world has gotten so evil that to save those who are still in relationship with Him, God must put them in a safe place, in this very large, very strong boat, in the ark. Then God will destroy every other person, every animal, everything that is left on the earth with a worldwide flood.

The rational, clear-thinking intellectuals of the world completely reject these unverifiable, unscientific claims. The intellectuals know that water has never fallen from the sky; the rivers have never overflowed their banks; there has never been rain or a flood on the earth; and there is no scientific indication that such a thing is even possible.

Therefore, the intellectuals reject the claims of Noah as simplistic, ignorant, and naïve.

The overtly religious people of the world have been busy developing and promoting their own worship program. They appreciate what God has created, the beautiful things of the world: the trees, the animals, the birds, and the people. These overtly religious people think so highly of the beauty that God has created that they think of these created objects as if they are representations of God *or* as if these created objects are gods themselves. They think of these created objects and creatures as if they have the same feelings, the same thoughts, the same ideas, the same actions, the same human characteristics as they themselves have: pride, envy, power seeking, lust, hatred, vengeance, greed, and violence.

Then they reversed the analogy. They turned this concept on its head and said, "If these beautiful objects that God has created, if these representations of gods have these human thoughts and ideas and actions—and they *are* gods, then it is certainly okay if *we* have these same thoughts and ideas and carry out these same actions of lust, greed, violence, etc." Thus, the obviously religious people reject the sinfulness of their own activities and proclaim that these activities are not sinful, not if the "gods" also think and act in this way. In fact, it would be totally unfair and out of character for God to punish these ideas and activities and to destroy His own creation. Therefore, the overtly religious people reject Noah as a religious simpleton, or worse—a fanatic.

In the beginning many of the crafts people, the farmers, the servant-class of the world, the ordinary citizens, as well as some of the intellectuals and some of the religious people believed Noah's preaching. His earnestness in building the boat impressed them. His fervent preaching pricked their consciences. But as time continued, public pressure built up against Noah and against those who believed his message. And now those who once believed have abandoned their belief in Noah's message and became the worst in laughing at Noah's foolishness.

In mercy and patience God did not immediately visit retribution on these rational intellectuals, these overtly religious people, these misguided and misled common masses. And they all have interpreted this to mean that God is not interested in their actions and will not punish them for their sins. Thus, they are emboldened even further to ignore God's commandments and, even more, to flagrantly violate them without fear.

So 120 years have passed.

During that time Noah has continued to build the ark, employing many of these same people in the construction process. And for 120 years Noah has preached, although in the last few years hardly anyone has even considered the possibility that he might be right.

And now Noah has become the local entertainment. It's fun to go up on the hill and watch him preach—and laugh at him. Everyone loves to laugh at a fool!

But today is different. The ark is finished. It has been loaded with food for both man and animals. Noah has sent the workers home with their last paycheck. Everyone wonders what he will do now. The boat is finished, and there is still no sign of any water to float it. What will be the next act in this 120-year-long drama/comedy? Nobody wants to miss the next exciting episode.

As the people gather on this beautiful morning, Noah again mounts his small hill that he has used for years to pour out his heart, to let these people know the calamity that is about to happen. But today Noah seems different. His words carry more power. His face is almost in agony as he pleads from his heart for the people to heed his warning and enter the God-given refuge from the coming storm and flood.

But they have rejected his message for so long that his earnestness only calls forth even more intense mocking and contempt.

Suddenly a hush falls over the crowd. The laughing stops. Noah stops preaching.

Someone says, "Look!" and points to the edge of the forest. They see, coming from among the trees, every sort of animal known to man deliberately marching toward the ark. Remarkably, they are actually lining up—by twos and sevens—to stride up the long ramp and into the darkness of this huge boat.

Suddenly every head turns at the sound of a rush of wind. From out of the clear sky every known kind of bird flocks toward the ark. They cover the sun like a cloud, and as people watch open-mouthed, they fly through the cavernous door.

No one has an explanation. The intellectuals and the religious people are called upon to explain it—and they can't. For just a moment everyone is stunned into silence as they watch the parade of animals and birds, as if guided by unseen hands, into the ark.

This is where we are in earth's history today.

I'm going to stop at this point in the story because this is where we are in earth's history today, right now—even as you and I are having this conversation. As we watch the world news unfold each day, as we observe the activities and events in our towns and neighborhoods, as we live out our lives in response to these news events (by which we daily witness to our friends and neighbors), you and I are watching and living a repeat of this story in today's world.

First of all, please notice:

Just like Noah, God has called out a special group—the "visible" Remnant—to preach the message that God is about to visit this world once again. And again, just as in Noah's day, God is about to bring the Plan of Salvation to a conclusion.

Just like Noah, the Remnant are to be preaching that God has already offered a substitute Lamb (John 1:29) for the sins of everyone in the whole world—if they will accept it.

Just like Noah, the Remnant are to be preaching that those who accept the first Gift need to *separate* themselves from the philosophies and the activities of those who have rejected the first Gift and accept God's second Gift (the Holy Spirit, Acts 2:38). Review Chapters 4–6 if you don't remember the Gifts and how they build the Covenant Grace-Faith Relationship. This second Gift will create the change of heart, internally (Ezekiel 36:26, 27), and the change of behavior to match, externally (Romans 12:2), so that everyone can be restored to the character of God—the third Gift (2 Peter 1:4)—if they will accept it.

And now, especially like Noah, the Remnant must be preaching that God is about to return to the earth and reveal who has accepted and who has rejected these three Gifts (John 5:28, 29). For God is about to cleanse the earth—this time with fire (2 Peter 3:7)—and eliminate the instigator of Sin, "the serpent of old called the devil and Satan" (Revelation 12:9). God is about to eliminate the Sin (separation from God, Isaiah 59:2) that Satan has caused and the final system that he put in place (Revelation 13; 17) in the Time of the End to promote the separation from God.

For those who have chosen to accept these three Gifts and the wonderful changes that these gifts bring, God is bringing the final manifestation of the third Gift—the physical changes of immortality and the reality of eternal life (see 1 Corinthians 15:51–53)—when Jesus returns at His Second Coming.

These are the Three Angels' Messages—in their practical form—that the visible Remnant are to be preaching. As we have discussed in previous conversations, the visible Remnant must stop being Laodicea, become the Remnant, and preach the message of Noah: The Time of the End is now and God is about to return to this earth in judgment.

Now please, make sure you understand that the visible Remnant will have had this life-changing experience themselves, and they will be preaching these messages out of their own experience, but not by their own physical or intellectual strength. By what power will this change and this preaching be possible, do you think? (Do you remember Ezekiel 36:26, 27 and Zechariah 4:6?) You should know this already. By the time we finish our conversation, you will know it. And I hope you will have discovered another answer to my curiously hard question: Do you know who you are?

Just as in Noah's day, the visible Remnant can expect rampant opposition.

Second, please notice: Just as in Noah's day, the visible Remnant can expect rampant opposition.

Just as in Noah's day, the rational intellectuals of our day have concluded that man is in charge of this world. The rational intellectuals have rejected the idea that God—if He exists—created this world. Therefore, He's certainly not going to destroy this world with a flood or fire or by any other means.

The rational intellectuals say that the whole concept of God and what He might or might not do is archaic, simplistic, ignorant, and naïve.

Just as in Noah's day, the overtly religious people of our day have chosen to worship gods they have created in *their own* image. And yes, they have names for their gods. Some of these names are *isms* that express their secular, humanistic, and ecumenical approach to religion. Some of these names are religious systems that depend on pre-scribed ritual and rote with meritorious rewards for compliance. However, every false religious deity has characteristics—thoughts, ideas, and actions—that are exactly like their creator's own human characteristics: pride, envy, power seeking, lust, hatred, vengeance, greed, and violence.

And just as in Noah's day, the overtly religious people assume that because their deity has these characteristics it is perfectly okay for the overtly religious people to have these same characteristics in their own lives. Therefore, the overtly religious people reject the sinfulness of their own activities.

The overtly religious people reject the visible Remnant and their message of a merciful God who is coming in judgment. They say that the visible Remnant are religious simpletons or worse—fanatics.

However, just as in Noah's day, there will be those who respond to the *messages* and the *ministry* of the visible Remnant. Some of the People of the World will hear about the offer of the Gifts of God. These people—the "invisible" Remnant—want a relationship with God. And these people of the invisible Remnant will understand that this is just what they have been looking for all their lives.

A few of these people will come from the rational intellectuals or from the overtly religious. But most will come from the common people, the people who admit that they have failed miserably at trying to be smart or at trying to be good. They know they need help of some kind since they have learned by their painfully human experiences that they can't change themselves.

Just like Noah, the visible Remnant must take this ministry of reconciliation, the three Gifts, to the world and seek out those who want a relationship with God. They must seek out the invisible Remnant—just as Philip sought out the eunuch. Again, the visible Remnant will not be carrying out this ministry of reconciliation in their own power. (By what power and guidance did Philip find the eunuch?) By what power will this search and rescue operation take place, do you think? Even if you're sure of the answer, please check the story of Philip and the eunuch in Acts 8:26–29. I'll give you a minute. Do have the answer?

Third, just as Noah did for the animals and all who *could* have come with him, the visible Remnant must build an Ark for these people to safely ride out the coming storm. Now I'm watching the changes on your face as questions cross your mind.

"An *ark*?" you ask. "You're obviously not talking about a wooden boat, but is it a structure of some kind? Exactly what *do* you mean?"

Let's look in the Scriptures and see. Jesus called this structure "His church" (Matthew 16:18). Paul called this structure "the body of Christ" (Ephesians 4:12). Peter called this structure a "spiritual house" built up of "living stones" (1 Peter 2:5).

As you can tell, we aren't talking about a physical structure of bricks and mortar, wood, or steel. We are speaking about a community made of people. Nevertheless, this Ark must be made *just like* and must function *just like* Noah's ark.

What do I mean: *just like*? Consider Noah's ark at the time of the Flood:

1. Noah's ark was a safe place to be.

2. The experience of entering into Noah's ark made it a place where faith could grow.

3. Being in Noah's ark caused all who were on board to come closer to each other and closer to God.

Imagine how your faith might have had to grow—in the face of so much opposition—to even enter Noah's ark. Imagine what you would have been doing while sitting in the ark waiting for the rain. Or, don't imagine. Consider what the disciples were doing in Acts 1:13, 14 in the upper room as they waited for the "rain."

The Ark that the visible Remnant will build must function in exactly the same way. The Ark for the Time of the End must be

- a safe place of acceptance

- where people can grow

- into the image of God.

Let me say that again with a little more detail. The Ark for the Time of the End must be

- a place where people feel safe— where they are accepted and protected

- a place where they can serve and be served—growing in grace and faith and love

- a place where they know they belong to and are included in the family of God.

How do the People of God go about building this Ark? Do you see that ark over there on the hill—450 feet long, 75 feet wide, 45 feet high? That ark was built in three ways: deliberately, radically, and compassionately.

"What do you mean?" you ask again.

In reply, let me ask you a series of questions: How was Noah's ark built? At what point did it begin? Was it when Noah began acquiring the tools he needed? Was it when the blueprint was being drawn up? Was it when God first gave the command and instructions for building it?

Look—yes, in that Bible you keep with you when we talk—look at Hebrews 11:7. Now notice how the verse begins. "By faith, Noah being warned by God about …" and it goes on with the details. But did you see how it began? The building of the ark began—*by Faith*.

Where did that Faith come from? Let me suggest to you that that Faith comes from the *deliberate* mindset of Noah—or Elijah or David or any Bible member of the visible Remnant that you want to name. Read with me. Go ahead. Open your Bible and read it for yourself. Yes, I know that you know it, but read it again. Nothing is so powerful as reading Scripture. Deuteronomy 6:5 says, "And you shall love the Lord your God with all your heart and with all your soul and with all your might."

Noah responded to God's love with a deliberate and intense love for the Lord that involved every fiber of his being. Out of this shared love grew the Covenant Grace-Faith Relationship that Noah shared with God. Therefore, Noah talked with God—just like you talk with someone with whom you are deeply in love and with whom you share a relationship.

Deliberately entering into this Loving Covenant Grace-Faith Relationship with God is a must if you are to be a part of the visible Remnant who are going to build the Ark for the Time of the End.

The visible Remnant must love the Lord their God just as much, just as intensely, and just as deliberately in order to begin building their Ark.

Personal question: Are you talking to God? Are you listening when He talks to you? Do you love the Lord your God with all your heart, all your soul, all your strength, and all your mind? Deliberately entering into this Loving Covenant Grace-Faith Relationship with God is a must if you are to be a part of the visible Remnant who are going to build the Ark for the Time of the End.

Again, do you see that ark over there on the hill? Of course you can, and likewise everyone else can see it as well. Can you imagine any-

thing so *radical* as building an ark on the hill where everyone can see what you are doing? It would be one thing to build it down in a valley hidden by tall trees, but to build it right up there where everyone can see—and everyone can wonder—and everyone can ridicule. Talk about *radical.*

The Ark of the Time of the End must be built just as radically, just as "in-your-face" as that ark up there on the hill. The visible Remnant's Ark must be right out in plain sight where everyone can see it. And remember, this is not a physical structure; this is a community of people.

Can you imagine anything so *radical* as a group of people out in plain sight living as if they really believed that the Holy Spirit is directing their lives? Imagine what that would look like.

Well, actually, don't imagine it. Look at Colossians 3, starting in verse 12: "And so, as those who have been chosen of God, holy and beloved, put on a heart of compassion, kindness, humility, gentleness, and patience; bearing with one another, and forgiving each other, whoever has a complaint against anyone; just as the Lord forgave you, so also should you. And beyond all these things put on love which is the perfect bond of unity. Let the word of Christ richly dwell within you, with all wisdom, teaching and admonishing one another with psalms and hymns and spiritual songs, singing in your hearts to God. And whatever you do in word or deed, do all in the name of the Lord Jesus, giving thanks through Him to God the Father."

Can you imagine anything so *radical*? Do you think it would stand out, do you think it would be noticed if an entire community of believers actually lived like this? These actions aren't going to happen externally, of course, unless the visible Remnant has allowed the Holy Spirit to change their heart internally. But imagine how in-your-face *radical* that would be.

Noah was just that radical. He put his ark where people would see it. He *wanted* to attract attention to it. He *wanted* people to get in it. The visible Remnant also want the invisible Remnant to see their Ark, to be attracted to their Ark, to want to get into their Ark.

Noah was just that radical. He put his ark where people would see it.

Why? Because the visible Remnant, like Noah, feel *compassionate* toward the people. The visible Remnant, like Noah, love the people who are not yet committed to the Ark, just like God loves these people.

You have that look on your face again, asking, "How do you know this?"

Look with me at Luke 10:30–37. Do you know this story? Who is the central character? Of course, the Samaritan man. Good, you *are* familiar with it. Look with me at verse 33. "But a certain Samaritan, who was on a journey, came upon him; and when he saw him, he felt compassion."

Jesus is the Good Samaritan. *Compassion* for the lost world is the driving force behind Jesus' ministry (see Matthew 9:36). After Jesus tells the story—note verse 37 of Luke 10—He instructs the lawyer and those who are listening, "Go and do the same."

Noah—on that last day, during that last sermon—wasn't angry with those who laughed at him. His voice wasn't in agony from rejection by the people. Noah spoke out of *compassion* for the people. And the visible Remnant must feel the same about those whom they are trying to reach—not anger, not holier-than-thou, not rejection, but compassion.

And this strength to express godly compassion for these people will come to them through what Agent? (The capitalization of the word "agent" should be your first clue.) If you have any doubts, look up Ephesians 3:16.

Have I painted the picture clearly enough for you? If not, let me outline the essential points. The situation that Noah faced is the same situation that the visible Remnant faces.

1. Just like Noah, the People of God have been called to deliver these messages in the Time of the End. This visible Remnant at the Time of the End is the Seventh-day Adventist Church. I don't have time now to do the Bible study to demonstrate this fact, but we covered this in Chapters 10 and 11. However, I leave it to you to compare the work of Elijah and John the Baptist with the work of the last Remnant as described in Revelation 12 and 14. Compare that with Malachi 4:5, 6.

2. Laodicea must wake up—now! She must discover that she is the visible Remnant. As the Remnant, she must deliberately, radically, compassionately demonstrate to, and share with, the invisible Remnant— those who are seeking—that a Covenant Grace-Faith Relationship with God is not only possible but is full of promise.

3. The visible Remnant must prepare a safe place of refuge, just like Noah did for the animals and any people who might have responded. When the invisible Remnant responds—

and some will—the Ark must be ready to receive them.

4. The visible Remnant must be inspired by, convicted by, motivated by, and directed by the Holy Spirit. Just in case you missed it, look one more time at Zechariah 4:6. Do you get it? Do you think it is time for us to follow the instructions of Jesus and ask for the Holy Spirit (Luke 11:13)?

5. Just as in the days of Noah—on that last day when the animals started coming—*the invisible Remnant has already started to appear.*

Yes, just as the animals came to Noah, the invisible Remnant are *already* coming. Haven't you seen them in your church? Some of them come to your Revelation Seminars. Some of them come to your health programs. Some come to your Community Services. And some come to your church on Sabbath morning in larger and larger numbers.

Look at Matthew 25:35, 36 for a description of them: "For I was hungry, and you gave Me something to eat; I was thirsty, and you gave Me something to drink; I was a stranger, and you invited Me in; naked, and you clothed Me; I was sick, and you visited Me; I was in prison, and you came to Me."

Can you see them coming?

• They are hungry for the Word

• They are thirsty for a better life

• They are strangers to acceptance

• They are naked and exposed to the ravages of this world

• They are sick and tired of their empty, sinful lives

• They are imprisoned by the bonds of their life choices and the temptations of the devil

And the King says: "When you did it unto one of the least of these, my brothers, you did it unto Me …"—deliberately, radically, compassionately.

Look around. The people are already starting to come.

Come stand with me—up here on the hill—where we have deliberately and radically and compassionately placed our church, our Ark. Look around. The people are already starting to come. The storm clouds are already gathering. The lightning is already flashing and the thunder is already speaking to us.

Yes, some who helped us build this Ark for the Time of the End will be some of the worst at mocking and laughing. But the crowd will stop denying our message, they will stop laughing at our lifestyle, they will be startled into silence when they see so many coming and when the rain begins to fall.

This is our last session, our last conversation together. I have been blessed in sharing with you because I have had to grow in my own understanding and I have had to ask myself: Do I know who I am? I hope and pray you have gained insight into the issues that face us as Seventh-day Adventist Christians. I pray you have come to understand the deeper meaning of and have been inspired to develop some of your own answers for the curiously hard question I've asked so many times: *Seventh-day Adventist Christian, do you know who you are?*

We could have covered many more topics in our conversations, such as the Latter Rain and Jacob's Time of Trouble. We could have spent a lot more time on the Sanctuary and Last Day Events. We could have explored Time-of-the-End parables like the "wedding garment" and the "cursing of the fig tree." However, as I said at the very beginning of our conversations, I wanted to cover the main elements of the Covenant Grace-Faith Relationship and sketch out the practical applications of that relationship in the life of a Seventh-day Adventist Christian, especially in the Three Angels' Messages in the Time of the End.

I am praying that I have piqued your curiosity, heightened your awareness, and—more importantly—motivated your desire for this Covenant Grace-Faith Relationship "and all the more, as you see the day drawing near" (Hebrews 10:25). My prayer is that you will walk through the Sanctuary, work through R-G-B, or utilize whatever metaphoric symbolism appeals to you to discover for yourself the Faith, Hope, and Love inherent in the Covenant Grace-Faith Relationship that God so deliberately, radically, and compassionately offers to you and me. I pray you will accept the three

Gifts and that you will give God permission to use them to work the greatest miracle of all in your life—the transformation of your being to "become [a] partaker of the divine nature" (2 Peter 1:4).

"For this reason I bow my knees before the Father, from whom every family in heaven and on earth derives its name, that He would grant you, according to the riches of His glory, to be strengthened with power through His Spirit in the inner man, so that Christ may dwell in your hearts through faith; and that you, being rooted and grounded in love, may be able to comprehend with all the saints what is the breadth and length and height and depth, and to know the love of Christ which surpasses knowledge, that you may be filled up to all the fullness of God.

"Now to Him who is able to do far more abundantly beyond all that we ask or think, according to the power that works within us, to Him be the glory in the church and in Christ Jesus to all generations forever and ever. Amen." (Ephesians 3:14–21)

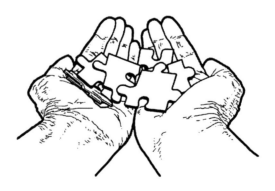

Epilogue

Dear friend,

Please excuse me for communicating with you in this way. I didn't know where to leave this note, but I decided to slip it under your door in hopes that you would see it and put it with your things. Whether you read it today as you leave or when you arrive home, I wanted to bring something to your attention.

Since our last conversation, I have overheard some Adventist Christians discussing a topic that made me think I should be abundantly clear about the basics of the Covenant Grace-Faith Relationship—how it is established, how it is maintained, and how it reaches its goal. I know that you will hear about many methodologies for establishing a relationship with God—from demonstrative Eastern mysticism, to secular social activism, to established puritanical works and rules-keeping. I want to be abundantly clear as to how God has outlined His plan for establishing and maintaining His forever relationship with you. And I want to reassure you that His method is none of the above.

God has always wanted to re-connect with us, His children. He wants us to understand these basic precepts. He is God. We are human. He is righteous. We are sinful. He loves us. We need Him.

Step #1: When we respond to the prompting of the Holy Spirit and choose to surrender to His love, He ratifies in our lives "personally" the merits of Christ's death on the cross, and we are considered a "new creature" in Christ. This is not a mystical concept. It is a transaction recorded in real books in a real place in heaven.

We confirm this transaction on earth by publicly announcing our transfer of allegiance from the world to the Father by our baptism.

Step #2: Jesus promised to send to those who accepted His substitutionary death the gift of the Holy Spirit. When we choose to place ourselves in His hands, the Holy Spirit will

1. change our hearts,

2. bring us to life spiritually as well as mentally, physically, and socially,

3. gift us and empower us for service,

4. put us to work with our Christian brothers and sisters in the church,

5. guide us to our place of ministry,

6. and, by all these methods combined, grow our character internally as we work with others and minister to others externally.

Again this is not a mystical concept. We do not need to seek an emotional, ecstatic, mysterious, obscure, metaphysical, unfathomable experience. The process that the Holy Spirit uses is at once practical in service to others and life-changing as it draws us closer to Him. The proof of the process is in the others-focused ministry and the change of character—the fruit of the Spirit—as described by Paul in Galatians 5:22, 23.

We confirm this transaction on earth by abiding with (staying close to) and walking with (obeying from that new heart) God in all the very practical ways – study of the Word, ministry to others, and intercessory prayer.

Step #3: God promised to begin a good work in us and to finish it. When we choose to allow God to do what He says He can do—change our heart and write on that heart His character such that we perfectly reflect it—He will do it. When Jesus returns the second time, He will not be looking for those who have had a mystical experience, or those who have sought the world's recognition, or those who have kept the rules. Jesus will be looking for those—the final Remnant—who "follow the Lamb" wherever He goes, think like the Lamb, and act like the Lamb.

We confirm this transaction on earth by "treasuring" the commandments of God and "reflecting" the faith of Jesus.

I know that we discussed all of this and that you understood it. And you know that much of what we discussed in our closing conversations was but the natural outworking of this Covenant Grace-Faith Relationship in very practical ways.

But I want to make sure that you know that God is a not a magician, not a conjurer. I want you to know that we are not involved in an enigmatic, mysterious ritual. God is very practical. His plans create real, lasting change in us so that we truly reflect His character. Yes, His process seems to be time-consuming, tedious, and fatiguing much of the time. And, yes, this process is not especially colorful, ecstatic, or showy—but it is effective.

Based on my own personal experience and the experience of many other Seventh-day Adventist Christians I know, I can tell you that the end product of this relationship with God is personally peaceful, belonging, exciting (at times), and rewarding. The reward? Eternal life with Him.

Thank you for talking with me. My prayers go with you on your journey and adventure with God.

Max Hammonds

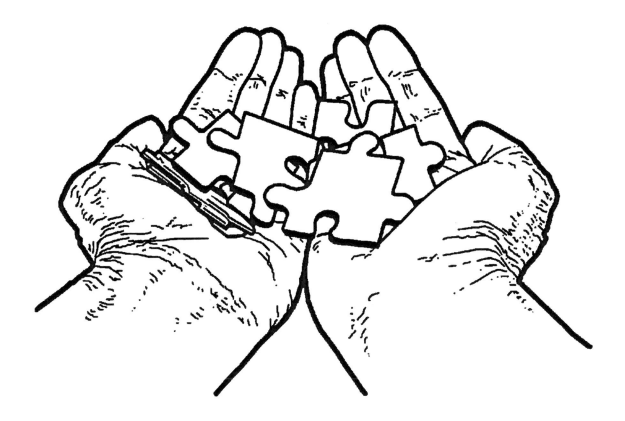

Appendix:

Discussion Questions

A Note to Teachers, Instructors, and Seminar Leaders

This book was initially written to be read by an individual person. It was my intention to have a close encounter, one-to-one conversation with the reader. However, this book can and has been used as the source material for a discussion group or for a seminar setting. And I have included the following section of discussion questions to be used in such a setting.

Of course, these questions could be used by an individual reader to review what he or she has read in the chapter to which the questions refer. But the discussion questions were designed particularly with a seminar setting in mind.

In fact, I have written an accompanying study guide with workbook pages for each chapter. The material in each study guide chapter leads the participant through the chapter in a programmed learning format, expanding on the book material and preparing the participant for the discussion questions. In my seminar, each chapter in the book and the accompanying study guide chapter were assigned and handed out as homework to be completed prior to coming to each seminar session. Then the discussion questions—located in the appendix—were used as the guide for the discussion session in the seminar setting. Note that I have also written a teacher or seminar leader's guide to the discussion questions for those who might need help in deciphering the author's intentioned meaning in asking specific questions.

Again, this was *my* methodology. Certainly, you as the seminar leader are free to design your presentations in any format that suits your style and skills. The discussion questions could be used as the guide to the seminar presentation without the supplemental study guide materials.

However, I found that many people were unfamiliar with the concepts in the book and benefited from filling out the study guide material prior to the seminar presentation and discussion.

My intention is to make available materials for you, the teacher or discussion leader, to conduct your own seminar. And as always you are certainly free to seek the Holy Spirit's guidance and assess your own leadership skills as to how best to present the material and to lead the discussion.

If you would like to see a sample of the material in the study guide or if you would like to order additional books or download the Participant's Study Guide or the Seminar Leader's Guide to the Discussion Questions to use in a seminar, visit http://1ref.us/doyouknow to examine a sample of the study guide materials or to download all of the study guide chapters or the leader's guide for FREE.

Chapter 1

Discussion Questions

1. Who are Seventh-day Adventists? Explain your answer.

    a.   A cult or sect   c.   A church denomination
    b.   Modern-day Millerites   d.   The Remnant

2. Have you ever had to tell someone who Seventh-day Adventists are? What did you tell them?

3. **Read** 1 Peter 3:15. Why is it important that we be able to tell people who Seventh-day Adventists are? Read 1 Peter 4:7, 17. What information is found here that brings this question into sharper focus?

4. **Read** Daniel 8:19. Do you believe that, in fact, we are living in the Time of the End? If so, what makes you think so? What effect does this knowledge have on your answer to Question 3?

5. **Read** Exodus 25:8; Leviticus 26:12; Jeremiah 24:7; 31:33; Ezekiel 11:20; 37:27; Zechariah 8:8; 2 Corinthians 6:16; Hebrews 8:10; Revelation 21:3. What has been, what is, and what will continue forever to be God's one and only goal for Himself and His people?

Take Home Thought Question

How often do you read your Bible?
    a.   Once a month   c.   Several days a week
    b.   Once a week   d.   Every day of the week

Whatever your answer, explain the reason (and perhaps the circumstances) for it.

Chapter 2

Discussion Questions

1. Which words best describe what saints are like, (a) or (b) below? Explain your answer.

   a. Faithful, holy, sanctified, set apart
   b. Passionate, imperfect, sinful, helpless

2. Which scripture reference best describes the "saints" as you know them at your church?

   Colossians 3:12–17; 1 Corinthians 5:1, 2; 11:18–22

   Why do you think so? Give a reason for your answer.

3. Think of a person who loves you. Get their name firmly in mind; close your eyes and see their face. With that face in mind, describe what it is like to be loved using words like "intense, unreserved, sacrificial" (in other words, use personal words).

4. How did the biblical giants David and Daniel differ?

   References for David: 1 Samuel 17:36, 37; 25:21, 22; 26:9; 2 Samuel 11

   References for Daniel: Daniel 2:26–28; 9:1–19; Ezekiel 14:14

5. How are David and Daniel alike? Compare 1 Kings 14:8 with Daniel 9:22, 23.

   Which one are you most like—David or Daniel? Give a reason for your answer.

6. **Read** Mark 1:11. Does God love Jesus?

   Does Jesus know He is loved? Mark 12:6

7. Does God love you—personally? Which scripture tells you that this is true?

8. **Read** Romans 1:7 and Jude 1:1, then answer the following questions:

   a. Do these scriptures describe you?
   b. Are you called by God? Romans 8:29, 30
   c. Are you loved by God? John 16:26, 27
   d. Are you a saint?

Take Home Thought Question

Who initiates the love relationship between God and His saints, God or the saints?

Chapter 3

Discussion Questions

1. True or False: The Seventh-day Adventist Church is a cult. (Be careful.)

   What is a cult? What are the characteristics of a cult?

   Now what do you think? Answer the question again.

2. True or False: The Seventh-day Adventist Church is Christian. Give reasons for your answer.

   What is a Christian? What does a Christian believe?

First "C"

3. Who is Jesus Christ? Compare Colossians 1:13–18; John 1:1–3; 6:68, 69; 1 John 4:2

   a. Why is this important to know? Acts 4:12; 1 John 5:12

   b. Do Seventh-day Adventists know who Jesus is? John 1:1–3

Second "C"

4. What is the significance of the Cross? 1 John 4:9; Mark 10:45; 1 John 2:2; 1 Peter 2:24; Romans 5:8; 1 Timothy 1:15

   a. What of significance was accomplished at the Cross? John 19:30

   b. What was finished? Revelation 12:10

   c. Do Seventh-day Adventists know the significance of the Cross? John 3:16

Third "C"

5. Is it necessary for us to obey the Commandments? Read Matthew 5:18 slowly and carefully

   a. Why? Give three reasons. Proverbs 7:2; Matthew 5:16; John 15:10–11

      b.   Are you able to do this—consistently? Romans 7:18–24

      c.   Where can you find help to do what you find impossible to do in your own power? Ezekiel 36:26, 27

      d.   Do Seventh-day Adventists believe in "keeping" the Commandments? John 15:10, 11

Fourth "C"

6.   Explain what is meant by the term "The Great Controversy." Read the Bible verses quickly and give your short answer.

      a.   Where did it begin? Revelation 12:7–9

      b.   How did it get transferred to earth? Genesis 3

      c.   What was the deciding battle? John 19:30

      d.   What's going on now? Ephesians 6:10–13; 1 Peter 5:8; Revelation 12:17

      e.   How will it end? Revelation 20

      f.   Do you think other denominations know about this concept? How do you know that they know?

      g.   Do Seventh-day Adventists know about and understand the Great Controversy?

Fifth "C"

7.   How do these Bible texts describe the Second Coming of Jesus?

      a.   Is it literal? Matthew 24:27–31

      b.   Is it visible? Matthew 24:27; Revelation 1:7

      c.   Audible? 1 Thessalonians 4:16, 17

      d.   How many will see this event happen? Revelation 1:7

     e.   What happens to the righteous? 1 Thessalonians 4:16, 17; 1 Corinthians 15:51, 52

     f.   What happens to the wicked? 2 Thessalonians 2:8, 10; Revelation 14:14–20; 19:11–21

8.   Why are there so many theories about what will happen at the Second Coming of Jesus?

9.   Do Seventh-day Adventists believe in the literal, visible, audible Second Coming?

Take Home Thought Question

Are you a Christian? Using information you have learned above, give reasons for your answer.

Chapter 4

Discussion Questions

1. What is a relationship? What essentials are needed to establish a relationship?

2. What are the two viewpoints of any relationship (including the God-Man Relationship)?

    From whose point of view can *you* visualize the relationship?

Description of Grace

3. Describe Grace using examples from the story of the paralytic.

    a. When did God's grace begin for the paralytic—and for you? Ephesians 1:4 and Jeremiah 31:3, if needed

    b. What was the Gift that God gave to the Paralytic? 1 John 4:10

    c. For how long are God's commands and promises valid? For how long will God's Grace continue to be available to you? Review Ephesians 1:4, 2:4

Description of Faith

4. Describe Faith using examples from the story of the paralytic.

    a. When did the paralytic first express his Faith in Jesus?

    b. When did you first express your Faith in God?

    c. How did Jesus describe the results of this experience? John 3:3

    d. By what public action do you make this *choice* known to the world? Romans 6:4

    e. When did the paralytic express his Faith in Jesus the second time?

    f. How can you express your Faith like this? Romans 6:12–19; John 15:5

g. Is this second expression of Faith harder to do than the first level? Why or why not?

h. When Jesus told the paralytic to stand up and walk, what did the paralytic *do* that was the same as what Abraham *did*? Be careful. This answer is critical. Consult Romans 4:9, 18–22

How can you "walk by the Spirit"? Galatians 5:25

5.   Name the three Gifts God gives and how we receive each of them.

How does *choice* play a role at each level of the Grace-Faith Relationship?

Take Home Thought Questions

What's the point of the Grace-Faith Relationship?

Is it about getting the work done (important as that is)?

Or being healthy (important as that is)?

Or going to heaven (important as that is)?

What's the point of the relationship with God really? Compare Exodus 25:8; Jeremiah 24:7; Isaiah 44:8

The Covenant Grace-Faith Relationship

<u>Grace</u>		<u>Faith</u>
God Gives the Gift (Cross)	⇄ (Choice)	Man Accepts and Submits (Baptism)
God Gives the Gift (Holy Spirit)	⇄ (Choice)	Man Abides and Trusts (Internal Change of Heart)
God Gives the Gift (Motive and Power to Do) (Character of the Father)	⇄ (Choice)	Man Loves and Acts (External Change—Empowered to Obey) (Change of Character and Personality)

Chapter 5

Discussion Questions

1. How many factors in her life did Eve consider when she allowed sin to come into the world? Count them. Genesis 3:6

    How many temptations did Jesus face in the wilderness? Matthew 4:3–10

    How many basic temptations does the enemy still use today? 1 John 2:16

    How many parts would you expect God to use in the Covenant Grace-Faith Relationship to solve the sin problem? 1 Corinthians 13:13

Part 1: Received From—Faith, the First Gift, and the Son

2. What gifts did the prodigal son receive on returning home? Did he deserve these gifts? Luke 15:22, 23

3. What is the first Gift offered by God to you? Do you deserve it? Then why does God offer this Gift? John 3:16; Romans 3:10–19

Part 2: Growing In—Hope, the Second Gift, and the Holy Spirit

4. What was the gift that the prodigal received, even while still at the pigsty? Compare John 16:8 with Ephesians 1:18

    Is that same Gift available to you? John 14:16

5. What does the prodigal son remember that would cause him to think that his Father will even give him the time of day, even as a servant? Luke 15:17, 18

    What else does he remember? verse 19

6. What is Hope; that is, Constant Expectancy? See Hebrews 10:22, 23

    According to the Scripture, in whom do you have Hope—yourself or God? Whom do you constantly expect to be faithful—you or God?

Part 3: Becoming Like—Love, the Third Gift, and the Father

7.   About whom was the Prodigal's father thinking as he watched the road, himself or his son?

     Whom did the Prodigal think he would embarrass, himself or his father? Luke 15:19

     Whom is the Prodigal becoming like?

8.   Whom does God want you to become like? 2 Peter 1:4

     How else is this state of things described? Galatians 5:22, 23; Ephesians 3:19

     Who is in charge of making this happen? Ezekiel 37:14; Romans 8:11; Ephesians 3:16

Take Home Thought Question:

In the Covenant Grace-Faith Relationship:

What has God promised to do? Ephesians 3:14–20

What have you promised to do? Genesis 15:6; Romans 4:20, 21

Chapter 6

Discussion Questions

1.   Explain how each of these situations makes it hard to be a Christian.

     a.   The world does not follow God.

     b.   We are trained to function like the world.

     c.   We don't know what to *do* after we confess.

     d.   We don't know how to *walk*.

2.   Draw a line from the phrase in Column A to the phrase in Column B that goes with it.

Column A	Column B	
Hope	Faith	Ephesians 2:8
Confess with the Mouth	Walk with God	Colossians 1:10
Pleasing to God	Abide	Hebrews 10:23; John 15:5
Grace	Believe in the Heart	Romans 10:9, 10

3.   Explain the relationship between the above word pairs.

4.   Where in the body is the biblical "heart"? Romans 12:2; see accompanying diagram.

     What critical, basic activity happens there? Joshua 24:15b

5.   What are the two options for the "set-of-the-mind" in the "human heart"?

     Explain each one.
     a.   1 John 2:16

     b.   Micah 6:8

6.   How does Paul describe the two options for a "mindset" in the human heart? Romans 8:6

     What is the result of each option?

7. Who has knowledge, patience, and skill to change our hearts? Ezekiel 36:26, 27

8. Who has the gifts, power, and life to enable us to do that which we cannot do on our own? Romans 8:11; Ezekiel 37:14; 2 Corinthians 3:6

9. How and when are we changed by the Holy Spirit? What does each of the following scriptures add to our understanding of this process?

   a. John 3:8

   b. Acts 2:38

   c. 2 Corinthians 3:18

   d. Romans 8:11

   e. Romans 12:2

   f. Ephesians 4:12

   g. Ephesians 3:16

10. In order to "please God" we must choose to:

    a. Give up our hu_ _ _ mi_ _ s_ _ (called submission) Ephesians 4:22, 23; Romans 8:5, 6

    b. Recognize that we (can vs. cannot—circle one) act on the decision we have made. Romans 7:18

11. How then are we able to "walk by the Spirit"? 2 Corinthians 3:18; Zechariah 4:6; Romans 8:11

Take Home Thought Question:

Why is *learning* to "walk by the Spirit" pleasing to God? Jeremiah 31:9; John 16:27; Colossians 1:10–12

THE HUMAN MIND

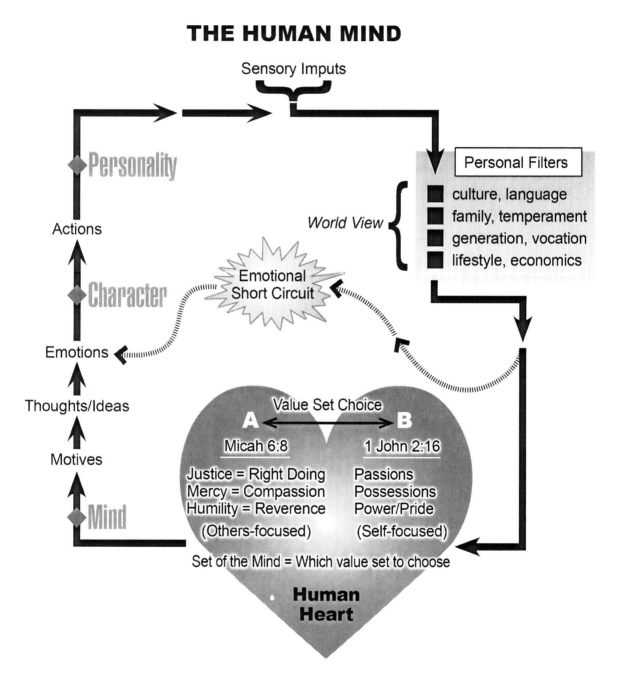

Chapter 7

Discussion Questions

1. What does the biblical word "keeping" mean? Choose only one answer; explain your choice.

    a. Obeying
    b. Holding close
    c. Hiding in secret

    d. Owning
    e. Remembering
    f. Treasuring

2. What person or thing in your life do you "treasure" and plan to "keep"?

Two Concepts

3. Describe how the Ten Commandments are a:

    a. Description of God. Deuteronomy 8:6

    b. Description of the People of God. Psalm 19:7–11

    c. Description of those who are in a relationship with God. 2 Peter 1:4

    d. Description of those who love God. John 15:10

4. What is God's will for you? Choose your own scripture and explain it.

Tying the Two Concepts Together

5. What motivator is strong enough to make the will of God happen in your life? Deuteronomy 6:5; Matthew 22:37–40

6. Why should love be this motivator? John 3:16; Luke 15:32; Luke 10:33

7. We "keep" the commandments:

    a. Not because we try hard, but because we _____ hard. Deuteronomy 6:5
    b. Because we treasure the _____. John 17:23
    c. Because it is an act of _____. Romans 12:1

Take Home Thought Questions

Three Basic Concepts:

Why do you "keep" the Sabbath holy?

Keeping the Commandments and Having the Faith of Jesus—are these two separate concepts or the same concept?

Basic Questions: Give a reason for each response.

Does God love you?

Do you love God?

Chapter 8

Discussion Questions

1.   Describe and explain the use of the articles and furniture found in the Old Testament wilderness Sanctuary: (If you need to, refer to the Sanctuary diagram for the discussion questions of Chapter 13.)

     a.   The Altar of Burnt Offering – Exodus 29:38, 39

     b.   The Laver – Exodus 30:18, 19

     c.   The Lampstand – Exodus 27:20, 21

     d.   The Table of Showbread – Exodus 25:23, 29, 30

     e.   The Altar of Incense – Exodus 30:6, 7

     f.   The Ark of the Covenant – Exodus 25:22

Altar of Burnt Offering

2.   Who brought an offering to the altar of burnt offering? Why? Leviticus 1:3; 4:20

3.   What more—beyond the offering for sin at the altar of burnt offering—did God promise to do with His people where the other people in the world could see? Exodus 19:4–6

     Does the Christian experience stop at the altar of burnt offering? What more does God ask of His people today? 1 Peter 2:9

Laver—Preparation to be Priests

4.   Why did the priests stop to wash at the laver? Exodus 30:18, 19

     What was the danger if they did not wash? Compare Isaiah 6:5 with Isaiah 33:14

5.   In the Ordinance of Humility what is symbolically being washed clean *again*? Compare John 13:10 and Matthew 15:17–20

     Why do we do this before ministering? Hebrews 12:28b, 29

First Apartment Duties—Lampstand, Table of Showbread, Altar of Incense

6.   With four layers of skins and cloth over the Tent of Meeting, what was the purpose of the lampstand in the first apartment? John 1:5

   a.   Who/what does the lampstand represent? Psalm 119:105; John 1:9–14

   b.   What does Light do for us? 2 Timothy 3:16, 17

   c.   As priests, what do we do with the Light? Matthew 5:16; 2 Timothy 4:1, 2; 1 Peter 3:15

7.   What did the priests do with the showbread? Leviticus 24:9

   a.   What did Jesus say was His bread, His food? John 4:34

   b.   What is to be our bread and our wine? Compare John 14:12 with John 6:53–57

   c.   As priests what burdens do we bear? Galatians 6:2; Leviticus 18:1

8.   Where and how is the altar of incense placed in the Sanctuary? Exodus 30:6

   a.   What activity takes place here just across "the Veil" from God? Revelation 8:3, 4

   b.   With Whom are you most closely aligned physically and spiritually when interceding on behalf of others?

9.   Which member of the Godhead has primary responsibility for the activities of the priests in the first apartment? John 16:13; Ephesians 4:7, 11; Romans 8:26, 27

Take Home Thought Questions:

As part of the Communion service, can you wash your own feet? Romans 12:2

Who needs the Light? Isaiah 60:2; Matthew 15:14

What are we promising to do when we partake of Communion? John 13:15

What does it mean to partake of Communion unworthily?
Compare 1 Corinthians 11:18–22, 27–29 with John 13:18

How close to God are you when you are praying for others? Exodus 30:6; Hebrews 9:4

Why did we need to establish the abiding of the Holy Spirit in us before embarking on this assignment as priests? Ephesians 3:16; Zechariah 4:6

Chapter 9

Discussion Questions

1.   What is a Steward? Choose only one answer; explain why you chose as you did.

   a.   A slave   d.   A servant
   b.   A manager   e.   An underling
   c.   A non-owner

   Review the story of Eliezer in Genesis 24.

2.   How do the following characteristics describe the role of a Steward as illustrated by Eliezer?

   a.   **Praying.** Whose God does Eliezer trust? Verse 27

   b.   **Persistent.** Whom does Eliezer represent? Whose mission? Verse 33, 34

   c.   **Persuasive.** How careful and focused is Eliezer? Verse 49–56

   Describe the mindset of a Steward. Luke 17:7–10; compare with Philippians 2:1–5

3.   Think about the characteristics of a Steward outlined above and about the lives of the men listed below. Describe what each man was given to manage. For each man describe the circumstance in which the man illustrated being a Steward.

Name	What he managed	Characteristic
Moses	Exodus 32:31–32	Numbers 12:3, 7
Joseph	Genesis 39:4–6	Hebrews 11:22
Abraham	Genesis 18:19	Genesis 15:6
Paul	Colossians 2:25–27	2 Timothy 4:7

   Summary: Matthew 24:45 and 25:21 – A Steward is f_ _ _ _ _ ul.

   What made it possible for each of these men to carry out their very difficult task?

   Romans 4:20, 21

4.   What does the word "faithful" mean? Webster's Dictionary

For God—Deuteronomy 7:9, 10

For Man—Isaiah 26:2–4

What Is the Covenant Grace-Faith Relationship Based on?

5. What was Enoch doing when he was taken up by God? Genesis 5:24

    Why was Enoch taken up? Hebrews 11:5

6. What does "pleasing" mean and how is it related to "walking with God"? 1 Thessalonians 4:1; Colossians 1:10

7. Compare God's faithfulness in Hebrews 10:23 with the human faith described in Hebrews 11. Explain what the word "faithful" means when applied to humans. Romans 4:18–22

8. How do we "please God" and "walk with God"? John 15:5, 10, 11

9. How is it that Enoch—and we—are made capable of such a walk? Who is responsible for making this happen? Romans 12:2; 2 Corinthians 3:18

Critical Question

10. In Whom does Enoch have faith? What two concepts does Enoch believe about God? Hebrews 11:6

11. Explain how Enoch—and Eliezer—are "faithful."

Take Home Thought Questions

Whom do you trust? What do you believe about God?

Since this is critical to being a good Steward, what is faithfulness?

Chapter 10

Discussion Questions

1. Why did the people not answer when Elijah told them to choose between God and Baal?

    a. Religion wasn't important to them.

    b. They didn't remember the Exodus stories.

    c. They were confused

    d. They didn't know who they were.

Make a copy of the outline of the book of Revelation, use the outline in Chapter 10 or the one at the end of these questions, or write out by hand your own copy. Be prepared to write on and make notes on this copy. Where the interludes occur on your outline, write the information given in each interlude.

Interlude 1

Revelation 7. Find Interlude 1 on your diagram.

2. **Read** Revelation 7:4.

Write in …

3. 144, 000. At this point in history when the 144,000 appear.

4. **Read** Revelation 7:2–4. What happens to this group (verse 2) just before the release of the four winds of destruction? Write this on your diagram at Interlude 1.

5. What does this sealing signify? Ephesians 1:13, 14; 2 Timothy 2:19

Note: This group of people is described as appearing between the Sixth and Seventh Seals.

Interlude 2a

Revelation 10. Find Interlude 2a on your diagram.

1. **Read** Revelation 10:1, 6.

2. What "time" has come to an end? Earth time? (Read verse 11.) Bible prophetic time?

    See Daniel 8:14

Write in all of the following …

3. Angel of the Loud Cry—end of prophetic time. At this time in history the Angel of the Loud Cry announces the end of prophetic time.

4. **Read** Daniel 8:17, 19; 12:4. Write in the name of the book that was closed and is now open that the Angel has in his hand.

    Write in what time period has now begun.

5. **Read** Revelation 10:7. What specifically is to be completed during this time?

    What does "mystery of God" mean? Colossians 1:26–29; 2:2, 3

6. **Read** Revelation 10:10. What does eating the little book do to John; that is, God's End Time People? **Write** this at Interlude 2a on your diagram.

7. **Read** Revelation 10:11. What must the People of God do after their indigestion problem? **Write** this also on your diagram at Interlude 2a.

Note: This same group of people appears between the Sixth and Seventh Trumpets. The time of their appearance is at the end of the 2300 year-day time prophecy. **Write in** the year of the end of this prophecy at Interlude 2a.

Interlude 2b

Revelation 11. Find Interlude 2b on your diagram.

1. **Read** Revelation 11:4, 11. Compare with Daniel 12:4. **Write in** who or what is resurrected at this time.

2. **Read** Revelation 11:2. **Write in** what time period—compare with Daniel 7:25; 12:7—comes to an end with an earthquake (see verse 13, similar to the Sixth Seal. Revelation 6:12.)

Note: This same group of people is confirmed as attached to the ending of the 1260 year-day time prophecy, along with the "resurrected" interest in Bible prophecy. **Write in** the historical date of the end of this prophecy.

Interlude 3

Revelation 12. Find Interlude 3 on your diagram.

1. **Read** Revelation 12:17.

Write in …

1. What group emerges after the 1260 years and how does Satan relate to them?

2. What two characteristics distinguish this group? Check Revelation 19:10 for a definition.

   Note: This same group of people is confirmed again as appearing at the end of the 1260 year-days with two specific characteristics. What was the historical date for the end of this prophecy?

Interlude 4

Revelation 14. Find Interlude 4. Write in the two purposes for the sealing of this group.

1. Verses 1 and 4:

2. Verse 6–12:

Think It Through: Note the historical time when all these activities are to take place. Check Revelation 12, comparing verses 12–16 with verse 17. From all the above interludes, make an inclusive, composite list of all the characteristics of these people—the same group of people who appear in every one of these interludes. Who are these people?

Big Question: If the world is poised between the Sixth and Seventh Seal and the Sixth and Seventh Trumpet, if all pieces are in place for the final events to happen, why is the process not moving forward?

Interlude 5

Revelation 3:14–22. Find Interlude 5 on the chart.

1. Where is the Interlude between the Sixth and Seventh Churches and what does it reveal?

2. **Write in** who or what is Interlude 5?

3. How will God get the process moving forward again? Hebrews 12:26, 27

4. How are these people like the people of Elijah's time? Compare 1 Kings 18:21 with Revelation 3:17.

Take Home Thought Questions

Is claiming that the Seventh-day Adventist Church is the Remnant a statement to be arrogant about or a statement to be ashamed of? Is there a third option?

Is the Seventh-day Adventist Church identified in the Bible? If so, is it by name or by function? Defend your answer.

Simplified Outline of the Book of Revelation

"Interludes"

Chapter 1—Introduction and purpose of the book

Chapter 2–3—The Seven Churches

> **Interlude 5**—Chapter 3:14–18—Laodicea

Chapter 4–5—The Heavenly Throne Room

Chapter 6—The Six Seals

> **Interlude 1**—Chapter 7—The 144,000 and the Great Multitude

Chapter 8:1—The Seventh Seal

Chapter 8–9—The Six Trumpets

> **Interlude 2a**—Chapter 10—The Angel of the Loud Cry

> **Interlude 2b**—Chapter 11:1–14—The Two Witnesses

Chapter 11:15–19—The Seventh Trumpet

Chapter 12—The History of the Great Controversy on Earth

> **Interlude 3**—Chapter 12:17—The Remnant (cf. Chapter 19:10)

Chapter 13—The Activities of the Unholy Trinity

Chapter 14—The Activities of the People of God

> **Interlude 4**—Chapter 14:1–12—The People of God and the Three Angels' Messages
>
> Cross-reference with Chapter 12:17

Chapter 15—The Close of Probation

Chapter 16—The Seven Last Plagues

Chapter 17–19—The Scarlet Woman, Battle of Armageddon, The Second Coming of Jesus

> Cross-reference Chapter 19:10 with Chapter 12:17

Chapter 20—The Millennium and the Final Great White Throne Judgment

Chapter 21–22—The New Heaven and New Earth

Chapter 11

Discussion Questions

The Remnant:

1. What is the biblical meaning of the Remnant? 2 Kings 19:30, 31

2. Arrange the experiences of the Remnant in the order of occurrence. Number them in the order you think they occur. Choose which one to label as 1, 2, etc. (Clue: check the chapter)

    a. Ezekiel 36:26, 27: Has a heart-changing experience—   #____
    b. Genesis 45:5–7: Assigned a task to provide for survival of others
        in the crisis—   #____
    c. Zechariah 4:6: Functions in the power of the Holy Spirit—   #____
    d. Hebrews 11:7: Endures and explains how to endure the crisis to others—   #____
    e. Joshua 24:15: Chooses to live in the Covenant Grace-Faith Relationship— #____
    f. 2 Peter 2:5: Delivers a message to the world about the choices and
        the coming crisis—   #____

    Why is it hard to arrange these events? Where do you place (c) above?

3. What prevents the Seventh-day Adventist Church from becoming the Remnant? Revelation 3:17

4. List four ways in which Elijah and John the Baptist were alike in their mission, ministry, message, and power. Clue: Question 2 above

    Note: In their reaction to adversity, they were also alike. They were both *painfully human.*

5. What did the dejected Elijah and the questioning John the Baptist—and the Remnant— have to remember to carry out the assignment given them? Jeremiah 23:6; Zechariah 4:6; 1 John 4:19

6. Who is going to help them remember this vital information? John 14:26

Being Painfully Human

In Matthew 13 Jesus tells the parable of the sower and the soils. The third soil describes being painfully human. In Matthew 13:22 Jesus explains this condition with two kinds of thorns.

Worries = loss of Hope

Riches = majority position, physical or economic power, spiritual arrogance

7. Which kind of "thorns" do you think is most dangerous to the spiritual life of the Remnant—loss of Hope or spiritual arrogance? Give the reason for your answer.

8. Describe the remedy for spiritual arrogance noted in each of the following scriptures.

    a.   Revelation 3:15–18

    b.   Matthew 24:15–22

    c.   Genesis 32:24

Which remedy do you think will be most effective to wake up apathetic, arrogant Laodicea?

9. What is the greatest weakness of the Remnant—in every age?

    Being painfully _____

10. What is the only way to address that weakness? You choose which scripture best describes this remedy. Give a reason for your choice.

Take Home Thought Question

What is Hope?

    From Jesus – 2 Corinthians 1:20

    From the Holy Spirit – Romans 15:13

    From the Father – 2 Peter 1:4

How does Hope address our painfully human condition?

Chapter 12

Discussion Questions

1. What is a Pro-test-ant? Define each segment of the word and discuss the historical meaning of the word as a whole.

2. What were the Protestants pro-testing? Isaiah 58:12; see Chapter 12 in the book

3. What do you think it means to be a Time-of-the-End Pro-test-ant? What are they protesting?

Time of the End Protestants

In each segment below, describe the man and his connection to the doctrine, then describe how Jesus is the central focus of the doctrine and what significance the doctrine has for the Time of the End.

Person	Doctrine	Jesus Focus	Time of the End Significance
William Miller	Second Coming		
Hiram Edson	Sanctuary		
Joseph Bates	Spirit of Prophecy		
James White	State of the Dead		
John Nevins Andrews	Sabbath		
Uriah Smith	Seraphim (Three Angels)		
A.T. Jones & E.J. Waggoner	Salvation by Faith		
Ellen G. White	*Sola Scriptura*		

4. Based on the study of Chapter 12 of the book, give two reasons why it is important to know our doctrinal history (how we grew doctrinally).

5. What is unique about these eight doctrinal positions for the Seventh-day Adventist Church?

6. Are we the only Christians who believe these teachings of the Bible?

Take Home Thought Question

Are Seventh-day Adventists a People of the Book? Give a reason(s) for your response.

See Revelation 12:17 and 14:12

Chapter 13

Discussion Questions

Orientation

Chapter 13 and 14 are two parts of a unit—the reality of the Third Angel's Message as Righteousness by Faith. Chapter 13 illustrates the concept by means of the Sanctuary. Chapter 14 illustrates the concept by means of the Three Angels' Messages.

1. How does the wilderness Sanctuary symbolize the Covenant Grace-Faith Relationship? Exodus 25:8; Revelation 21:3

2. How confident should we be as we approach the Sanctuary? Hebrews 10:19–23

Keep this in mind as we study this chapter.

The Wilderness Sanctuary

What is our High Priest, Jesus Christ, actually doing in the heavenly Sanctuary? Hebrews 8:1, 2

To find the answer, concentrate on two aspects: 1) where the sins reside in each part of the sanctuary and 2) how the Covenant Grace-Faith Relationship is illustrated in the sanctuary activity—your connection to God. Use the accompanying outline of the Covenant Grace-Faith Relationship as you work through these questions.

To get oriented to sanctuary language and references, look at the accompanying diagram of the wilderness Sanctuary. On this diagram you will find—with the approximate size and placement—the implements in the courtyard, the furniture in the first apartment, and the furniture, including the extra items added later, in the second apartment.

The Courtyard — Review: See Chapters 4–6 for details.

1. On your diagram in the **courtyard,** find the altar of burnt offering and label it. On the line to the right, write what Gift of God this symbolizes. Below the line to the right, write the Faith response of the Covenant Grace-Faith Relationship. Also find and label the laver.

2. What function does Jesus our High Priest perform in this area? John 1:29

Thinking of the Time of the End in which we live—is He still doing this for sinners today?

The First Apartment — Review: Chapter 8

3.   On your diagram, next to the **first apartment**, find each article of furniture and label them. On the line to the left write what each article symbolizes. (They are all parts of the Gift of the Holy Spirit.)

4.   How are the activities of this apartment described in Hebrews 9:6? Use NASB or KJV.

5.   What two functions is Jesus performing as High Priest in this area?

John 14:16, 17; Luke 11:13

Revelation 12:10; Zechariah 3:2

6.   On the line to the right of the first apartment, write what Gift of God this symbolizes. Below the line write the Faith response to these gifts.

Second Apartment

7.   Where is "the Veil" located in the sanctuary? Exodus 26:33

Label it on your diagram.

  a.   Who resides behind the Veil? Exodus 30:6; Hebrews 12:29
  b.   What does the Veil symbolize? Isaiah 59:2; Hebrews 10:20

8.   Where do your forgiven sins reside as of now? Leviticus 4:6, 34; 6:24, 25; Numbers 18:1

9.   Who is represented by all of these sanctuary locations where your sins currently reside?

10.   Why is Jesus carrying all of our sins? Genesis 4:13; Romans 3:10; Isaiah 53:5, 6; Hebrews 8:1, 2

11.   Find each article that is found in or near the ark of the covenant and label them. In the line to the left, write how Jesus is symbolized in each of these articles. Hebrews 9:4

The Ten Commandments – John 1:1–3; 17:4; see Chapter 7

The Jar of Manna – Colossians 1:17

Aaron's Rod – Numbers 17:5; Matthew 12:18–21; 28:18

12. What does Jesus intend to do during the "cleansing of the sanctuary"? (Daniel 8:14)

1 John 3:5

1 John 3:8; Leviticus 16:21, 22; Revelation 20:1–3

Leviticus 16:30; 1 John 1:9

Matthew 27:51; Hebrews 10:20; Ephesians 5:26, 27; Jude 1:24

Psalm 24:3, 4

13. On the line to the right of the **second apartment**, write the Gift of God symbolized. Below the line write the Faith response to this gift.

Take Home Thought Question

Locate the item found in the middle of the ark of the covenant and label it (Exodus 25:17). Draw a line to the left and write what this article symbolizes in the Covenant Grace-Faith Relationship. Hebrews 10:19–23

1. Do you believe that Jesus is faithful to *you* personally?

2. Do you believe Hebrews 10:22, 23 applies to *you* personally?

3. Do you believe that Jesus is cleansing *your* sin from the heavenly Sanctuary?

4. Are you moving toward the Light or away from the Light? John 3:19–21

THE WILDERNESS SANCTUARY

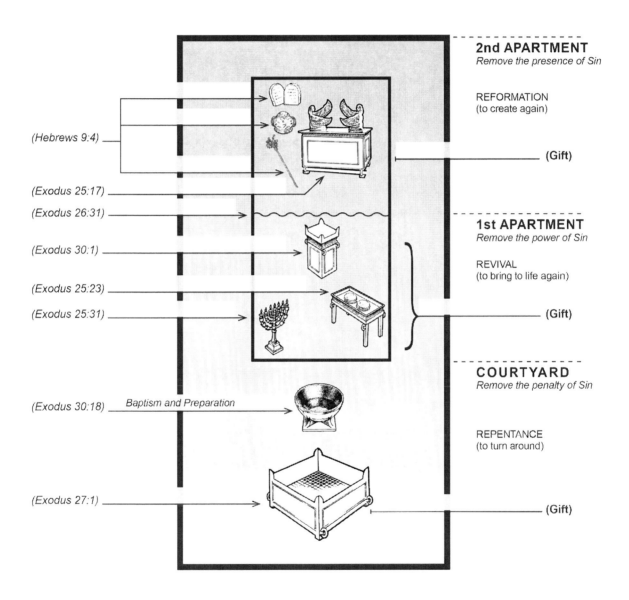

Chapter 14

Discussion Questions

Orientation

Chapter 13 and 14 are two parts of a Unit—the reality of the Third Angel's Message as Righteousness by Faith. Chapter 13 illustrates the concept by means of the Sanctuary and is intended for us personally. Chapter 14 illustrates the concept by means of the Three Angels' Messages and is intended for us to share with others.

Use the outline of the Covenant Grace-Faith Relationship as you answer these questions.

The Millerite Understanding

1. Draw a line between the Angel's Message and its Millerite understanding.

First Angel   1. Consequences of rejecting the imminent Second Coming

Second Angel   2. Gospel, Obedience, and Judgment

Third Angel   3. Rejection of Second Coming by churches constitutes Babylon

Time of the End: Expanded Understanding

1. **Review**: See Chapters 4–6. Describe the First Angel's Message in Covenant Grace-Faith Relationship terms.

    a. Gospel—Ephesians 2:4–7. What Gifts are you to "receive"?

    b. Glory—Ezekiel 37:14; Ephesians 4:12–16. How will you "grow"?

    c. Judgment—Psalm 24:2, 3. Whom will you "become like" in order to stand?

    d. What is the confirmation and assurance that this angel's message can be believed? Revelation 14:7b

    e. Is God to be trusted to do what He promises? Hebrews 11:6. Do you believe Him?

    f. How should this message be delivered to "those who dwell on the earth, and to every nation and tribe and tongue and people"?

2. **Review:** See especially Chapter 6. Describe the two choices presented in the Second Angel's message—in Covenant Grace-Faith Relationship terms. Micah 6:8; 1 John 2:16

    a. How did Jesus describe these two choices in John 3:19–21?

    b. Using the intimacy terms of the Covenant Grace-Faith Relationship describe the role of the Sabbath/Sunday choice in the Second Angel's Message.

        Is this about which day you go to church—or is it more?

    c. Which choice have you made? Explain why you answered as you did.

The Third Angel

1. The Third Angel's Message points out the consequences of the choice made under the Second Angel, concentrating on the negative, devastating consequences of choosing not to follow God. What are the positive results of choosing to follow God? (Revelation 14:12)

    a. 2 Peter 1:4

    b. Revelation 3:12

    c. Romans 1:17; 3:22; 4:5; Galatians 5:5; Philippians 3:9

2. So what's so hard about preaching the Three Angels' Messages? What events are taking place that make the "tribulation" so difficult?

    a. Matthew 24:42–44

    b. Matthew 24:21

    c. 2 Thessalonians 2:10; Revelation 13:14

    d. Revelation 13:15

    e. Zechariah 13:6

3. What is this crisis time called? Hebrews 12:26–29

What do you think it is that "can be shaken"? What is it that "cannot be shaken"?

4. What does *living in* the Covenant Grace-Faith Relationship look like when every earthly support is taken away, do you think? Job 13:15; Romans 4:20-22; Hebrews 10:19–23; Daniel 3:17, 18; Philippians 4:13

5. Is this who you are—by Faith?

Take Home Thought Questions

1. Write a statement of your commitment to living in the Covenant Grace-Faith Relationship of the Three Angels' Messages.

    First Angel

    Second Angel

    Third Angel

2. What's the connection between Chapter 13 and Chapter 14? Why are they considered as part of a unit?

The Covenant Grace-Faith Relationship

Grace		Faith
God Gives the Gift	⇄	Man Accepts and Submits
(Cross)	(Choice)	(Baptism)
God Gives the Gift	⇄	Man Abides and Trusts
(Holy Spirit)	(Choice)	(Internal Change of Heart)
God Gives the Gift	⇄	Man Loves and Acts
(Motive and Power to Do)	(Choice)	(External Change—Empowered to Obey)
(Character of the Father)		(Change of Character and Personality)

Chapter 15

Discussion Questions

How do we make practical what we have learned in the last two studies? The next four studies will cover:

Making Disciples

Being a Witness

Being one of the Sheep

Building an Ark

We begin with a paradigm of how one does long-range planning.

1. Draw a line and match the items in the left-hand column with those on the right.

The "Why"   the main task, the mission

The "What"   three or four focused steps to achieve the main task

The "How"   the shared values

2. What is the "main task" of the Seventh-day Adventist Church, do you think?

Abraham's Covenant Grace-Faith Relationship With God

3. What was Abraham's response to God's call to leave Ur? Genesis 12:1–5

4. Why did Abraham respond as he did? Genesis 15:6

5. Think in Covenant Grace-Faith Relationship terms: Romans 4:18–21. What has God promised to do for Abraham? What was Abraham's Faith response?

6. What is the basis of your Covenant Grace-Faith Relationship with God?

   Do you believe that God will do as He has promised? What is your Faith response?

7. **Review** "obedience from the heart". See Chapter 4 and Romans 6:17

   Choosing to let the Holy Spirit change the heart. Ezekiel 36:26, 27

Choosing a Spirit mindset. Romans 8:5, 6

Choosing to allow the Spirit to write on the heart. Jeremiah 31:33

Choosing to allow the Spirit to make us new in the "divine nature." 2 Peter 1:4

This is the "Why" of Abraham—which looks very much like our value set.

8. "What" was Abraham's assigned "main task"? Genesis 12:2; 17:4

9. Note the three phrases that describe "what" Abraham will focus on with his "obedience from the heart"? Genesis 18:19. Fill in the blanks from the book chapter.

    Abraham was focused on making a family who would—by trusting in God:

    Fill in the words.

    "Command his children after him …" See Philippians 3:17. f_ _ _ _ w a_ _ _ r h_ _

    "Keep the way of the Lord …" See book Chapter 7. d_ a_ h_ d _d

    "Doing righteousness and justice …" See Micah 6:8. c _ _ _ y o_ w_ _n h_ w_ _ g_ _ e

10. What do we call those whom we train to do the above three things?

    Abraham called them _____ Genesis 18:19

    Jesus called them _____ Mark 3:34, 35

    Jesus also called them _____ Matthew 10:1a

11. What did Jesus say was the "main task" of His church? Matthew 28:19

12. What do you think is the "main task" of the Remnant church at the Time of the End?

In the Time of the End

13. When God gives us a task to do, how can we follow Abraham's model? Romans 4:21; Matthew 28:19; Revelation 14:12a; Romans 5:3–5; Ephesians 2:10

    Because we want to make disciples who, by trusting God like us, will (from the book chapter):

Revelation 14:4b. f_ _ _ _w a_ _ _r J_ _ _s

John 13:15. d_ a_ J_ _ _s d_d

2 Timothy 4:5–7. c_ _ _ y _n w_ _ n J_ _ _s i_ g_ _e

Take Home Thought Questions

Sitting on the church board, you hear about a particular church activity. You think it is not focused on making disciples. What questions would you ask to find out if the activity has as its "main task" to make disciples?

When thinking about how to carry out the "main task" of being a Seventh-day Adventist Christian:

Should you quit your job and become a Bible worker? Why or why not?

Should you not go to the Ladies Night Out next Thursday evening, but instead set up a Bible study? Why or why not?

As a Seventh-day Adventist Christian, what is your "main task?" Where would you start, do you think? Give a reason why you would start there.

Chapter 16

Discussion Questions

Reviewing Last Week's Study—Making Disciples

1. How did Abraham respond when he was called of God?

   a. Genesis 15:6—When God promised, Abraham _____ Him.

   b. Genesis 12:2—When assigned his task, Abraham _____ the assignment.

   c. Hebrews 11:8—Abraham _____ on the task at hand, even when faced with the necessity of Isaac's resurrection.

2. What three things did Abraham train his family (disciples) to do? Genesis 18:19

   a. Follow _____ _____

   b. Do what ___ _____

   c. Carry __ _____ ___ ___ gone

How Jesus Makes Disciples—Making a Witness

A. **Believe and Follow**—Mark 5:1–15

1. After Jesus intervened for the Wild Man and saved him from his demons, do you think Jesus and the Wild Man had a relationship?

   Do you think the Wild Man believed in Jesus?

   Was he willing to follow Jesus anywhere? Mark 5:18

   Give the reason for your answer. Luke 7:42, 43

2. Circle the statement that is correct for you. Why did you choose as you did?

    a. I follow Jesus because it is the right thing to do.

    b. I follow Jesus because He loved me and I believe in Him.

A loving Covenant Grace-Faith Relationship is stronger that doing the right thing. Doing the "loving" thing always leads to the "right" thing. Doing the "right" thing does *not* always lead to the "loving" thing. We believe and follow because—it is the *loving thing* to do.

3. Circle the correct answer about believing and following. Give a reason for why you chose as you did.

    T F You don't have to be careful about whom you follow if they are nice to you.

    T F Disciples shouldn't believe in you; you must lead them to believe in God.

    T F You don't have to be a disciple to make a disciple.

B. **Accept the Assignment and Do as Jesus Does**

What was the Wild Man's assignment?

1.   Did he accept his assignment? Mark 5:18, 19

2.   What did he tell the people where he lived? Mark 5:18

3.   Do you have a story to tell? Circle one: Yes   No
        What is your story?

We accept our assignment and do as He did because—everyone has at least one evangelistic sermon that they can preach—*their own story.*

The Disciple Has Become a Witness

1. To what four kinds of people will the new Witness tell his story?

    a. Those who _____ him and will _____ to him.

    b. Those who ____ him and will _____ him.

    c. Those who are _____ of his experience and will _____ him.

    d. Those who _____ him and will not _____ to him.

2. To what four kinds of people will you tell your story?

3. If the Wild Man (and you) do what Jesus did, what will be the purpose of his (and your) assignment to tell his (and your) story? Luke 4:18, 19

4. How do you think you will do this? What specific, practical things do you think you will be doing?

C. Focused on the Task and Carrying on After Jesus Is Gone

1. Does the Wild Man go and do his assignment? Mark 5:20

   Will you? Why? This answer is critically important.

2. Did the Wild Man have to go and do his assignment alone? John 14:16–18

3. Are you ever alone on God's assignment?

   We focus and carry on when Jesus is gone because—we are *never alone*.

Pressing the Point Home (one word answer for both questions)

4. The word "Christian" means _____ of Christ.

5. To be a Christian you must not only accept Jesus as Savior, you must also be a _____ of Jesus as Lord.

Take Home Thought Question

Is Jesus calling you to be a disciple and a witness? Isaiah 43:10; Acts 1:8

What assignment has He given you? Mark 5:18

How do you think it will be received by those to whom you reach out? Does that matter to you?

Chapter 17

Discussion Questions

On the Mount of Olives—Matthew 24:1–14

Part 1: Signs of the End

1. On the Mount of Olives that last night, what basic question did the disciples ask Jesus? Matthew 24:3

2. What were the first three answers that Jesus gave them? Matthew 24:4, 8, 14

3. What events do the Seventh-day Adventists of your church usually focus on when they start talking about the Time of the End or the Second Coming?

4. What event is to be the one all-consuming event for the Remnant that truly marks the Second Coming of the Lord? Matthew 24:14

Part 2: Watching

Three Groups Who Were Not Watching: See Chapter 17

5. The Unknowing—Matthew 24:38, 39. These people are consumed with l _ _ e.

    They don't *know* the ev _ _ t. They don't even *know* that it's c _ m _ _ g.

6. The Unwatchful—Matthew 24:43. These people are not paying at _ _ _ t _ _ _. They don't know w_ _ n to watch. They don't know the t _ m _ _ g.

7. The Unexpectant—Matthew 24:45–47, 48–51. Two groups: The first group expects the master at any time. They are always r _ _ _ y. The second group does not expect the master any time soon. They are not r _ _ _ y. They do not realize the im _ _ d _ _ cy of His return.

8. Is it enough to know the Signs of the Times? What three lessons are we to learn from these three groups in Part 2 of the Sermon?

Part 3: Preaching the Word

9. What World?

    a. What world are the disciples to witness to? Acts 1:8. Where do they start? Then go where?

    b. What world are the Time of the End Remnant to witness to? Where do they begin? And then where do they go?

10. What Gospel? In practical terms—three parables.

    a. The First Parable: The Ten Virgins *know* and *expect* the Bridegroom. What's the critical element that's missing? Zechariah 4:6; Ezekiel 37:14.

        The Gospel is *Spirit-given* and *Spirit-driven*.

    b. The Second Parable: What is the difference in *attitude* between the first two servants and the third servant? Compare Hebrews 11:6 with Matthew 25:24, 25.

        See Chapter 9 of this book. Faith vs. Fear and Fruitful vs. Unfruitful.

        a) Do the first two servants believe Hebrews 11:6 about the master?

        b) What is the reward for loving and trusting the master in this life and in the life to come? (This answer is critical to see if you have been paying attention in all of these studies. For help, see Chapter 4.)

        c) As a result, what will be missing in the lives of those who "fear" as the third servant did? A one-word answer: John 15:5; Matthew 7:20

    c. The Third Parable: Which group—the sheep or the goats—were surprised that the people in great need represented Jesus?

        Others-focused vs. Self-focused

        a) Describe the difference in attitude between that of the sheep and that of the goats toward those in great need. Goats: Luke 6:32–34; Sheep: Matthew 9:36

        b) What criteria does Jesus use to separate the Sheep and the Goats? Matthew 9:36; 25:40

Part 4: The Time of the End

1. Who will deliver this Gospel to the whole world for a witness? Isaiah 43:10; 44:8; Matthew 24:14

2. According to the three parables, in what three ways will they do that?

Take Home Thought Questions

1. Has the "gospel to the whole world" already begun in your part of Jerusalem?

2. What are the Three R's that God uses to get us ready to participate? How did we describe them in our Covenant Grace-Faith Relationship? See Chapters 4–6.

    Re _____   (to turn around)   Rec_____ from

    Re _____   (make alive again)   Gr_____ in

    Re _____   (create anew)   Bec_____ like

3. Which of these three must we have a part in?

4. How do we partake of these three Gifts? Romans 1:17; see Chapters 13–14

Chapter 18

Discussion Questions

In Chapter 13 and 14 we discovered Good News for the Time of the End. In the Sanctuary, in the last days we can trust Jesus to take care of the barrier that separates from the Father—the penalty, the power, and the presence of sin. That's good news for us personally. In the Three Angels' Messages, we have this same Good News to share with the world: "A return to a relationship with God will do for you what it has done for me." These two concepts were the result of everything else we studied.

Chapters 15, 16, 17 explain **how** this is to be done by the Remnant: Make Disciples, Be a Witness, "Preach the Gospel to the Whole World as a Witness" like one of the Sheep.

Chapter 18 adds the fourth segment: Build an Ark

Part 1: The concept of the Remnant—Visible and Invisible

1. What were the five parts of our definition of the Remnant? This is a review from Chapter 11. Check there for the words and concepts—the characteristics of all Remnants.

    a.   John 16:8; Ezekiel 36:26, 27

    b.   Revelation 14:6–12; Zechariah 1:3

    c.   Revelation 14:12a; Jeremiah 4:18–22

    d.   Isaiah 37:32

    e.   Zechariah 4:6; Matthew 25:1–4

2. How is the Remnant of the Time of the End described in Revelation 12:17?

3. Why is the Dragon angry with the Remnant? (Not the Woman, not the Seed, but the Remnant.) Revelation 12:17

    What is the Remnant doing that makes the Dragon angry? Revelation 14:1–4

    What is the Remnant proclaiming? Revelation 14:6–12

4. How is the invisible Remnant described? In the Old Testament: Zechariah 8:22, 23; in the New Testament: John 12:20, 21

Do you see why the answer to our question, "Do you know who you are?" is so important? This is who we are as Seventh-day Adventist Christians. We are the "visible" Remnant. And we are calling out to whom? Yes, everyone. But who responds? Those who want what the Remnant has found for themselves and for others. These are the "invisible" Remnant who respond and join with the "visible" Remnant to make the "final" Remnant People of God in the Time of the End.

5. List—by group or by name—the "invisible" Remnant (those in the world who responded) to the messages of the "visible" Remnant listed below. Use the Bible or the Internet, etc. to help find your answers.

Noah	Abraham
Elijah	John the Baptist
Martin Luther	John Wesley
Joseph Wolfe	William Miller
Mark Finley	

If you are part of the visible Remnant church, what invisible Remnant are you hoping will respond to your messages?

Part 2: Noah

What three messages (similar to Noah's messages) are the visible Remnant to be preaching in the Time of the End?

1. Noah #1—God **loves** you and wants to **rescue** you.

    Time of the End #1—What is the message? John 3:16

    What name does the visible Remnant use to describe what God is offering with this first gift? Revelation 14:6, 7; Romans 1:16

2. Noah #2—God is giving you a choice.

    Time of the End #2—What is the message? 2 Kings 18:21

    a. John 14:16 vs. Ephesians 2:2. What's the contrast? What two powers can we choose from?

        Micah 6:8 vs. 1 John 2:16. What's the contrast? What two life focuses can we choose from?

        b.   From where does God call people to be transformed by this second gift? Revelation 14:8

            Out of what? 2 Thessalonians 2:9, 10; Revelation 13:13, 14. What does "Babylon" mean?

            Into what? John 14:16, 17; 15:5

3.   Noah #3—The consequences of your choice.

      Time of the End #3—What is the message? Revelation 22:12

      What did Jesus say are the two consequences? John 5:28, 29

Revelation 14:9–11 graphically describes the negative consequences of choosing to **not** live in a Covenant Grace-Faith Relationship with God.

4.   What do those who respond positively to the first two messages develop under the guidance of Gift #2? See Revelation 14:12; compare to 2 Peter 1:4

5.   What is the purpose of the Special Emphasis Message? Revelation 18:2–4

      What *is* the Special Emphasis Message? 2 Peter 3:9. Why is it given?

Remember what business God is in: the Salvation Business—always.

Critical Question: By what process and by what power is the visible Remnant able to do this? Ezekiel 37:14; Zechariah 4:6. **You must know this answer to the very core of your being.**

6.   What kind of opposition should the visible Remnant expect to these messages?

      Colossians 2:8; Matthew 15:8, 9; Micah 7:6

7.   If the whole world is described in the above three categories, who are the visible Remnant looking for? Who is there left to talk to? Acts 8:26–29

8.   In the Time of the End, what does an "Ethiopian" mean? Acts 8:27

9.   What is the "Ethiopian" looking for? 1 John 1:1–3; Romans 8:14

Part 3: The Ark

1. While the Remnant are making disciples (Chapter 15), being witnesses (Chapter 16), and serving others (Chapter 17), what is the fourth task they have to carry out? Genesis 7:1

2. What is the New Testament equivalent of Noah's ark? Ephesians 4:12; 1 Peter 2:5 Matthew 16:18

3. What three characteristics must this Ark have—just as Noah's ark had? (see Chapter 18)

    (Received From) Psalm 119:114, 117

    (Growing In) Ephesians 4:15

    (Becoming Like) Ephesians 4:13, 16

4. How do you build an "Ark" at the Time of the End?" Reminder: you studied this in Chapter 6. Frame your answer in accordance with the three sections of Micah 6:8.

    Deuteronomy 6:5; Romans 8:5; Joshua 24:15b

    Acts 4:23–30; Matthew 5:16; Colossians 3:12–17

    Matthew 9:36; Galatians 5:22, 23; 2 Peter 1:4

Before we can "build an Ark" where people 1) are safe, 2) to grow, and 3) become like Jesus—we must do the following in our own experience:

Establish the Covenant Grace-Faith Relationship by faith in Jesus

Establish "obedience from the heart" by hope in the Holy Spirit

Establish "the power of the Holy Spirit" by love of the Father in a functioning church

5. Describe in some detail how you would build this kind of Ark at your church

    Deliberately

    Radically

    Compassionately

Take Home Thought Questions

Matthew 25:35, 36 gives the description of those whom Jesus intended for His people to reach out to, and is listed below. Following each word, the two-word description of the literal meaning of the word is given. Write a two-word description of the *metaphorical* meaning of the word. Remember: two words only.

Can you picture, are you aware of, "those who dwell on the earth," those who are:

	Literal	**Metaphorical**
"hungry" (Amos 8:11; John 6:35)	without food	
"thirsty" (Isaiah 55:1; John 4:14)	without water	
"strangers" (Ephesians 2:12–14)	not known	
"naked" and exposed (Psalm 32:1; 9:14)	without clothing	
"sick" and tired (Isaiah 1:5, 6; Jeremiah 3:22) (Matthew 11:28, 29)	ill and dying	
"imprisoned" (Isaiah 49:8–10)	in jail, in captivity	

How will you respond to these needs?

What kind of Ark will you build?

Who will help you?

What will it look like?

Will it look like your current church?

Bibliography

Edson, Hiram. Untitled Manuscript. Heritage Room, James White Library, Andrews University.

Loughborough, John Norton. *The Great Second Advent Movement: Its Rise and Progress.* 1905. Reprint, Ringgold, GA: TEACH Services, Inc., 2013.

Miller, William. *Wm Miller's Apology and Defence.* Boston, MA: J. V. Himes, 1845.

White, Ellen G. "A Missionary Appeal." *The Review and Herald*, December 15, 1885.

———. *The Desire of Age.* Mountain View, CA: Pacific Press Publishing Association, 1898.

———. *Early Writings.* Washington, DC: Review and Herald Publishing Association, 1882.

———. *The Great Controversy.* Mountain View, CA: Pacific Press Publishing Association, 1911.

———. *Letter* 130, 1901.

———. *Manuscript 43*, 1901.

———. *Testimonies for the Church.* Vol. 5. Mountain View, CA: Pacific Press Publishing Association, 1889.

We invite you to view the complete
selection of titles we publish at:

www.TEACHServices.com

Scan with your mobile
device to go directly
to our website.

Please write or email us your praises, reactions, or
thoughts about this or any other book we publish at:

TEACH Services, Inc.
PUBLISHING
www.TEACHServices.com • (800) 367-1844

P.O. Box 954
Ringgold, GA 30736

info@TEACHServices.com

TEACH Services, Inc., titles may be purchased in bulk for
educational, business, fund-raising, or sales promotional use.
For information, please e-mail:

BulkSales@TEACHServices.com

Finally, if you are interested in seeing
your own book in print, please contact us at

publishing@TEACHServices.com

We would be happy to review your manuscript for free.

CPSIA information can be obtained at www.ICGtesting.com
Printed in the USA
LVOW09s0955310815

452077LV00005B/13/P